THE CHILD IN CINEMA

THE CHILD IN CINEMA

Edited by Karen Lury

THE BRITISH FILM INSTITUTE
Bloomsbury Publishing Plc
50 Bedford Square, London, WC1B 3DP, UK
1385 Broadway, New York, NY 10018, USA
29 Earlsfort Terrace, Dublin 2, Ireland

BLOOMSBURY is a trademark of Bloomsbury Publishing Plc

First published in Great Britain 2022 by Bloomsbury
on behalf of the
British Film Institute
21 Stephen Street, London W1T 1LN
www.bfi.org.uk

The BFI is the lead organisation for film in the UK and the distributor of Lottery funds for film. Our mission is to ensure that film is central to our cultural life, in particular by supporting and nurturing the next generation of filmmakers and audiences. We serve a public role which covers the cultural, creative and economic aspects of film in the UK.

Copyright © Karen Lury, 2022

Karen Lury has asserted her right under the Copyright, Designs and Patents Act, 1988, to be identified as editor of this work.

For legal purposes the Acknowledgements on p. xi constitute an extension of this copyright page.

Cover design by Louise Dugdale
Cover image: *The Year My Parents Went on Vacation*, 2006. Gullane Filmes/Caos Producoes Cinematograficas/Miravista/Alamy Stock Photo

All rights reserved. No part of this publication may be reproduced or transmitted in any form or by any means, electronic or mechanical, including photocopying, recording, or any information storage or retrieval system, without prior permission in writing from the publishers.

Bloomsbury Publishing Plc does not have any control over, or responsibility for, any third-party websites referred to or in this book. All internet addresses given in this book were correct at the time of going to press. The author and publisher regret any inconvenience caused if addresses have changed or sites have ceased to exist, but can accept no responsibility for any such changes.

A catalogue record for this book is available from the British Library.

A catalog record for this book is available from the Library of Congress.

ISBN:	HB:	978-1-8445-7513-8
	PB:	978-1-8445-7512-1
	ePDF:	978-1-8390-2495-5
	eBook:	978-1-8445-7724-8

Typeset by Integra Software Services Pvt. Ltd.
Printed and bound in Great Britain

To find out more about our authors and books visit www.bloomsbury.com and sign up for our newsletters.

CONTENTS

List of Illustrations vii
List of Contributors viii
Acknowledgements xi

Introduction   *Karen Lury* 1

PART ONE SPACE AND TIME 19

1 The dream house   *Amelie Hastie* 21

2 Children's right to space, place and home
   Owain Jones 35

3 Synchrony in the work of Hayao Miyazaki
   Robert Maslen 49

PART TWO SCREEN PERFORMANCE 69

4 The achievement of Janis Wilson, Hollywood juvenile supporting actor   *Martin Shingler* 71

5 Performing black boyhood, quiet and *Moonlight*
   Karen Lury 85

6 Children in documentaries: or, the camera never lies
   Stella Bruzzi 101

PART THREE HISTORIES 119

7 Kusturica's children: the bubble that bursts history
Dimitris Eleftheriotis 121

8 The child imprisoned in history: crystalline community building in *O Ano em Que Meus Pais Saíram de Férias* (Brazil, 2006)   *David Martin-Jones* 139

9 Beginnings and children   *Lalitha Gopalan* 157

PART FOUR BEYOND CINEMA 169

10 The child in surrealism: Bellmer, Cornell, Hiller
David Hopkins 171

11 Mind how you go: children and the public information film   *Andrew Burke* 187

12 'We know what it's actually like': voice, dialect and self-efficacy in Scotland's *Understanding Cinema* project   *Jamie Chambers* 203

Index 224

LIST OF ILLUSTRATIONS

1.1 'The burning dollhouse'. *Badlands* directed by Terence Malick 23

1.2 Mason (Marc Donato) in *The Sweet Hereafter* directed by Atom Egoyan 29

2.1 'In between spaces'. *Boyhood* directed by Richard Linklater 41

2.2 Mason (Ellar Coltrane) in the car moving home. *Boyhood* directed by Richard Linklater 44

3.1 A 'mobile home'. *Howl's Moving Castle* directed by Hayao Miyazaki 61

3.2 In flight. *Howl's Moving Castle* directed by Hayao Miyazaki 66

4.1 Janis Wilson distraught as 'Tina' in *Now, Voyager* directed by Irving Rapper 76

4.2 The 'make over' of Janis Wilson as 'Tina' in *Now, Voyager* directed by Irving Rapper 79

5.1 Alex Hibbert as 'Little' in *Moonlight* directed by Barry Jenkins 90

5.2 Ashton Sanders as teen Chiron looking back through the camera in *Moonlight* directed by Barry Jenkins 91

5.3 'What's a faggot?' Little's question in *Moonlight* directed by Barry Jenkins 94

6.1 In the queue for the cinema. *Seven Up!* 107

6.2 At the photocopier. *Être et avoir* directed by Nicolas Philibert 111

7.1 On the trailer in *When Father Was Away on Business* directed by Emir Kusturica 128

7.2 The disruptive 'bubble' of childhood in *When Father Was Away on Business* directed by Emir Kusturica 130

LIST OF CONTRIBUTORS

Stella Bruzzi is a professor and Executive Dean of Arts and Humanities at the University of Central London. Her research and publications include work on documentary film and television; costume, fashion and film; masculinity and cinema; and representations of the law and true crime in film and television. Following on from the Leverhulme Major Research Fellowship 'Approximation: Documentary, History and the Staging of Reality', a monograph of the same title has been published by Routledge (2020).

Andrew Burke is a professor in the Department of English at the University of Winnipeg, Canada. His book *Hinterland Remixed: Media, Memory, and the Canadian 1970s* was published by McGill-Queen's University Press in 2019.

Jamie Chambers is a lecturer in film and television at Edinburgh College of Art. He is the founding editor of the *Film Education Journal* and has worked as a film education practitioner with *Understanding Cinema* and *Cinéma Cent Ans De Jeunesse* since 2013. He is the curator of the Folk Film Gathering (the world's first folk film festival (www.folkfilmgathering.com) and is the director of the award-winning, BAFTA-nominated films *When the Song Dies* (2012) and *Blackbird* (2013).

Dimitris Eleftheriotis is Professor of Film Studies at the University of Glasgow. He was an editor of *Screen* between 2012 and 2021. His publications include the monographs *Popular Cinemas of Europe* and *Cinematic Journeys*. He is currently working on film and cosmopolitanism and has published a series of articles on the subject.

Lalitha Gopalan is Associate Professor in the Department of Radio-Television-Film, affiliate faculty in the Department of Asian Studies, South Asia Institute, and Core Faculty in the Center for Women and Gender Studies at the University of Texas in Austin, USA. She is the author of *Cinema of Interruptions: Action Genres in Contemporary Indian Cinema* (2002) and *Bombay* (2005), and editor of *Cinema of India* (2010). She is a member of the editorial collective *Camera*

Obscura: Feminism, Culture, and Media Studies. Her most recent book, *Cinemas Dark and Slow in Digital India* (2020), explores various experimental film and video practices in India.

Amelie Hastie is the author of *Cupboards of Curiosity: Women, Recollection and Film History* (2007), *The Bigamist* (BFI Film Classics, 2009), a forthcoming volume on *Columbo* (Duke University Press), and essays on film/television theory and historiography, feminism, and material cultures, including 'The Vulnerable Spectator' column in *Film Quarterly*. She teaches at Amherst College in the United States.

David Hopkins is Emeritus Professor of Art History and Research Fellow at the University of Glasgow. His books include *Dada's Boys: Masculinity after Duchamp* (2007), *Virgin Microbe: Essays on Dada* (co-edited, 2014) and *After Modern Art 1945–2017* (2nd edition, 2018). His latest book is *Dark Toys: Surrealism and the Culture of Childhood* (2021).

Owain Jones trained as cultural geographer and became the first Professor of Environmental Humanities in the UK in 2014 at Bath Spa University. He gained a PhD in the geographies of rural childhood at the University of Bristol; conducted an Arts and Humanities Research Council project into depictions of childhood and has published many scholarly articles on various aspects of children's geographies. He was a founding associate editor of the *Children's Geographies* journal, and chair of the Royal Geographical Society's Children, Youth and Families Research Group from 2009 to 2014.

Karen Lury is Professor of Film and Television Studies at the University of Glasgow. She has published widely in film and television studies, focusing particularly on aesthetics, childhood and performance. She is the author of *The Child in Film: Tears, Fears and Fairytales* (2010) and, most recently, co-editor of *Discourses of Care: Media Practices and Cultures* (2020). She is an editor of the international film and television studies journal *Screen*.

David Martin-Jones is Professor of Film Studies at the University of Glasgow. His work explores the question of what it means to study a world of cinemas. He is the author/editor of nine books, including *Cinema Against Doublethink* (2018) and *Columbo: Paying Attention 24/7* (2021).

Robert Maslen is a senior lecturer in English Literature at the University of Glasgow and founded the MLitt English Literature: Fantasy, dedicated to the study of fantasy and the fantastic. He is the author of *Elizabethan Fictions* (1997), *Shakespeare and Comedy* (2005), and *The Shakespeare Handbook* (2008), and has edited Sir Philip Sidney's *Apology for Poetry* (2002) and Mervyn Peake's *Collected Poems* (2008) and *Complete Nonsense* (2011). He has written many essays on early modern literature and twentieth-century fantasy and science fiction, with subjects ranging from fake translations to books and reading in Japanese anime. He also blogs at 'The City of Lost Books'.

Martin Shingler is an independent scholar and freelance writer/editor who previously lectured on film and media at the universities of Staffordshire (1990–2005) and Sunderland (2005–2019). In addition to co-editing the BFI *Film Stars* book series (2012–2019), he has published books on radio, film melodrama, star studies and Warner Bros.

ACKNOWLEDGEMENTS

This anthology has been in limbo for a long time. I particularly want to acknowledge all those contributors who did make it this far, even when it meant you had to provide new material. Of these patient fellows, my close colleagues at Glasgow, Dimitris Eleftheriotis and David Martin-Jones, made particular efforts to keep the anthology on track. You and your fellow contributors have been endlessly sympathetic and kind. I want to offer special thanks to Amy Holdsworth and Michael Lawrence, who – of course, when I was now suddenly 'in a rush' – both provided a final critical reading of my contributions, enabling me to just 'finish the thing'. As ever, I am also indebted to Caroline Beven who made the business of pulling everything together so much easier and who added stylistic elegance and coherence to my and other contributors' chapters. I'd also like to thank Rebecca Barden, who initiated the project (how she must rue the day) and ultimately came back to see it finally completed. I'd also like to thank my husband, Tim Niel and our daughters – Delilah, Alice and Edie – all of whom in different ways made suggestions and offered encouragement along the way.

Finally, I'd like to dedicate the book to the late Elizabeth Lebas, whose contribution sadly could not be completed – however, her passion, humour, scholarship and sense of style made a huge impression on me in the brief time I knew her.

INTRODUCTION

Karen Lury

This collection is, as its title suggests, about the child in cinema: its central ambition is not just to think about the representation of the child on screen, but to expand this critical domain to include the child as they appear in non-fiction and non-theatrical films (documentaries, art installations and public information films), to develop the global reach of the texts discussed (including the former Yugoslavia, Brazil and India) and to explore the labour of the child both in front of and behind the camera (as actors and filmmakers.) Despite the diversity of texts discussed, the anthology provides an overlapping series of arguments, in which key themes and preoccupations recur: the spaces and places children inhabit and imagine; a concern for children's rights and agency; the affective power of the child as a locus for memory and history; and the complexity and ambiguity of the child figure itself. Since the book was originally commissioned, it would be fair to say that there has been an explosion of popular and academic writing on the child in cinema and, to a lesser degree perhaps, on children's films.[1] Previously overlooked, the child is now a subject of interest across a wide range of different film analyses, which employ the child to expose the under-explored nooks and crannies within the architecture of cinema.[2] In the chapters in this volume and elsewhere, the majority of film analyses focus – understandably – on how the child is depicted and represented: in the closing section of this introduction, I will highlight how my various contributors (and I) similarly explore questions of representation and agency. In opening up the discussion, however, in the first section of this introduction, I want, perversely perhaps, to take the opportunity to reflect on my increasing ambivalence about the child as a critical lens.

This is, I suspect, because this anthology has had – even more than most academic anthologies – a very long gestation, and it has been neglected, in large part due to the distractions of other commitments, both domestic and professional. Over this period, my own interest in the child has also waxed and waned, although I am not sure whether I want, or am even able, to let go of the child's grasp on my attention. I suspect that the child will still manage to get its 'sticky fingers' into everything and anything I write. However, having now spent over fifteen years thinking and writing about the child in film, television and amateur media, I want to be a bit disruptive – to make some noise, to stir things up a bit – by reflecting on my ambivalence about the exploitation of the child as critical lens in film; in doing so, I know that I share these concerns with many of my peers. The following is therefore both a rebuke and a challenge to myself and others. I will start simply, with a list of statements that make me anxious when people (and by 'people' I mean adults, like me) use them to explain or justify their focus and 'expertise' in relation to the child.

'We were all children once'

Well, yes I guess, in a sense 'we all' were. But surely the point is that we were no more alike (or unalike) as children as we are now as adults. Children, like other non-human animals, are universalised (and homogenized) not so much because they share characteristics or perspectives amongst themselves but because they are both unknowable and vulnerable. It can often be a mistake to recognize the child 'you once were' on screen, or project fantasies about your own children (about whom you probably know very little) in order to understand child characters, or to use your own memories as a way of understanding or legitimizing 'childish' behaviour and attitudes that are depicted on screen. As Chris Philo observed, while it may seem to be the only viable approach, adult researchers must take great care not to colonize children's space or identity.[3]

'The child and … ' or 'The child in … ' or 'The child on … '

I am as guilty as anyone here (see, for instance, the title of this anthology and my previous book on 'the child in film'). My admonition here is to myself as much as it is to other authors thinking of writing about the child figure. The child really shouldn't be a cookie-cutter metaphor that is picked up and slapped onto a series of films to make them more appealing. Each time I see 'The Child and … (national cinema, genre of filmmaking, auteur)' as a book or essay title, I think about Richard Benjamin's 1990 film adaptation of Patty Dan's novel *Mermaids*, featuring Cher as the bad/'good enough' mother, Rachel, who, in one memorable scene uses a cookie-cutter on white bread and ham, creating a star-shaped sandwich (she only makes childlike 'party food') for her embarrassed teenage daughter Charlotte (played by Winona Ryder). All of us should have the ambition to make more than another ham sandwich.

'The child's point of view'

Or 'objects in the rear view mirror may appear closer than they are'. Film directors and academics generally accept that they cannot see the world as children do, but are sometimes guilty of thinking that if they look back carefully enough – in the rear view mirror provided via psychoanalysis perhaps – or if they are willing to 'get down' physically to the child's presumed eye level, then they will be closer to, or even be able to adopt, the child's 'point of view' (perspective.) No, I don't think so. Taking the time to do this can create more interesting stories, and the films and analyses produced are often illuminating and moving. Ultimately, however, they are still stories (films and/or critique) by adults for adults, or – at best, or sometimes at worst – by adults 'as if' they were able to speak for children (they rarely, if ever, speak *to* children, but that can be even more excruciating). 'As if', in my childhood at least, was used as an alternative phrasing to the provocative and sarcastic use of 'yeah … right' – meaning that the speculation or possible solution being promoted by the storyteller would and could never happen, and in fact was actively prevented from ever happening, in that particular way, however much it might have been wished for – 'as *if*'. (By the way, see my first point – my childhood was not your childhood and as an explanation this may make little sense to you.)

The child as 'becoming', the child in 'transition', the 'liminal child'

This is difficult, as I am pretty certain I have also used all those descriptors myself at one time or another (and both Owain Jones and David Martin-Jones, along with some of my other contributors, use the same kind of descriptive terms to good effect). The concept of 'becoming' is often drawn from Deleuze, whereas the term 'transition' is often framed, at least initially, as sociological; the 'liminality' of the child more frequently emerges from literary studies and close textual analysis – and all are used in film studies.[4] Like many approaches to the conception or description of childhood, it comes with the best of intentions. After all, it is evidently true that (most) children are not fixed as categories or as individuals (since most children grow and are growing), meaning that the child figure as a theoretical, social and psychological construct has a useful slipperiness, where it appears vividly, as neither one thing nor the other, delightfully, scarily plastic. But, as ever with the child, there is a danger of fetishization here, and, as I have indicated, even the conception of 'growth', which may appear as a biological certainty, excludes those fictional and actual children who may not, for various reasons, 'grow' as other children appear to do.

The growing child is in fact rather difficult to capture – even filmmakers who follow the child over a number of months or years (see, for instance, Hirokazu Kore-eda, Michael Winterbottom, Richard Linklater or the *7 Up!* documentary team)[5] – necessarily fail to capture growth as it is actually happening. For this reason, perhaps, critics are drawn again and again to instances exemplified by the ambivalent meaning of a 'freeze-frame' (usually at the end of a film), a clever, two-faced image, looking back and forward, although in reality this is more often true of the filmmaker and adult spectator than of the child character. The most cited version of this image is the much discussed ending from *400 Blows/Les Quatre Cents Coups* (Francois Truffaut, 1959), where Antoine Doinel (Jean Paul Leaud) is running to the sea but is stranded, or stilled, in the final shot of the film, looking back at the camera, in a freeze-frame. This is a position and gesture directly referenced by other little boys in *This is England* (Shane Meadows, 2006) and *Moonlight* (Barry Jenkins, 2016), both of which also feature a final image of the boy on a beach, looking out to the horizon and/or back at the camera. My point is not that the readings of the child as 'becoming', or in 'transition', or as 'liminal' are wrong, but rather that as adult critics we invest too much in these instances or this positioning of the child as 'betwixt and between' and as a figure of potential (a fulcrum between the past and the future). This leads me to my final anxiety about whether or not we should:

'Fuck the child'

Lee Edelman has offered a profound and provocative critique of the 'sacred status' of the child in social and political discourse. In his summary of his own argument, he suggests:

> *No Future* argued that social relations that imagine an end to their structural antagonism in a tomorrow perpetually deferred invoke the future as guarantee of meaning's realization. Such a future, in its status as supplement, as the empty placeholder of totalization, works at once to preclude and assure the social system's closure, denying its totalization in the present while filling the gap that denial opens with the pledge of the yet-to-come. The Child, as the privileged figure of that pledge – one with no markers of identity in advance, such that any child, in the proper context, can instantiate its logic – compels us take our social value from our various relations to it and to make ourselves, in whatever way, the guardians of its future.[6]

I am pretty sure that Edelman would be fully aware of how that last line chimes with the nauseatingly sentimental (and retrospectively contaminated) line from Michael Jackson's recording of 'The Greatest Love of All' (written by Michael Masser/Linda Creed): 'I believe the children are our future.' Edelman's provocative critique is sophisticated and complex; however, it makes two simple things very clear. Firstly, that the child is a political hostage through which we (well certainly, 'I', as a mother of three daughters) are all hoodwinked into saving and preparing for a future-yet-to-come and which, of course, never actually arrives. This prompts an inevitable recollection (another cultural earworm, if you like) that it feels impossible to avoid, this time from Lewis Carroll's *Alice*, a real and fictional little girl who seems inescapable, either within academic studies of childhood or in numerous adaptations in film, television and other media forms. The deniability of today and the forfeiting of the present to the future is, after all, neatly summarized by the White Queen's rule: 'jam tomorrow and jam yesterday – but never jam today'.[7]

Secondly, within the bio-political framework described by Edelman, the child is othered, since as a child they must always be to one side, or on the outside, awaiting this unknown and anticipated future, so that they are therefore 'other' to the society they presently inhabit. Ironically, perhaps, this then aligns the child with those 'other' individuals ('queers') who refuse to participate in the relentless merry-go-round of reproduction and child-worship.[8] Or, as Edelman famously puts it:

> Fuck the social order and the Child in whose name we're collectively terrorized; fuck Annie; fuck the waif from Les Mis; fuck the poor, innocent kid on the Net; fuck Laws both with capital ls and small; fuck the whole network of Symbolic relations and the future that serves as its prop.[9]

What Edelman's critique exposes, I think, is that the child – as metaphor, as metonymic figure, or featuring otherwise in our various shared fantasies – is hollow, much like the cookie-cutter I described earlier. It can seemingly be used for almost any purpose, filled by and shaping whatever ideology is desired and it can be used – at this point in time and certainly since the late twentieth century – as the 'trump card' in any political debate.[10] The importance of the child appears, at the current time, to be a given; it is almost always possible to describe work or research on the child as urgent, inclusive and universal. It is more difficult, I have discovered, when facing a number of rejected grant applications, to make it interesting. In addition, as many others have noted, the sanctity of the child as political subject (as future citizen) does not, despite the rhetoric, appear to hold for actual children (those annoyingly material, solid, messy and frequently noisy beings). However, this final switcheroo – replacing the child-figure with the actual child – is another familiar conceit, since *real* children *really* matter, don't they? So it is good, isn't it, to do 'work' on the child? Edelman's point is not, however, that children don't matter, just that they don't matter 'more' – that is, more than the old, the queer, the childless, the disabled, the dying and those other individuals we deem to be 'adult'.

Writing this now, in the second year of a global pandemic, the sacred status of the child is employed in popular discourse and political debate in various, and often confused, ways. COVID-19 and its variants is highly infectious but it seems (predominantly) to kill old people (and this is acceptable? Although *when*, exactly, are we suggesting someone is 'old'?) But even young children can be infected, some with lasting effects. So whom do we vaccinate and whom do we expose? Do we vaccinate children to protect them, or is it to protect their parents, adult carers, siblings, grandparents and others? And if we decided to do this, whom can we ask for permission to administer that vaccination? (The child or, perhaps, their 'anti-vaxxer' parents?) What are the consequences, for all of us, as the normal patterns and routines for schooling and socializing children continue to be disrupted? It seems that there is no escaping the question of who 'matters most', since it is becoming clear, finally, in the discussion around 'key workers' that 'everyone' does.

A virus that attacks everyone explodes the tidiness of our antiquated and toxic taxonomies, established through our fetishization of biological 'difference' rather than an appreciation of the similarities and intra-dependencies that exist between humans of all ages, as well as with other entities of all kinds, such as non-human animals, microbes and bacteria. In her fascinating book, *Infrahumanisms: Science, Culture and the Making of Non/Personhood*, Megan H. Glick provides a cogent account of the various ways in which the child emerged in the late nineteenth and early twentieth centuries as a convenient vehicle for and the primary 'exception' within medical and psychological doctrine.

> Imagining the child as unique in soma and psyche, in dietary consumption and patterns of rest and activity, in health and illness – in short, imagining the child as infrahuman – seemed to allay fears about human progress, of which there was still so much to learn. The consideration of the child as a special case, in the rise of both child psychology and paediatric physiology, animated fantasies of control and quantifiable difference.[11]

As Glick goes on to demonstrate, the result is that the child is employed (once again) as both the exceptional proof of, and thus the rationale for, a racist and anthropocentric world view.

It may seem that I have come a long way from thinking about film or media representations of children. However, my point is to look forward to what might be the next step in our thinking about children/childhood and their various ways of being, and seeming, both on and off screen. It seems to me that one way forward might be to consider the heterogeneous, and apparently eccentric, relations shared between children; between the child and adult; between children and those others (non-human animals, viruses, machines, atmospheres, climates) with which we share our screens and our world.

In an essay I am still struggling to write, I try to articulate what it might mean to think about how one set of relations between children and these kinds of inhuman entities are captured on film, focusing on three 'devices' that appear frequently in films for and about children: the balloon, the kite and the bicycle. Using work by the geographers Derek McCormack and Sasha Engelmann, and their attempts to imagine and reveal a 'geo-poetics of air' – in Engelmann's words, 'an awareness of the simultaneous material, affective and aesthetic impressions of air'[12] – I suggest that the kite, balloon and bicycle can be determined not simply as children's playthings, but as McCormack suggests, following arguments by Jane Bennett, that they are objects with 'thing power'.[13] All three devices use, employ or pass through the atmosphere and the air, and in doing so they bring the child into a material, aesthetic and affective relationship with air and atmosphere, provoking scary, necessary and delightful experiences of flight, breath and lift. The kite flies because of heat and wind; the balloon is made up of, and rises and falls through, the air; even the bicycle, the most 'grounded' of these devices, is a machine that can be 'punctured' and which will not work with deflated tyres (meaning that tyres are dependent on air and air pressure). The bicycle is also a machine that frighteningly and excitingly propels its operator and/or passenger through the air, making the air audible, tangible (it hums, it is cold or hot, feels soft, fluid, prickling or harsh as you pass through the air and it rushes over your skin.) Air and atmosphere are part of the experience of the bike, the kite and the balloon: whether this is the air rushing past as you descend down a hill, the tug of the wind as you pull at the strings of a kite, or the envelopment of your exhaled breath within the rubber skin of the balloon.

The significance of these different objects is not just because these three airborne or air-filled devices are symbolically loaded with cultural associations that are related to childhood, to parent–child relationships, or that they rehearse child-related concepts of attachment and loss. They are of interest and importance because they facilitate an openness and expose a series of relations between child and world or 'sensing-spaces' as McCormack describes them.[14] They allow for a moment of animation, the instance of lift, the possibility of untethering, the intake or expulsion of breath, of making yourself heard or making yourself present, to the just-before, the just-after, suggesting a momentum anywhere between balance, falling and moving forward. In film, therefore, these relational moments provide instances of affective force, a sense of being in and of the world, in which the child on screen and the audience participates.[15] To award these objects agency in this way also acknowledges the humility that can be experienced by the child in these relations – a give and take that is not always or only about 'mastering' a new skill. It can be difficult to try and think in this way (I find it appealing, sometimes appalling and often just a little bit silly) but perhaps there is something, in considering not just what the balloon, the kite and the bicycle mean to the child, but how they work together.[16] As McCormack suggests: 'It's about how movement and thought think you: about how ideas have you; about how things work you out.'[17] It isn't going to be easy, but surely in a world in which a virus can destroy national economies and when climate change 'changes' everything, we should consider how to work things out so that we recognize the child less as a hostage to our future and more as an ally in our present.

The book

The anthology is divided into four parts: Space and Time; Screen Performance; Histories; and Beyond Cinema.

Space and time

In this first part, the essays overlap in their focus on the spaces, places and temporalities that children occupy, imagine and travel through with a specific focus on the idea and material qualities of the house and home. In the first chapter, the film scholar Amelie Hastie's writing, in terms of its poetic phrasing and eye for detail, is both informed by and resonates with Gaston Bachelard's sensitivity to the child's experiences and memories of home in his series of remarkable essays in *The Poetics of Space*.[18] Looking at three films, Terence Malick's *Badlands* (1973), Lynn Ramsay's *Ratcatcher* (1999) and Atom Egoyan's *The Sweet Hereafter* (1997), Hastie asks us to reflect on how these films are alert to the way in which children use the space they live in, and how what may seem to be mundane spaces (the nooks and crannies of the home which are both found and created) are, for the child, also places of fantasy. She illustrates, through close analysis, how key images from each film – a burning house; a boy wrapped in a white lace curtain; children, who we know to be actually dead, apparently alive and safely asleep in their beds – demonstrate that these filmed houses become dream houses, places of fantasy, sometimes offering comfort but also provoking fear.

In Owain Jones's chapter, which focuses primarily on Richard Linklater's *Boyhood* (2014), he boldly sidesteps what is perhaps best known about this film (which is that it was filmed over twelve years as the central protagonist/child actor Ellar Coltrane grew up) and, rather than reflecting on the passage of time, he considers the child's desire, or indeed their right, to place – and specifically to a 'home'. What, he writes provocatively, 'if we were to ask questions of how seriously children's aspirations should be heeded', and further asks us to consider how doing so might transform 'the conditions of both children's and adult lives, the interactions between them, as well as their spatial out-playings in everyday life'. As he notes, the controversial United Nations Convention on the Rights of the Child Charter (1989) apparently offers a series of rights to the child, which many national governments (including the United Kingdom but not the United States) have ratified. However, as Jones indicates, what this means in practice is variable, with the child's wishes (for example the desire not to move home) often overruled by adult pressures, desires and life choices. By focusing on the instances when the children are moved (by their mother who relocates several times in the film) he is able to illustrate how the child's movements in space (often reflected in purposeless, mundane activities such as 'lying about daydreaming', fidgeting and farting) create a kind of affective choreography in which children can be seen to attune themselves to and sometimes subtly resist the adult 'patternings and orderings' of their environment. In both these chapters, then, albeit with some ambiguity, the child's ability and indeed their right to occupy, make use of and control spaces and places, to subvert the apparent meaning of the corner of a room or the otherwise redundant space between houses, is seen as important to their well-being.

In the final chapter of this section, Robert Maslen, a literary and fantasy scholar, brings together the concerns of both Hastie and Jones when he considers the possibility of 'synchrony' in relation to the child's experiences of time and space. He asks how it might be possible to create a cinematic experience that could play to an 'auditorium as a complex web of experiences governed both by the constantly shifting dynamics of biological development and by distinct but overlapping perspectives on the object of attention, variously oriented towards past, present or future'. Examining, in detail, three animated films by Hayao Miyazaki – *My Neighbour Totoro* (1988), *Whisper of the Heart* (1995) and *Howl's Moving Castle* (2004) – Maslen demonstrates how the overlapping chronologies of the characters, their mutability (in terms of appearance, age and species) as well as the plastic and frequently magical properties of the spaces and places they inhabit (however mundane these places might at first appear) facilitates a cinema for children and adults in which the child's experience is foregrounded but, significantly, is not detached (or 'othered') from that of other generations, or indeed other species and hybrid figures (animals, gods, monsters or machines). Miyazaki's artwork – indebted still to the traditions of cel (hand-drawn) animation and using very little computer-generated imagery (CGI) – has a very light touch, and appears, in some senses 'simple'. However, Maslen's absorbed and absorbing analysis illustrates quite how detailed and frequently dark the artwork and themes of Miyazaki's films actually are. Taking us from the playful, melancholy terrain of *Totoro* (with its memorable hybrid, the 'cat-bus') through the temporally complicated romance of the protagonists in *Whisper of the Heart*, he brings us finally to the eccentric and time-travelling occupants of *Howl's Moving Castle*. With a focus on time and intergenerational relationships, it may seem that his focus is solely on the significance of time for the child. Yet in the final images of the *moving* castle, delightfully described by Maslen as a 'poignantly rickety structure', children (and adults) are provided with a 'mobile' home, a home full of nooks and crannies, that can move through and with time – a mutable, hopeful place of nostalgia and anticipation – that becomes, as Maslen suggests, a 'blueprint for co-habitation'.

Screen performance

In this part, the essays variously address the agency of the child in relation to their performance on screen. The first two chapters, by Martin Shingler and myself, concentrate squarely on the labour of the child actor in fictional film. Shingler draws on his vast expertise in Hollywood cinema (and the work of Bette Davis) to reflect on the acting choices and performance of the child actor Janis Wilson, in the Bette Davis star vehicle, *Now, Voyager* (Irving Rapper, 1942). He demonstrates, via close textual analysis (drawing on an analytic model provided by Cynthia Baron and Sharon Carnicke, along with work by Andrew Klevan) how Wilson's overlooked performance (both at the time and now) can be seen not only as an exemplary 'supporting performance' but as distinctive in its deliberate opposition to the performances of the 'cute' child characters and child stars that dominated Hollywood cinema in the 1930s. Indeed, via his close analysis of specific scenes, it becomes possible to discern how Wilson offers a prototype for the anxious, unhappy (sometimes anorexic) teen character that was the precursor to the 'sullen' teenage girls that moved centre stage in various films from the 1990s on, such as

Girl, Interrupted (James Mangold, 1999), *Thirteen* (Catherine Hardwicke, 2003) and perhaps even *Ladybird* (Greta Gerwig, 2017).

In my chapter, I also focus on the acting choices made and the resulting performances of the child actors who portray the character of 'Little'/Chiron (Alex Hibbert and Ashton Sanders) in Barry Jenkins's 2016 film, *Moonlight*. Originating from a discussion with students from my Screen Performance class in the spring of 2020, I employ Kevin Quashie's concept of 'quiet' in relation to black masculinity, and here black boyhood, as part of a strategy to do justice to the child actors' minimalist but hugely affective performances in the film. In doing so, I touch on the various racist discourses and practices at work in cinema, largely arising from the expectations that are raised between the black actor and spectator, but also, following work by Richard Dyer and Mary Ann Doane, as they are consolidated by apparently neutral technological processes such as lighting, cinematography and specifically, in this context, the formal properties of the close-up. In doing so, I challenge some of our assumptions about how we 'read' faces and, like Shingler, ask that we grant the child actor an agency and power that is often overlooked.

In Stella Bruzzi's chapter on the 'performative' child in non-fiction cinema, the performance of the child is understood not as work in which the child produces a fictional character, but as how the child in these non-fiction contexts – such as the documentaries *Être et Avoir* (Nicolas Philibert, 2002), *Seven Up!* (Granada/BBC, 1964–), *Tarnation* (Jonathan Caouette, 2003) and *Capturing the Friedmans* (Andrew Jarecki, 2003) – oscillates, and actively manages the distinction between their apparent unselfconsciousness in front of the camera, and other times in which they are clearly acutely aware of their 'to-be-looked-at-ness'. In teasing out the discomfort experienced by audiences viewing the 'home movie' footage in the latter two documentaries, and the related exposure of the documentarist's unhealthily obsessive interest in and necessary exploitation of their subjects, the child's presence on screen – their labour if you like – is to problematize, as Bruzzi suggests, 'so many received ideas about documentary and how nonfictional images function'. As her chapter further illustrates, the child's mutability (at times beguiling yet capable of acting with guile) provokes larger questions about the work of performance of 'self' on screen.

Histories

In the third part of the book, the child as a social, historical and political figure is examined in three chapters that explore the child's articulation of cinematic histories – histories as they are refracted through cinema, in films about significant historical periods and events and, in Lalitha Gopalan's essay, in relation to the history of cinema in India.

In Dimitris Eleftheriotis's elegant and playful chapter, he engages with the earlier work of the controversial Serbian film director Emir Kusturica. Focusing on three of his films – *Do You Remember Dolly Bell* (1981), *When Father Was*

Away on Business (1985) and *Time of the Gypsies* (1989) – he examines the role of the child and children in these films, observing that the child's 'messy' agency constantly disrupts attempts to construct 'smooth' master narratives of official history. In developing this argument, he conceives of the child as inhabiting a 'bubble' – porous, fragile, yet beguiling and distracting. These bubbles, or microhistories, enclose each child's unique experience, their sense of chronology, their sense of place, as well as their intimate desires and distractions. Having established this model, through close analysis the films reveal, in Eleftheriotis's words, a '"bubbling-up" of agency that disturbs the powerful, linear surface of dominant history's symbolic violence'. Employing quotations from Reif Larsen's *The Selected Works of T. S. Spivet* as sub-headings, Eleftheriotis encourages the reader to recognize how the messy approach of this narrative (the book is full of maps, notes in the margin, souvenirs, drawings, the 'detritus' of observation rather than ordered note-taking or storytelling) resonates exactly with the impermanent, marginal, distracting and (from an adult perspective) frequently irritating activities of the children in these films. If paid proper attention, these could 'constitute a mighty centrifugal force that confuses simplistic and reductive versions of Yugoslavian history'.

In the second chapter in this part, David Martin-Jones explores a violent and turbulent period in Brazilian history, in his analysis of the child's role in the film *O Ano em Que Meus Pais Saíram de Férias/The Year My Parents went on Vacation* (Cao Hamburger, 2006). The film, set in 1970, reflects the exuberance of the few intense weeks during that summer when the Brazilian football team won the World Cup, while at the same time, it depicts the ongoing struggles of a diverse population subject to the violence imposed by the ruling military dictatorship. This is further complicated by the way in which that dictatorship, unsurprisingly, attempted to align the national team's success with their political authority and a 'banal' nationalism, an ideology that could never articulate or comfortably incorporate the diverse individuals and communities we see in the film. Drawing on Deleuze, Martin-Jones establishes the child protagonist here as not simply the Deleuzian 'seer' or privileged witness to events, but rather as the 'seed/environment' through and around which the recreated 'crystal of time' (that fraught summer of 1970 in Brazil) oscillates. Initially imprisoned in this layer of history, the child – Mauro – ultimately acts as the locus through which the diverse community he inhabits (left-wing radicals, the older Jewish community, the various individuals of Polish, Greek, Italian and African descent) are temporarily drawn together to establish, in this reconstructed past, a possible (virtual) future that might be imagined (by the viewer in 2006 and beyond). In a delicate and detailed analysis of the social and historical context for the film, alongside a careful observation of the film's aesthetics (its many reflecting surfaces, windows, windscreens and mirrors embodying the crystalline qualities of the image) Martin-Jones demonstrates Mauro's affective agency. Although the film does not provide a 'happy ending' for the child in 1970 – Mauro's father is killed, his mother injured and they are forced into exile – Martin-Jones demonstrates how the film, and specifically Mauro, are nonetheless able to 'reclaim the past, in the service of the future'.

In the final chapter of this part, Lalitha Gopalan provides a fascinating account of the significance of the child – as character, as metaphor, as audience – within the history of Indian cinema. Taking us from early cinema where the child features as a god – Krishna as child in Dadasaheb Phalke's *Kaaliya Mardan* (1919) – and the magical metamorphosis achieved in this film by double exposure, she traces the way in which the child's presence has continually inspired some of the most interesting and transformative moments within Indian cinema. Whether this is in relation to film form – for example, the low-angle framing and illusion it creates in Satyajit Ray's *Pather Panchali* (1955) – or in relation to making films specifically for children – via the creation of the Calcutta Film Society in 1947 – or its significance in 'New Wave' filmmaking (here the Kannada New Wave in the 1970s and 1980s), Indian cinema can be seen to echo and often pre-empt the way in which the child has been employed in other national cinemas or filmmaking movements. As she notes, children 'similarly crowd popular cinema' in India and are employed in a variety of genres, both in those we might expect, such as romance, socials and melodrama but also as rhetorical figures in the gangster film and within the Tamil 'Cruel Cinema', in which conflicts related to toxic masculinity, caste, class and religion are refracted through the child's birth, death and position within the extended and blended 'families' depicted on screen. Ending with a brief but evocative insight into the difficulties of filming children (specifically the pressures on the child actor and on the adult filmmakers who must accommodate the difference that a child makes) she embraces the ambition of this anthology, which is, in part, to recognize the child's value and agency both on *and* 'off' screen.

Beyond cinema

In this part, the final three chapters of the anthology pay attention to the child as they appear and function outside mainstream cinemas. Firstly, David Hopkins introduces us to the child as used, imagined and dreamed, in artworks such as surrealist films and contemporary video installations. Secondly, in Andrew Burke's chapter, his focus is on children as they appear in another kind of non-theatrical cinema, and he reflects on the powerful imagery and legacy of a series of short public information films produced in the UK during the 1970s. Appropriately, the last chapter of this section and of the book itself, written by Jamie Chambers – himself both a filmmaker and educator – looks even further beyond the child on screen and takes seriously the question of how and in what ways children themselves can become filmmakers.

In his chapter, David Hopkins reflects on the child's relationship to and exploitation within surrealism, initially focusing on artworks by the German artist Hans Bellmer, which were preoccupied by the figure of the pre-pubescent girl-child as a doll (sometimes as mannequin, in photographs and in drawings). Hopkins then contrasts Bellmer's explicitly paedophilic interest in the child with the no less problematic but less overtly expressed desires, fantasies and ambiguous relations to childhood that recur in films made by Joseph Cornell, specifically, the trilogy of 'Collage films', produced in collaboration with the filmmaker Larry Jordan, between the 1940s and 1960s, *The Children's Party, The Midnight Party* and *Cotillion*. As an art historian, Hopkins expertly guides the reader through Bellmer's obsessions, and provides a detailed analysis of several of Cornell's films, in which the child figures are often retrieved and displayed via short fragments of 'found footage' – an interesting parallel to Bruzzi's earlier chapter, in which she focuses on the use of 'home movies' in documentaries featuring children. He traces the origins of these artists' fascination with childhood to Goethe's 'Mignon' (the boy-girl acrobat, previously the subject of Carolyn Steedman's book, *Strange Dislocations: Childhood and the Idea of Human Interiority*),[19] as well as within Freudian psychoanalysis. Read alongside the wider surrealist interest with 'primitive cultures' and 'child's play', the chapter necessarily takes us into some uncomfortable territory. As a coda to this complicated legacy, Hopkins provides evidence for the significance of this earlier history for the contemporary female artist, Susan Hiller, and specifically, her powerful video installation 'An Entertainment' (1990) which explores and explodes the child abuse, sexual violence and misogyny at work within the traditional 'children's' puppet show, 'Punch and Judy'. We might tentatively suggest therefore, that since the installation interrogates, in a far more critical (and as Hopkins suggests, in a far more censorious) manner than the earlier surrealists, society's ongoing fascination with child/adult sexuality and associated fantasies of neglect and violence, Hiller's installation succeeds in de-sublimating, to an extent, some of the more troubling associations related to the exploitation of the child in the history of surrealism.

In Andrew Burke's chapter there is another kind of violence at work, as he examines an eccentric series of public information films produced in the United Kingdom in the 1970s. Including a detailed analysis of three films – *Mind How You Go*, (1973) *Apaches* (1977) and *Lonely Water* (1973), amongst other films from that era – Burke demonstrates how, in the 1970s in the UK, the peripheral, unregulated spaces and places that were, in some senses, celebrated in earlier chapters by Hastie and Jones, are depicted in these films as dangerous, risky places, in which the incautious child could be maimed, electrocuted or drowned. As he carefully reveals, the films – now long remembered by many adults in the UK with a kind of bemused nostalgia – were already articulating a contemporaneous nostalgic version of childhood, perceived to be under threat not just by the dangers of under-supervised farmyards and waste sites, or because these cautionary tales reflected the generic conventions of the then emergent 'slasher' series of horror films. He suggests that this threat emerges because the children in the films were also (crudely) aligned with other indigenous 'others' (such as Native Americans) who were similarly fantasized or more comfortably 'imagined' just as they were apparently 'vanishing' from the landscape. In his conclusion, he speaks not just to these films, but to very many versions of the cinematic child, when he suggests, 'These films persist in memory, they haunt the present, not because they represent an idealised safe world, but because they imagine a world in which adventure, imagination, and possibility goes hand-in-hand with risk, danger, and uncertainty.'

In the last chapter in this part, and the book, Jamie Chambers reflects on his experience as a practitioner and tutor for Scotland's *Understanding Cinema* project (2014), modelled upon the *Cinémathèque Français Cinéma Cent Ans De Jeunesse* programme (CCADJ).[20] Working with children (9 to 12 year olds) in a number of different primary schools across Scotland, Chambers details his struggle to convince the children of the value of learning the 'language of cinema' (largely informed by the writings of André Bazin and, latterly, the work and pedagogy of the French film critic Alain Bergala.)[21] By encouraging them to adopt a neorealist process, his hope was that they might make short films that were more authentic to their actual life experience – and might thereby find their own voice and 'dialect'. Aware that to privilege authenticity (as understood from the adult's point of view) and even to suggest that the children ought to prioritize 'finding their voice' can be understood as a contentious ambition (indeed it is one I interrogate in my own chapter in this anthology), Chambers is both passionate and pragmatic in his description of his work with the children and their responses to his (self-acknowledged) paternalistic and 'teacherly' interventions. Nonetheless, Chambers provides persuasive evidence of the localized but very real impact that learning to make films had on those children involved. While in the end, as he ruefully notes, he was unable to completely eradicate the desire of many of the children to emulate (whether in relation to film form or in terms of performance and accent) the Hollywood cinema they were most familiar with, at the same time many of the students recognized how the apparently mundane characters, locations and events in their own lives (hard-working mothers, forbidden sweets, the wider school environment, and girls they fancied) might be successfully captured in all their 'local' specificity and made interesting to an audience wider than their immediate peers. Here, the children's work in and on film – as camera operators, writers, directors and performers – may arguably be seen as compromised, but is still justifiably celebrated.

The chapters in this anthology are not intended to be a direct or comprehensive response to my personal ambivalence about the models of analysis and the framing of our enquiry around the child in cinema. They do, I hope, make a distinctive contribution and broaden the scope of popular and academic debate in terms of geography and disciplinary perspective as well as in thinking about the different kinds of cinema in which children participate. More by accident than design, many of the chapters overlap in terms of their concerns, interests and certain key references (such as the UN Convention on the Rights of the Child, Deleuze and Freud.) Read together, they establish the complexity but also the centrality of the child to a wide range of different modes of cinema and filmmaking activity. Approached holistically, or read separately, I hope the reader will find the different chapters useful, entertaining and at times, discomfiting.

Notes

1. This is a necessary distinction made by nearly every author discussing this topic – many films feature children which are not intended for child audiences; many films (but not all) that are made for children are also intended for adult audiences, and there is, of course, despite the need for clarification, some degree of overlap between these categories. Excellent work on children's films has been done, for instance, by Noel Brown; see his *The Children's Film: Genre, Nation and Narrative* (New York: Columbia University Press, 2017), *British Children's Cinema: From The Thief of Bagdad to Wallace and Gromit* (London: I.B. Tauris, 2016), *The Hollywood Family Film: A History, from Shirley Temple to Harry Potter* (London: I.B. Tauris, 2012) and *Family Films in Global Cinema: The World Beyond Disney* (London: I.B. Tauris, 2015). Other work which manages to discuss both, while maintaining the distinction between the child on screen and the child spectator, includes Pamela Robertson Wojcik, *Fantasies of Neglect: Imagining the Urban Child in American Film and Fiction* (New Brunswick, NJ: Rutgers University Press, 2016).
2. Pre-empting my own research and publications on the child and film, Vicky Lebeau's *Childhood and Cinema* (London: Reaktion Books, 2008) is now a foundational book in the field, as is Emma Wilson's earlier but equally inspiring *Cinema's Missing Children* (London: Wallflower Press, 2003). An exemplary but not exhaustive list of later publications includes Daniela Berghahn, *Far-Flung Families in Film: The Diasporic Family in Contemporary European Cinema* (Edinburgh: Edinburgh University Press, 2013), Andrew Scahill, *The Revolting Child in Horror Film: Youth Rebellion and Queer Spectatorship* (New York: Palgrave Macmillan, 2015), Sarah Wright, *The Child in Spanish Cinema* (Manchester: Manchester University Press, 2016) and Stephanie Hemelryk Donald, *There's No Place Like Home: The Migrant Child in World Cinema* (London: I.B. Tauris, 2018). Edited collections include Debbie C. Olson and Andrew Scahill (eds), *Lost and Othered Children in Contemporary Cinema* (Washington, DC: Lexington Books, 2012), Debbie C. Olson (ed.), *Children in the Films of Alfred Hitchcock* (New York: Palgrave Macmillan, 2014) as well as many on different national cinemas, such as Carolina Rocha and Georgia Seminet (eds), *Screening Minors in Latin American Cinema* (Washington, DC: Lexington Books, 2014) and Stephanie Hemelryk Donald, Emma Wilson and Sarah Wright (eds), *Childhood and Nation in Contemporary World Cinema: Borders and Encounters* (London and New York: Bloomsbury Academic, 2017). There are also collections exploring both film and television for and about children; for instance, Casie Hermansson and Janet Zepernick (eds), *The Palgrave Handbook of Children's Film and Television* (New York: Palgrave Macmillan, 2019).
3. Chris Philo 'To go back up the side hill': memories, imaginations and reveries of childhood', *Children's Geographies*, vol. 1, no. 1 (2003), pp. 7–23.
4. For Deleuze and the child, see Anna Catherine Hickey-Moody, 'Deleuze's children', *Educational Philosophy and Theory*, vol. 45, no. 3 (2013), pp. 272–86. As an example of the use of 'transition' along with 'transdisciplinary', see Sandra Dinter and Ralf Schneider (eds), *Transdisciplinary Perspectives on Childhood in Contemporary*

Britain: Literature, Media and Society (London: Routledge, 2018); for transition as it relates to both the child and a historical 'transition', see Sarah Thomas, *Inhabiting the In-Between: Childhood and Cinema in Spain's Long Transition* (Toronto: University of Toronto Press, 2019); for work in which the child is conceived as 'liminal', see my *The Child in Film: Tears, Fears and Fairytales* (London: I.B. Tauris, 2010), and Linda C. Ehrlich, *The Films of Kore-eda Hirokazu: An Elemental Cinema* (New York: Palgrave Macmillan, 2019).

5 Long-term filming of children was employed (over the course of a year) in Hirokazu Kore-eda's film *Nobody Knows* (2004), over a five-year period in Michael Winterbottom's *Everyday* (2012) and over twelve years in Richard Linklater's *Boyhood* (2014). The documentary series, *Seven Up!* (Granada/BBC, 1964–) has filmed the same group of children, now adults, every seven years since the initial episodes, first broadcast by Granada TV in 1964.

6 Lee Edelman, 'Learning nothing: *Bad Education*', *differences: A Journal of Feminist Cultural Studies*, vol. 28, no. 1 (2017), pp. 124–73, p. 124.

7 Lewis Carroll, *Alice's Adventures in Wonderland and Through the Looking Glass: The Centenary Edition* (London: Penguin, 2003) first published as *Through the Looking-Glass, and What Alice Found There* (London: Macmillan, 1871).

8 The definitive examination of alliance of children, childhood and 'queerness' can be found in Kathryn Bond Stockton, *The Queer Child, or Growing Sideways in the Twentieth Century* (Durham, NC: Duke University Press, 2009).

9 Lee Edelman, *No Future: Queer Theory and the Death Drive* (Durham, NC: Duke University Press, 2004) p. 29.

10 Here I am conscious that I am echoing in a slightly different guise arguments first about the 'innocence' of the child initiated by James Kincaid in both his books, *Child-Loving: The Erotic Child and Victorian Literature* (London: Routledge, 1994) and his later book, *Erotic Innocence: The Culture of Child Molesting* (Durham, NC: Duke University Press, 1998).

11 Megan H. Glick, *Infrahumanisms: Science, Culture and the Making of Non/personhood* (Durham, NC: Duke University Press, 2018) p. 54.

12 Sasha Engelmann, 'Towards a poetics of air: sequencing and surfacing breath', *Transactions*, no. 40 (2015), pp. 430–44, p. 430; see also Derek P. McCormack, 'Aerostatic spacing: on things becoming lighter than air', *Transactions*, no. 34 (2009), pp. 25–41 and his book, *Atmospheric Things: On the Allure of Elemental Envelopment*, (Durham, NC: Duke University Press, 2018).

13 McCormack cites Jane Bennett, 'The force of things: steps to an ecology of matter', *Political Theory*, no. 32 (2004), pp. 347–72.

14 McCormack, 'Aerostatic spacing', p. 38.

15 The possibility of understanding and engaging with the world in this manner is aligned with Tim Ingold's work; see, for instance, his *The Perception of the Environment: Essays on Livelihood, Dwelling and Skill* (London: Routledge, 2000).

16 One version of this work in progress, 'Children, objects and motion... balloons, bikes, kites and tethered flight' is available as an audio recording along with the Powerpoint slides. These can be retrieved, thanks to the Leverhulme funded network, whose co-investigators (Sarah Wright, Stephanie Hemelryk Donald and Emma Wilson) organized the conference 'Childhood and Nation in World Cinema' at Royal Holloway, in London in 2018, https://backdoorbroadcasting.net/2016/04/karen-lury-children-objects-and-motion-balloons-bikes-kites-and-tethered-flight/ (accessed July 2021).

17 Derek McCormack, 'Devices for doing atmospheric things', in Philip Vannini (ed.), *Nonrepresentational Methodologies: Re-Envisioning Research* (London: Routledge, 2015), pp. 89–111, p. 102.

18 Gaston Bachelard, *The Poetics of Space*, trans. Maria Jolas (Boston, MA: Beacon Press, 1994).
19 Carolyn Steedman, *Strange Dislocations: Childhood and the Idea of Human Interiority 1780–1930* (Cambridge, MA: Harvard University Press, 1994).
20 For more on Bergala's pedagogy and responses to this (including my own critique) see the recording of a 2017 symposium held by the BFI in London, 'Alain Bergala: The Cinema Hypothesis', https://www.youtube.com/watch?v=C0H74quQWJ8 (accessed July 2021).
21 Alain Bergala, *The Cinema Hypothesis – Teaching Cinema in the Classroom and Beyond* (Vienna: Austrian Film Museum, 2016).

PART ONE

SPACE AND TIME

1 THE DREAM HOUSE

Amelie Hastie

The present tense is the one in which wishes are represented as fulfilled.
SIGMUND FREUD

Nights now I can sit in my living room alone, looking at the glass of the picture window, with the reflection of my body and the drink in my hand and the chair and the lamp beside me glaring flat and white back at me, and I am in no way as real in that room as I am in my memories of my wife and children.
BILLY, *THE SWEET HEREAFTER*[1]

Inhabited geometry

I have always loved nooks and crannies. They are perfect places for both hiding and displaying things, whether sacred or ordinary objects, or children small enough to burrow into them. They are places of sanctuary: a kind of house within a house. As a child, I both explored the nooks and crevices of houses and sometimes made my own, whether through my cupboard of miniatures or through composing new corners in my own space. In my bedroom, for instance, I had a giant closet with three doors: I could open the doors and form them to make an enclosed triangle, multiplying myself across the mirrors. When I imagine doing this now, I don't believe I stared at my own seeming infinite reflections for long but rather looked inwards, eyes almost closed, comforted by this tiny space where three corners met. I don't exactly remember what I daydreamed in these moments of reverie, though today I rather believe that I imagined being somewhere else, transported in and by this tiny space.

    Such imaginings and desires are hardly unusual for a child (and such acts of selective memory and forgetting are common for an adult). Children seek to duplicate or reimagine their own living spaces in other manners, sometimes in miniature and certainly in narrative form. The miniature object or the small space of a nook allow for both a means of possession and control as well as a projection of oneself into another world that's physically impossible to inhabit, at least for long. Films are like miniature worlds in this way. While as viewers we cannot order them ourselves, we might unconsciously imagine ourselves controlling their universes.[2] But of course we also cannot inhabit a film. It enters us more than we enter into it.

In *The Poetics of Space*, Gaston Bachelard understands the house as a space for dreaming. Corners are particularly fertile spaces for the imagination, he tells us. 'The corner is a haven that ensures us one of the things we prize most highly – immobility', Bachelard writes; 'We have to designate the space of our immobility by making it the space of our being.'[3] This is a way of saying 'I don't want to leave here. Let me inhabit this space forever.' Solitude also allows us, as 'corner-readers', the opportunity to see forgotten details – the things or dreams that might be overlooked or tucked away, lost in the crevices between the inside and outside, the past and the future.

Perhaps, then, cinema is more like a corner than a miniature world. The screen, after all, is made up of four corners – whether it's in a movie house or whether we watch it on a small screen in another abode. Those corners register an inside and an outside, a space between imagination and physical reality – all the more blurred because film, in the strictest sense, has its roots in physical reality. I want to take advantage of these corners and of 'corner reading' to think about both physical and imaginary houses of childhood in three narrative films: *Badlands*, *Ratcatcher*, and *The Sweet Hereafter*. Via a controlled, even restrained, exposition, each film narrates a trauma, explicitly or implicitly, from a child's point of view. Resonant moments in each also reveal a house that holds the child's memories but that also incites the child's imagination of the future. In this medium defined by mobility – *the moving image* – we can see how images of nooks and corners of houses invite us to dream of their own imaginary dwellers inhabiting those spaces forever. I want to home in on the details of the houses the children inhabit, paying attention to the crevices between reality, memory and fantasy in the films themselves.

Playing house

In Terrence Malick's 1973 film *Badlands* our protagonist and narrator, 14-year-old Holly, falls in love with the bad-boy Kit, and they decide to run away together. In an act of finality that begins their new life, Kit kills Holly's father and sets fire to her house. He begins by dousing the piano, then wildly throws gasoline atop the furniture throughout the perimeter of the living room. We briefly watch him continue through a hall towards another room and then cut to see Holly leaving the house with a box of treasures while Kit sets up a record player, the album spinning, telling his tale for the District Attorney to find – 'gamblin' for time', Holly tells us. He tosses a match to ignite the fire, then runs jig-jaggedly to the car. As Kit and Holly flee we stay with the burning house. The sequence in which her house burns haunts this essay, begetting my own reverie regarding the latter films.

First we see the flames beginning to engulf an old photograph of a child, and then we move through the house to see the fire surround other objects and furniture. The camera itself doesn't move: instead, our gaze shifts with each slow cut. The image holds still on various objects as the flames take flight around them: fallen dolls, Holly's bed, the doll's house in her room, her father dead on the floor. The space which contained her childhood and those things which measured and, indeed, constrained her age now topple, melt and burn.

It is the burning doll's house that particularly haunts me (Fig 1.1). At once terrifying and beautiful, it signifies the end of Holly's childhood, quite literally and doubly refusing a sense of immobility that would allow anyone to dwell in it forever. The burning house is liberating in its signal to start anew whilst simultaneously terrifying in the sense of loss that it invokes. The coincidence of beauty and terror and of loss and liberation is uncanny; in fact, its coincidence is in some ways definitive of the very essence of the term, itself based in a paradox. In his essay on 'The uncanny', Sigmund Freud traces the etymological origins of *heimlich* and *unheimlich*, ultimately noting that the former 'becomes increasingly ambivalent, until it finally merges with its antonym'.[4] Thus, in its act of destruction, the home begins its act of haunting the film, its characters and, as I suggest above, my own reading. Perhaps this is inevitable; as Freud tells us, 'in some modern languages the German phrase *ein unheimliches Haus* [an uncanny house] can be rendered only by the periphrasis "a haunted house"'.[5] As the flames engulf Holly's house, we stand in the moment of the present, between the past and future: we catch a glimpse both of what might have been and the possibility for something else, even as we know that something-else is also surely doomed. But at first, of course, this possibility persists; or at least the characters try to insist on a new possibility as the story goes on.

FIGURE 1.1 'The burning dollhouse'. *Badlands* directed by Terence Malick © Warner Bros. 1973. All Rights Reserved.

The loss of Holly's home and her house-within-a-house initiates a series of attempts for our characters to play house in other *unheimlich* spaces. First – and most elegiac – is the treehouse the runaways build. A fantastic structure fitted with pulleys and booby traps, Holly and Kit occupy it like storybook children and, perhaps inevitably, like an old married couple (as our narrator tells us). Such dual roles are not surprising. In 'The creative writer and daydreaming', Freud asserts that 'the child's play is governed by its desires, in fact by the one desire that contributes to its upbringing – the desire to be big and grown up'.[6] In their treehouse in the woods, they begin their days by coming up with a new password between them – a childish game of playing captives and spies – yet Holly also dons ladies' curlers and Kit shaves before a makeshift bathroom mirror as part of their morning ritual (Kit, after all, has entered adulthood, even as he acts impulsively like a child).[7] After their hideaway in the forest is discovered, the runaways first head to Kit's friend Cato's shack, and then they briefly take over a wealthy man's house, Kit stealing the man's hat and seersucker jacket, so that he is now dressing as well as performing the part of a grown-up.

The performance of adulthood resonates within Holly's narration, which throughout the film pointedly has the earnest sophistication of an adolescent who imagines herself older than she is. Her narration is therefore also like that of the children in Carolyn Steedman's study of children's storytelling in *The Tidy House*. Remarking on a fictional story that a group of schoolchildren wrote collaboratively, Steedman claims:

> The children's text is a *dramatisation* of the circumstances they describe, not to be confused with the narration of a particular event. For the children, the text asserted that they were *not* there, were *not* witnesses. It is as if, projected onto a screen, the events of the story take place *out there*, out of real time; and the children briefly watch them, involved and fascinated, considering them and perhaps denying that this will be their future, that they will have children they don't really want, and spend their days in irritation and regret.[8]

Steedman's remarks might also apply to Holly's narration throughout the film, but especially to one of the film's most poignant scenes, in which she looks at a series of images through her father's stereopticon. Over photographs of famous sites or of anonymous figures, which narrate the possibility of other spaces or events, she says,

> Where would I be this very moment if Kit had never met me, or killed anybody – this very moment – if my mom had never met my dad, if she'd never died? And what's the man I'll marry gonna look like? What's he doing right this minute? Is he thinking about me now, by some coincidence, even though he doesn't know me? Does it show on his face?

And after this revelation, Holly tells us, she lived in dread, fantasizing about being taking away to a 'magical land, and this never happened'. As Barbara Jane Brickman notes, 'In this one small interlude, we see the female teen simultaneously as spectator *and as* storyteller'[9] tying her further to the children in Steedman's work.[10]

But while Steedman suggests that the children had a sense of the function of narrative (which arguably Holly does here, too) – to 'objecti[fy], deny, and transmut[e]' – I want to consider these remarks as pertinent not just to children's written stories but also, as Steedman herself directs us here, to film: 'projected onto a screen, the events of the story take place *out there*, out of real time'. And here, of course, the corners return, as in this moment in *Badlands*, when Holly's daydreams over the images we share with her take us to another place and time. In the 'tidy house' of film, we are left to imagine that which seems possible, because it has its ontological foundation in the real, physical world. It is possible not just because we have lived in that world in some way, too, but also because through it we dream in and of another world.

Escape hatch

Lynne Ramsay's 1999 *Ratcatcher* lures us back into Malick's world. It takes place in 1973 during the garbage workers' strike in Glasgow, the year that *Badlands* was released, and it is also set in a similar aesthetic and emotional landscape as Malick's 1970s films (both of which, like Ramsay's work, are themselves placed in an earlier historical period). Like *Badlands*, *Ratcatcher* is grounded in a traumatic experience and the attempt to escape from it. The film begins with a staggeringly beautiful image: a white lace curtain is wrapped about a body that twists around slowly in the light of the window. But within a few minutes, this child, Ryan Quinn, drowns in the canal near his home, pushed in rough play by his friend James Gillespie. We remain with James for the rest of the film, silent witnesses to his part in his friend's death and, implicitly, to his own quiet guilt and grief.

James's family lives in council housing, garbage building up all around them, but they dream of a new home. It is on that dream that I wish to focus here. About a third of the way into the film, James hops on a bus, with the intention of finding out where his older sister secretly goes. Instead of finding her, he simply rides to the end of the line, where he almost magically comes upon a modern estate under construction. The ride itself is a kind of daydream, the film cutting between shots of the outside world passing by (the garbage beginning to recede as he gets deeper into the countryside), close-ups of James seated (doubled by his faint reflection in the window), and long shots of James standing in the aisle, as if he were not on a city bus but rather on a ferry, looking out at the sea before him. The bus enables a kind of immobility for its lone passenger, even as it moves through space itself. The inside of the bus appears perfectly still; this is, indeed, a safe passage.

Reality and imagination converge throughout the following scenes. In her BFI Film Classic volume on *Ratcatcher*, Annette Kuhn comments on just this convergence: as it integrates stillness and movement, the film 'draws on the indexical qualities of the photographic image to conjure a world that resembles the one we normally inhabit, and yet is at the same time self-evidently virtual'.[11] She notes shortly after that the film 'weaves together [...] several realities in an extraordinarily complex manner [... to] bring together and explore the relationships and rifts between outer and inner worlds, worlds of external reality and worlds of imagination and fantasy'.[12] These relationships are particularly resonant in those moments when James – and the film – encounters his dream house. Thus, when the bus finally stops and James disembarks, he walks away from it and towards us; the scene cuts mid-action, and suddenly James appears again, coming around a gate towards a building. He enters into what appears a kind of make-believe world but one, like the film, that is clearly grounded in reality.[13] In an act of play, the objects of this construction site fluidly become other things: James runs an obstacle course around a bunch of pipes, he stares through a giant tube as if it were a telescope, he rests on a set of scaffolding like a ship captain exploring the sea.

Once inside the house, he treats the unfinished space as if it were complete, the house where he luxuriously lives. He lies in the tub (covered in plastic), turns the un-plumbed faucet handles, pees in the unconnected toilet (then watches it seep out onto the floor). And why not dream here as if it is real – indeed, as if it is really his? For our fictional character, the unfinished house is like a materialized dream – or, from our point of view, the materialization of a film. All the pieces of the house are a part of physical reality, even if they are, for now, only representations of daily life. Like the children in Steedman's essay or Holly with her stereopticon, he watches this other story himself – the events take place 'out there, out of real time' – but he also enters into it as if it were his world. James here is what Bachelard calls a corner dweller: 'For to great dreamers of corners and holes nothing is ever empty, the dialectics of full and empty only correspond to two geometrical non-realities. The function of inhabiting constitutes the link between full and empty. A living creature fills an empty refuge, images inhabit, and all corners are haunted, if not inhabited.'[14]

This 'as if' is the very ontological, phenomenological, and, of course, technological premise of film. In the epilogue to his treatise of film's relation to physical reality, Siegfried Kracauer draws on the aesthetic theories of Alfred North Whitehead to describe our perception of art: our will towards experience. Kracauer writes, 'In experiencing an object, we not only broaden our knowledge of its diverse qualities but in a manner of speaking incorporate it into us so that we grasp its being and its dynamics from within – a sort of blood transfusion, as it were.' And he goes on, 'What we want, then, is to touch reality not only with the fingertips but to seize it and shake hands with it.'[15] In this scene from *Ratcatcher* before us, James seizes and shakes hands with the reality before him, the space itself – and the dream it encompasses for him – becoming incorporated into him. For Kracauer, of course, this is our potential (and ideal) experience of film: in its revelation of actual physical existence, moving in space and evolving through time, film invites our touch, even if we almost never move our actual bodies to attempt to shake its hand.

This dream house – both real and unreal – becomes increasingly parallel with the cinema (both the physical space and the film on the screen) as James moves through it. Thus, when he opens a door, we are situated inside as he pauses in the entrance, as if he is sneaking from behind the curtain to enter the screen. But it is also as if he is sneaking into a movie theatre. In fact, the film cuts from his act of looking to the 'screen' itself: a rectangular window frame without the pane inside, revealing an open field before it.[16] Here the outside world is literally framed by the dream house. James then climbs onto the window sill, swings his legs over the ledge, and stares into a field of wheat before he jumps through the empty window. At once he enters the film screen and abandons it for the real world, so that in this brief moment the two become – for us – one and the same. (As a nice twist on this simultaneity, in another neat, if avowedly unintended, nod to Terrence Malick, James seems to enter the very fields of *Days of Heaven*.) Once outside, the frame disappears, and James runs through the field before us with the sort of abandon we never see him experience in the rest of the film.[17]

Towards the end of the film, after a series of disquieting events, James returns to the house in the country, but the doors and windows are now locked. When he gets back home, the yard outside the tenements has been cleared by scabs working to break the strike. As James walks through the yard he eventually comes upon his friend Kenny, who sing-songs that he saw James kill Ryan Quinn. Kenny's pronouncement rings into the next scene, which opens with an image shot from above of James lying across the family sofa. The couch is wrapped in white and James's body is so still, the image briefly looks like a boy lying in a coffin. In a seemingly hypnogogic (or dreamlike) state, James's younger sister Anne Marie enters the room and joins him on the sofa, throwing her arm across his chest. James eventually embraces her as well, though quickly thereafter the scene cuts to one that echoes an image from earlier in the film, in which James replaces his mother's torn stockings over her big toe. From there we see him standing next to the canal where Ryan Quinn died (and where Kenny also nearly drowned). He removes his jacket and lightly jumps in. We watch the air bubbles on the surface of the water and then enter the water with him, witnessing his body float downwards. But as James's body continues down, the film cuts again: now we see his family and their friends walking across the field that James had earlier visited, transporting their possessions, seemingly on the way to their new home. At first James isn't visible, but the last shot in the field is of him, smiling towards the camera. And then it cuts again, back to James in the water, as the credits begin to roll.

In a fiction that ventures so close to reality – and one in which James himself experiences a kind of materialization of a cinematic dream – it's quite tempting to see this double ending as a form of ambiguity. Does he eventually leave the water and move with the family into their new home, or is this merely a fantasy as he drowns and thus ends his life? Ramsay herself claims that she meant for it to be 'ambiguous': 'It was meant to be a *dream*, well, not a dream – it's surrealistic. For me it was always that he's going down in the water and what is projected for him is like his fantasy.'[18] In spite of her initial claims of ambiguity, Ramsay actually suggests that there is a difference here between reality (James's death) and fantasy (what he imagines as he slips through the water). The fantasy provides a potentially happy ending for viewers, but given the bookends of James's sinking body, it's far less ambiguous than Ramsay (or other viewers) might suggest.[19] Perhaps, then, as with the convergence of '*heimlich*' merging with its antonym *unheimlich*, it's more accurate to call the ending *ambivalent* rather than ambiguous. The fantasy of a happy ending is briefly proffered to us, but it is markedly still a fantasy for us and for our primary character. In the end, however, I would suggest what is more important than the question of the film's ambiguity is the fact that we share a fantasy with the character James. And in that very shared fantasy between us, we the viewers can 'grasp its being and its dynamics from within'. In this way, images inhabit us.

Corner dwellers

While James occupies an empty dream house in *Ratcatcher*, the children of Atom Egoyan's 1997 *The Sweet Hereafter* daydream in the corners of their own homes. Adapted from Russell Banks's 1991 novel, Egoyan's film is the devastating story of a school bus crash that kills nearly all of its riders, save for 14-year-old Nicole and the bus driver Dolores.[20] Banks's novel, in which there are other survivors besides these two, is narrated by four of the central characters: Dolores, Billy Ansel (father of twins killed in the crash), Mitchell Stevens (the lawyer who attempts to organize victims to sue for compensation), and Nicole. Egoyan's adaptation retains these central voices, yet with the exception of Nicole's intermittent voice-over, he does so much less explicitly than in the novel; moreover, rather than following the organization of the four distinct narrations of the events (ending with a coda from Dolores's point of view), the film cuts across moments in time. This temporal structure not only elides a clear sense of chronological time, effectively refusing a stable conclusion to the story, but it also raises the question of what time, exactly, comprises the present. In a sense, rather than merely following a design of a clear diegetic past, present or future, the narrative's present coincides with our own present time of viewing. And in this present resides the possibility of what Bachelard might call the 'immobility' of time – the collapsing of dream and reality, memory and imagination.

To reveal this state of its being, I want to focus on one particular scene, which wends its way across other key moments in the film. Before we witness the bus accident – in fact, diegetically speaking, the night before it takes place – Nicole goes to Billy's house to babysit his twins, Jessica and Mason. Her arrival at his home is interrupted by a cut first to Billy in his gas station, playing guitar, and then to his assignation with his lover Risa, in room 11 of the Bide-a-Wile Motel, which Risa owns with her husband Wendell. As we return to Billy's house, Nicole is putting the children to bed, reading to them the story of *The Pied Piper*, a fairy tale that connects, through this scene, disparate parts of the film's narrative. The children's shared room is a nook of sorts, which is likely what draws me to it: each child has a twin bed tucked in a corner, and Nicole leans against a chest of drawers between them as she reads. In this way, the children 'take possession of a border or boundary zone in the house', as Karen Lury describes children's spaces in mid-century amateur films.[21] Together they occupy this corner of the house – a liminal space, as Lury would describe it or, as Bachelard might put it, a house within a house.

The scene begins with a full-screen image of the book itself – its title page and the one thereafter – as the story opens. We cut to the three children tucked away in their shared corner: the twins in their beds and Nicole against the dresser, with the window behind her. Both children look at her and listen, Jessica quietly leaning towards the end of her bed closest to Nicole, Mason in the middle of his, in an almost uncanny repose of sophisticated attention towards this girl he clearly loves. The camera moves continuously closer to Nicole – attending to her reading as do the children – initially without losing Mason or Jessica from the frame, who each briefly occupy a corner of the bottom of the screen. Nicole begins the book, at first interrupted by Mason's questions: 'What's a ditty?' and 'What's vermin?' As she answers and then goes on, the camera continues closer towards her, and the children disappear, though we hear them giggle and we see Nicole gesture to each as she reads. This shot of Nicole reading continues to be alternated with full-screen shots of pages of the book. We follow along with her, occupying her point of view in these moments. Then, as Nicole descends deeper into the book, Mason's questions become increasingly serious.

He interrupts once more, and this image of this little boy, tucked in a corner alongside a teddy bear, with a photograph of his dead mother behind him (Fig 1.2), fills the screen. 'Nicole?' 'Yes, Mason?' 'Can I sit beside you on the bus tomorrow?' Nicole asks whether he wouldn't rather sit at the back of the bus, where he can wave to his father, who follows behind them in his truck. No, he says, he wants to

FIGURE 1.2 Mason (Marc Donato) in *The Sweet Hereafter* directed by Atom Egoyan © Alliance Communications Corporation 1997. All Rights Reserved.

sit beside Nicole. And then he pauses for another question: 'Nicole, did the Pied Piper take the children away because he was mad the town didn't pay him?' 'That's right,' she answers. 'Well, if he knew magic, if he could get the children into the mountain, then why couldn't he use his magic pipe to make the town pay him for taking away the rats?' 'Because he wanted them to be punished.' 'So he was mean?' 'No, not mean,' and here Nicole pauses. 'Just very – very angry.' Nicole asks if she should keep reading. He replies yes, and we cut briefly to Jessica beginning to close her eyes on the other side of Nicole. And then we shift back to the motel room where Billy and Risa are in the quiet throes of passion.

The (non-diegetic) song, a cover of 'Courage', that plays while Billy's mouth moves across Risa's body is sung by Nicole/Sarah Polley. It continues to play as a bridge into the next scene, where Nicole is dressing in the hallway, the children now sleeping in their room. She swaps her jeans for a tight T-shirt dress, seeming to prepare for a date. I would argue that the connection between the initial two scenes – Nicole with the children and Billy with Risa – is not a means of sexualizing Nicole's relationship with the kids, though perhaps it is a means of suggesting a similar sort of affection between Billy and Risa to that which the three children share with one another. Both scenes are also, of course, ones of respite or sanctuary, allowing for a feeling of courage amidst foreboding sadness: in each, Nicole and Billy occupy corners of sorts – spaces of imagination or fantasy, spaces which briefly stop, or immobilize, time. What takes place shortly afterwards, after Nicole leaves Billy's house, however, is surely informed by the alternating scenes which come before it, complicated further by the now-atemporal sound bridge of Nicole reading the children's story. Nicole's 'date' is with her own father – who has already played this role in the opening scene of the film, presenting himself as more of teenage boyfriend or rockstar groupie than a dad. And though he drives his daughter home, he takes her instead to the barn behind the house.

As they step out of the car, her father Sam going ahead of her, Nicole pauses behind and the children's story begins again. Sam waits near the entrance to the barn and turns to look back at his daughter. She stands in the moonlight wrapped in a red blanket – resembling Red Riding Hood in her cape, thus offering another reference to a nightmarish fairy tale about children and their predators – while the narration of 'The Pied Piper' sets the scene. In fact, we return here to an image of the pages of the book: the children 'tripping and skipping, ran merrily after' the magical musician, with eerie music playing alongside Nicole's reading voice. Again, we see a shot of Nicole behind her father, who carries his guitar case as he walks towards the barn, and her reading voice softly echoes: 'When lo, as they reached the mountain-side, a wondrous portal opened wide, as if a cavern were suddenly hollowed, and the piper advanced, and the children followed.' Now father and daughter are inside the barn.

> When all were in and the mountain shut fast. Did I say all? No, one was lame. And could not dance the whole of the way. And in after years if you would

blame his sadness, he would say, 'It's dull in my town since my playmates left and I can't forget that I'm bereft of all the pleasant sights they see, which the piper also promised me'.

The story continues as we watch them settle into this candlelit scene – too tender, too intimate between father and daughter, which then becomes even more explicitly sexualized as Nicole's father kisses her.

This scene is confusing. Confusing because it seems to suggest some culpability on Nicole's part – her change into her pink T-shirt dress looks like part of an act of desire, for one, and the story read over the set of images notwithstanding, she seems a willing participant in this sexual fantasy when she leans into the kiss with her father. But of course the voice-over narration is hardly 'notwithstanding', for it is part of the very confusion of the scene; hypnotized by her own childish trust in her father's paternal authority, she follows when he beckons. (Banks's book is much clearer on this sexual abuse. There are no scenes of candlelight and tender kisses; rather, Nicole fears her father, knows what he is doing with her is wrong, and is caught in his trap, only to be released – as in the film – when she becomes paralysed from the accident.) And then, from the father's kiss, we cut to the bus on the snowy road and the terrifying accident that follows. Obviously the tale of the Pied Piper – which does not appear in Banks's novel – does double duty here: it is the story of Nicole's father and also the story of the bus, in which children are drawn into cavernous mountains, shut off from the world and, it seems, from childhood itself. With her playmates gone and her future altered, Nicole is left bereft. But drawn into her downstairs room after the crash, with a lock on the door that allows her to be shut off from the rest of the house, so is she also safe.

The Pied Piper returns at the end of the film, after Nicole gives a false deposition as part of Mitchell Stephens's organized suit with the townspeople. By claiming that Dolores the bus driver was going too fast, she effectively ends the lawsuits, eliminating the need for Billy Ansel to be deposed (and thus saving him from reliving the grief of the loss of his children before his eyes). Simultaneously, of course, Nicole is also punishing her father. But one look at Nicole and we know she is not mean, just 'very – very angry'. We leave this site of the deposition and turn to Mitch Stephens, whose plane ride to see his own troubled daughter – sometime in the future – has ended. Outside the airport, he sees Dolores boarding passengers on a hotel shuttle, and Nicole's voice returns. But now she is commenting directly on the scene of the film itself, with words drawn quite explicitly from the novel's final chapter (itself set in Dolores's voice, shortly after the deposition, in which the town watches a demolition derby together, cheering first the seeming destruction of Dolores's old station wagon and then its victory). Nicole's voice-over continues, as the scene shifts to Billy watching the school bus loaded on a truck, to be taken away. After Nicole announces that this is 'a town of people living in the sweet hereafter', we draw back again to *The Pied Piper*: 'where waters gushed and flowers grew and everything was strange and new. Everything was strange and new.' And now Nicole sits at the fairground where a whirling ride spins behind her; from this near close-up, we return again to Mason and Jessica's bedroom, at the moment when Nicole closes the book. She kisses the children, turns off their lights, and then heads into the hallway, standing before a window that lights her from the traffic passing outside. The film ends.

This house and its children, to which Nicole and the film return, leave us in another present tense. Perhaps this is the present tense 'in which wishes are fulfilled', as Freud tells us. The psychoanalyst's claim appears in his narration of a father's dream: his child has died, and he dreams that the child wakes him from sleep to announce that he is on fire: 'Father, don't you see I'm burning?' Freud tells us that the father then actually awakens to find that his dead child's arm has caught fire from a candle that has fallen on him. As frightening as it is, Freud offers us this dream as another case of wish-fulfilment: 'The dead child behaved in the dream like a living one: he himself warned his father, came to his bed, and caught him by the arm, just as he had probably done on an occasion in his life ... For the sake of the fulfillment of this wish the father prolonged his sleep by one moment.'[22] Freud compares this dream to a waking moment, perceived about a present incident, concluding, 'Thus dreams make use of the present tense in the same manner and by the same right as day-dreams. The present tense is the one in which wishes are represented as fulfilled.'

I believe that the conclusion of *The Sweet Hereafter*, a film about a nearly unspeakable tragedy, also fulfils a wish.[23] In the end, the children have returned to us; they occupy here not the past, but the present in our viewing. Is this to be conflated with the present-ness of memory (which is, by nature, of the past)? Perhaps, given that the final scene with the children follows Nicole's own beatific face at the fairground, seemingly at a moment after the accident. But if this is a fantasy in which Mason and Jessica are still alive – in fact, are merely sleeping in their beds after storytime – it is one that is very real in the images of the film, collapsing a sharp line between imagination and reality.[24] Banks's novel remarks on this blurred line (which is likely the origin of the blurriness in the film) in commentaries by both Billy and Mitch who have, albeit in different forms, lost their children. In fact, when Billy recounts the scene of the accident, he appears to be retelling the dream, or at least the wish, that Freud narrates about the father's burning child:

> we received one child after another from the divers and wrapped them in blankets and dispatched them on stretchers up the steep slope to the road and the waiting ambulances, as if by doing that I could somehow prolong this part of the nightmare and postpone waking up to what I knew would be the inescapable and endless reality of it.[25]

The film offers a version of this sensation for Billy: after identifying his children on stretchers, he turns and sees them laughing and playing, running in the snow.

In that scene, they are as real in that moment as living children, playing before us in our present witnessing of the film. Or in Mitchell Stephens's words, in relation to his own living but troubled daughter, 'It's the other child, the dreamed baby, the remembered one, that for a few lovely moments we think exists.'

I watch this film, on the edge of my seat, and I think, 'These children are still alive.' A wish fulfilled, they appear in the space and the image of the film before me, set in place by the four corners of the screen. Together, these corners make up a dream house of my own.

Epilogue

By looking across these three films, which arguably come together largely through my own interests or predilections than through consistent inherent connections between them, I wonder if writing this essay is my own act of daydreaming. And here I return to those three mirrors that surrounded me as a child. Building my own little sanctuary in my family's house, one might say I was retreating 'into myself'. But if my memory is right, and I did not just see the mirrors as reflecting myself, I might say the mirror could be like a screen – rather than the other way around. With my eyes turned away from myself, these were screens of other images, of a somewhere-else I would rather be. Therefore I might now imagine these three mirrors to screen one of each of the three films. Surrounded today by these mirror-screens, these films first take my place in the glass, and then they enter into me. And this is my blood transfusion.

Notes

1. Russell Banks, *The Sweet Hereafter* (New York: HarperCollins, 1991) p. 43.
2. This is a nod, of course, to the work of Christian Metz.
3. Gaston Bachelard, *The Poetics of Space*, trans. Maria Jolas (Boston, MA: Beacon Press, 1994) p. 137.
4. Sigmund Freud, *The Uncanny*, trans. David McClintock (London: Penguin Books, 2003) p. 134.
5. Ibid., p. 148.
6. Ibid., p. 27. This understanding of the play-acting within the film might also be informed and complicated by Karen Lury's discussion of 'acting and not-acting', as well as in relation to our knowledge of the actual age of the actors Sissy Spacek and Martin Sheen. See Lury, 'The impropriety of performance', in *The Child in Film: Tears, Fears and Fairy Tales* (New Brunswick: Rutgers University Press, 2010), pp. 145–89.
7. Karen Lury considers how amateur family films indicate how 'children apparently occupy the same places in the home as adults but they may experience and employ them differently — as else*where* and even as else*when*'. Lury, 'Halfway down the stairs: children's space in amateur family films from the 1930s to the 1960s', *Home Cultures: The Journal of Architecture, Design and Domestic Space*, vol. 10, no. 3 (2013), p. 271.
8. Carolyn Steedman, *Past Tenses: Essays on Writing, Autobiography and History* (London: Rivers Oram Press, 1992) p. 82 (emphasis in original). See also Carolyn Steedman, *The Tidy House: Little Girls Writing* (London: Virago, 1983).

9   Barbara Jane Brickman, 'Coming of age in the 70s: revision, fantasy and rage in the teen-girl *Badlands*', *Camera Obscura*, no. 66 (2007), p. 26.
10 Brickman goes on to suggest that 'the scene is expressing a female viewpoint and a female consciousness', which had not primarily been recognized in critical work preceding her own about Malick's film.
11 Annette Kuhn, *Ratcatcher* (London: Palgrave Macmillan, 2008) p. 12
12 Ibid., p. 18.
13 Kuhn remarks: 'Significantly, this place is figured as James's own discovery, its *mise-en-scène* the fulfilment of his desire.' Ibid., p. 61.
14 Bachelard, *The Poetics of Space*, p. 140.
15 Siegfried Kracauer, *Theory of Film: The Redemption of Physical Reality* (Princeton, NJ: Princeton University Press, 1997) p. 297.
16 See Pascal Bonitzer, 'Off-screen space', *Cahiers du cinéma*, nos 234/235 (1971/72).
17 Interestingly, the next scene shows James and his family in front of the television, watching Tom Jones; following this is a lengthy scene involving his friend Kenny, who ultimately sends his pet rat out of the window, tied to a balloon and headed to the moon. In the only purely fantastic sequence of the film, the rat appears actually to land there, accompanied by 'Gassenhauer' from Carl Orff's Schulwerk, a tune written for children also used in the score to *Badlands*, framing the building of the treehouse. Soon the scene shifts to a televised image of rats on the moon, which subsequently transforms into the 'snow' in the TV screen, with the screen itself coming into view in the film.
18 Kuhn, *Ratcatcher*, p. 86.
19 In his treatise on *The Fantastic*, Tzvetan Todorov sees the uncanny as that which can also be explained. He writes, 'The fantastic, we have seen, lasts only as long as a certain hesitation: a hesitation common to reader and character, who must decide whether or not what they perceive derives from "reality" as it exists in the common opinion. At the story's end, the reader makes a decision even if the character does not; he opts for one solution or the other, and thereby emerges the fantastic. If he decides that the laws of reality remain intact and permit an explanation of the phenomena described, we say that the work belongs to another genre: the uncanny.' Tzvetan Todorov, *The Fantastic: A Structural Approach to a Literary Genre*, trans. Richard Howard (Ithaca, NY: Cornell University Press, 1975) p. 41.
20 This is at once a very simple and a very complicated emotional film. It is quite literally about the grief of parents over the death of their children, but each loss also, as Lury puts it in her discussion of children and war films, 'stand[s] in for many deaths'. Lury, *The Child in Film*, p. 107.
21 Lury, 'Halfway down the stairs', p. 271.
22 Sigmund Freud, *The Interpretation of Dreams*, trans. James Strachey (New York: Avon Books, 1965) p. 548.
23 While I am describing a dream of the life rather than the death of the children, I would refer the reader to Vicky Lebeau's chapter on 'The child, from death', in her *Childhood and Cinema* (London: Reaktion Books, 2008) esp. pp. 136–7.
24 The scene also precedes Nicole's father's abuse of her.
25 Freud, *The Interpretation of Dreams*, p. 70.

2 CHILDREN'S RIGHT TO SPACE, PLACE AND HOME

Owain Jones

No, Mother, we're not moving. Nope, Nope
OLIVIA (Lorelei Linklater) in *Boyhood*
(Richard Linklater, 2014)

What might society (that is, modern, 'developed world' societies) look like if children had rights – or rather, if the rights that they do have, on paper – were fully actualized in their everyday life: in their home, neighbourhood and in their schooling? Another, follow-on question might be – should, or could, children have rights to place and home? Children (in some social classes in the developed world) do have rights. The United Nations Convention on the Rights of the Child is the most ratified UN treaty in history.[1] Some enlightened administrations are trying to enshrine children's right to play in all aspects of their governance: for example, see the Welsh Government's Play Sufficiency Duty, enacted in two stages – 2012 (assessment) and in 2014 (implementation of measures).[2] But what would it be like if children's *desires* – say, not to go to school; not to move house; to go out and associate and play unsupervised; to continue to live with their birth parents (or not); not to live in zones of conflict or ecological violence – were taken seriously as rights? What would the world look like then? If, in other words, children were 'put first' in society?[3]

This chapter was in part prompted by watching the film *Boyhood* (Richard Linklater, 2014). In one key early scene – when the mother of two children, one being the boy in question, is planning to move house in response to domestic tribulations (her separation from her partner, insufficient income and lack of career opportunities) – the boy's elder sister, Olivia, insists that she does not want to move.

I am a parent (of two boys, now adults). I am not saying that what children say they want is automatically right, and/or should be delivered as a right. But I feel to ask questions of how seriously children's aspirations should be heeded is helpful in understandings the conditions of both children's *and* adult lives, the interactions between them, as well as their spatial out-playings in everyday life. We (my partner and I) chose not to move home in the time between our children being conceived, born and leaving home as adults. We have been lucky insofar as circumstances have allowed us to do that. Across the world it is only too apparent that millions of families are forced to move and/or to split up. But it is also obvious that many families, or rather many parents/adults, choose to move home for a whole range of reasons: for the sake of their careers, or a change of setting, or in the pursuit of gain through house sale and purchase. The children, whatever their views, have to tag along.

Children's rights

Before we go any further, let us remind ourselves about some aspects of children rights as articulated by the UN. These do, after all, exert at least some force on society. For example, they explicitly underpin the aforementioned Play Sufficiency Measures implemented by the Welsh Government. Children's rights were enshrined in the UN Conventions on the Rights of the Child Charter (1989) and as stated, this is (or was) 'the most ratified human rights treaty in history'.[4] But I think this widespread ratification is partly lip service and easy to do, as the comeback for governments and adults is minimal despite the routine flouting of these rights. Indeed, this is symptomatic of what has been termed the adult-centrism of modern society. In fact, rights may be nominally or prescriptively bestowed often as a form of domination and entrenchment of power.[5] Having said that, the language of rights has to look good, or sound right and maybe there are genuine aspirational political sentiments here too.

Of the forty-five Articles in the Charter, I highlight four for the purposes of this discussion:

> Article 2 (non-discrimination). 'The Convention applies to every child without discrimination, whatever their ethnicity, gender, religion, language, abilities or any other status, whatever they think or say, whatever their family background'.

The convention is universal. *All* children's views should be heeded – *'whatever they think or say'*.

> Article 3 (best interests of the child). 'The best interests of the child must be a top priority in all decisions and actions that affect children'.

This immediately becomes highly problematic for all governments and any adult authorities making decisions that change society. It is difficult to think of any decision that does not have immediate or deferred impacts on children. For example, decisions about the economy; planning; foreign, welfare, transport or health policies.

> Article 12 (respect for the views of the child). 'Every child has the right to express their views, feelings and wishes in all matters affecting them, and to have their views considered and taken seriously. This right applies at all times,

for example during immigration proceedings, *housing decisions or the child's day-to-day home life*'.

(Emphasis added)

Housing decisions and the child's day-to-day home life are the key focus of this chapter. In the light of this right, what weight should be given to the heart-felt assertion of Olivia in *Boyhood* that she does not want to leave her home?

> Article 4 (implementation of the Convention). 'Governments must do all they can to make sure every child can enjoy their rights by creating systems and passing laws that promote and protect children's rights'.

The Welsh Government Play Sufficiency Measures represent an effort to do this in relation to children's rights to play. But, generally, this Article is not realistically implementable in the current context of our adult-centric forms of power.

Children, space and the importance of place and home

As set out above, it is recognized that place and home are key elements of children's lives and rights. Place and home are, of course, important to everybody insofar as we are bodies in space with all the affective, material and social ecology that emerge as part of this experience. But place, I suggest, is particularly important to children. For where they are born, and where and how they spend their first years, inevitably becomes the underpinning foundation of their affective ecology of becoming. Humans are creatures of memory and self-narrative that build through experience and time.[6]

The poet and critic Tom Paulin states, 'I believe there are primal, original landscapes of the imagination. Often they are the places in which we grew up and which remain important to us throughout adulthood.'[7] More recently, J. Douglas Porteous and Sandra E. Smith similarly suggest that

> Home is significant at all times in our lives, but particularly when we are children. Home is the centre, the mould, to family and friends; it is [*or should be*] our place in the community and the place where acculturation occurs. Feelings towards home include psychological territoriality, rootedness, a sense of security, irrational attachment, and refuge.[8]

And around the home is the locale, the home territory, or as Mike Pearson and Michael Shanks put it, 'the square mile' of one's first home.

> In our earliest years we know a patch of ground in a detail we will never know anywhere again – a site of discovery and putting names to things – people and

places – working with difference and similitude – favourite places, places to avoid – neighbours and their habits, gestures and stories – textures, smells – also of play, imagination, experiment – finding the best location for doing things – creating worlds under our own control, fantasy landscapes – a place of exaggeration and irrelevance, making rules and breaking rules … of learning to distinguish between 'do and 'don't do', of improvised response, rules of thumb.[9]

In the prize-winning novel, *So Long, See You Tomorrow*, author William Maxwell sets out just how central to the child's becoming is the rich, everyday fabric of home and what might happen if children are removed from it:

Whether they are part of home or home is part of them is not a question children are prepared to answer … Take away the pitcher and bowl, both of them dry and dusty. Take away the cow barn where the cats, sitting all in a row, wait with their mouths wide open for someone to squirt milk down their throats. Take away the horse barn too – the smell of hay and dust and horse piss and old sweat-stained leather, and the rain beating down on the plowed field beyond the open door. Take all this away and what have you done to him? In the face of deprivation so great, what is the use of asking him to go on being the boy he was? He might as well start life over again as some other boy instead.[10]

The poet and landscape writer Kathleen Jamie said she was jealous when a student told her that in the Shetland dialect there is a word for childhood/spiritual homelands – 'Bonhoga'.

I was envious, [I thought] I haven't got one, and I want one. And then I thought about it, and thought – there is nothing I can think of except the back lane where we played, behind the houses, and there is a particular old tyre tree at the bottom of the lane, and I thought – that tree, that was my Bonhoga.[11]

Whatever landscapes children are born into, and first grow up in, even if these landscapes, and the times of them, are very 'ordinary' such as that Jamie describes, or even if they leave much to be desired, children have the skills to *make the most of them*. And in turn this will mark children and enter their very being.

Even in zones of conflict, children find ways of becoming, and playing, becoming embedded in the ruins and in the paraphernalia of war. This is depicted in a range of films such as *Turtles Can Fly* (Bahman Ghobadi, 2004) and *The Grave of the FireFlies* (Isao Takahata, 1988). Of course, war can never benefit children in general terms, but it is testament to the striations of modern adult space – such as the city – that the disruptions of war can open it up for childhood, as described by Cloke and Jones in relation to the Second World War ruins of London as playground.[12]

The affective affordances of home for the otherness of children

I have suggested elsewhere[13] that childhood studies needs to a) engage with challenges of recognizing the 'otherness' of children, and b) do so through the lenses of the 'the affective turn'.[14] Although the concept of affect cannot and should not be pinned down to one clear definition or approach, it is clear that it encompasses all the richness of bodily being(s) in place, with the interplay of the senses, emotions, memory and materiality making the weave of what life actually is, moment to moment. A weave that is mostly invisible to the conscious self. Most of our mind–body functions, our relations of being in the world, physically and emotionally, are not easily known to us in thought or language. Research that is based upon representational accounts of thought and language alone therefore struggle to delve into this realm of affect. That is why the 'affective turn' demands research approaches that are 'non-representational'.[15] As Melissa Gregg and Gregory J. Seigworth put it, 'affect emerges out of muddy, unmediated, relatedness and not in some dialectical reconciliation of cleanly oppositional elements or primary units'.[16] I think the otherness of children is largely located in affective becoming, in differing sets of affective attunement to adults, and this can been seen in the way children move, play and interact with other things and beings (animals, people, toys and the materiality of space, such as the home and neighbourhood).

That is why film has an advantage here: it can show children's *bodies* in action. Glimpses of this kind of activity are shown in films such as *I Was Born But…* (Yasujiro Ozu, 1931) and in the remake *Good Morning* (1959) by the same director. Here the camera focuses on how children 'fidget' when sitting in chairs; how they move through the local environment; and their interest and delight in 'bodily functions' (e.g. farting); and the always (it seems) vexed interactions with often dismissive adult authority. Lury has also commented on the extent to which child actors' abilities to bring such behaviour to the screen is an element in the degree to which these performances are 'good' or represent the spirit of everyday childhood.[17]

In her article, 'Deleuze's children', Catherine Hickey-Moody employs Deleuze and Guattari to reflect further on the nature of the child's becoming

> Children are Spinozists. When Little Hans talks about a 'pee-pee-maker', he is referring not to an organ or an organic function but basically to a material, in other words, to an aggregate whose elements vary according to its connections, its relations of movement and rest, the different individuated assemblages it enters … Children's questions are poorly understood … they are not understood as question-machines; that is why indefinite articles play so important a role in their questions (*a* belly, *a* child, *a* horse, *a* chair, 'how is *a* person made?'). Spinozism is the becoming-child of the philosopher.[18]

Spinoza, as the quote implies, is one of the founding thinkers employed by affect theory. As Julie Henry suggests, he also addressed the challenges of the otherness between child and adult becoming. Henry concludes, for instance, that even though the

> change is so radical between being a child and being an adult, that it seems to be a real transformation, in the strong sense of the word: that is a mutation, a change from one form (and so a nature) to another ... becoming an adult can't involve destroying the child's form to replace it with a grown up form, even if the body and the mind of a child and of an adult seem to be incommensurable.[19]

In Hickey-Moody's essay, she further quotes Deleuze to demonstrate how the becoming of the child and their perceived otherness is spatial:

> Children never stop talking about what they are doing or trying to do: exploring milieus, by means of dynamic trajectories, and drawing up maps of them. The maps of these trajectories are essential to psychic activity.[20]

Importantly, this emphasis on the spatio-materiality of the child's becoming speaks to the affordances of home and home territory. This, for me, is what the filmic depiction of children's lives, the choreographing of figures in landscapes, can show.[21]

Movements in space: playing as being other

To add further support to this ongoing idea of the otherness of the child and the challenges to portraying their lives in film – and in academic research – I point to the suggestion by Sarah Scott, a writer on architecture and children, that 'children are a unique client [for architects] with heightened sensory needs, special scale considerations *and a totally different way of moving through and perceiving space to adults*'.[22] As previously stated, I am not convinced that such differences in (spatial) becomings have been fully appreciated in many areas of childhood studies. However, I do think some films have portrayed this quite movingly, for example Bryan Forbes's *Whistle Down the Wind* (1961). Here the children are seen in their own worlds, which are in part constructed by lying to adults and therefore as secret realms, while at the same time moving through Pearson and Shanks's concept of the 'square mile', moving through the landscape using hedges as cover and an old barn as a key space to the narrative.

I think *Boyhood* shows similar aspects of the affective otherness of childhood in play and its spatial outplaying. As I focus here on space rather than time, the much vaunted fact that the same actors were used to make the film over an eleven-year period (2002–13) is actually an irrelevant distraction of my reading of this film.

FIGURE 2.1 'In between spaces'. *Boyhood* directed by Richard Linklater © IFC Production 2014. All Rights Reserved.

There are a few shots in *Boyhood* which remind me of classic scenes which underpin the figure of the 'child in the environment' as featured in the books of Colin Ward (1970) and Robin Moore (1986).[23] For example, when Mason (the central boy protagonist) finds a space of solitude between a fence and the side of a house, the space is derelict or abandoned by adult power and thus becomes 'other space' for childhood becoming (Fig 2.1).[24]

The trouble with place and home

The fundamental problem facing the delivery of the rights of the child, and the wider suite of rights in the Charter, is that the modern world is overwhelmingly prioritized, scaled and ordered to adult agendas, ideologies and desires. This poses deep challenges to children's relationships to place. And within that overarching adult structuring, there are competing and conflicting sets of adult ideologies, which, in their battles, certainly do not put children first. Children have to fit into the adult patternings of society whether these are material, economic, cultural or political. Or they are forced into it, and through it, by all sorts of political, institutional, commercial and other means.

This raises a number of profound questions about children's experiences, children's rights, and how adult societies construct, instruct, coerce and oppress children and childhood; not least though systems of education.[25] As Ivan Illich states

> School has become the planned process which tools man for a planned world, the principal tool to trap man in man's trap. It is supposed to shape each man to

an adequate level for playing a part in this world game. Inexorably we cultivate, treat, produce, and school the world out of existence.[26]

The plight of children and young people is particularly sombre, in the light of the fact that adult orderings of the modern world are so often highly dysfunctional in social, political and ecological terms. Violence, injustice, degradation and 'cleansing' of rich cultural and biological ecologies are all too common.

As Felix Guattari suggests, the dominant powers of subjugation, embedded in capitalist systems and modernist world views, create conditions hostile not only to children but to human well-being more generally.

> In all its forms (family, school, factories, army, codes, discourse...) it continues to subjugate all desires, sexuality, and affects to the dictatorship of its totalitarian organization, founded on exploitation, property, male power, profit, productivity... Tirelessly it continues its dirty work of castrating, suppressing, torturing and dividing up our bodies in order to inscribe its laws on our flesh, in order to rivet our subconscious [into] its mechanisms for reproducing this system of enslavement.[27]

I add that this power has adult-centrism, as well as andro-centrism, at its core. Another aspect of modernity key to this discussion, and alluded to in relation to Article 12 above, is modernity's indifference or (at best) hostility to ideas and practices of place and home.[28] Places are expendable in relation to, and act as an impediment to, mobility, economic restructuring as well as military, ideological and economic imperialism. In considering this alliance between the adult-centrism of modernity and its associated hostility to place and home, we can see that quite a challenging picture for the well-being of children develops.

Moving home

A theme that rather jumped out at me from *Boyhood* – which has been nagging away at me for some time now, not least through film, and which might pertain to a reconstituted society *for* children – is therefore the idea of 'homeland', of 'rights to place' and particularly '*children's* right to place and home'. *Boyhood* revolves around three periods in Mason's (and his older sister Olivia's) lives, which are created by moves from one home to the next. These moves are precipitated, as is so often the case by marital/relationship breakdown and new partnering, domestic financial pressures and adults/parents seeking employment and/or looking to better their career or self-development.

The socio-spatial fabric of the children's lives, their affective terrains of becoming – represented by a sense of home, neighbourhood, peer group and school – are ripped up at each move. The children do not want to move – they express this very clearly and forcibly, especially during the first move when they are younger. In particular it is Mason's older, more voluble sister Olivia, who states on a number of occasions 'we are not moving'.

Although forcefully expressed, such statements do not register as objections that should be considered seriously by the parent and – one assumes, though less confidently, by those, presumably mostly adults, watching the narrative. Children have to fit into their parent(s)' lives. Home, from the parents' perspective is where *they* choose to live. Not a place in itself. Mobility is one of the hallmarks of modernity and as Leslie Van Gelder suggests 'contemporary western culture has discouraged people from maintaining articulating deep relationships with place. Few of us live in the homes we were raised in.'[29] Children therefore live within this adult modern world of 'mobility' – whether this is mobility afforded to highly resourced affluent adults moving regionally, nationally and internationally for the sake of career, power and so on, to adults who are forced to move due to conflict, economic and ecological violence and degradation. As such, our relations to home and our children's relations to home are more often in a state of rupture than continuity.

As an academic (geographer) of now some twenty years in the UK, I have witnessed the career paths of many other academic colleagues, both those with children and those without. Moving universities, cities, even countries, to secure a post and often simply a better post, is common. And I always wonder: did their children want to move? Is it just taken for granted that the parent's interests are paramount? Did these geographers consider the geographies of their children, apart from – perhaps – a careful scrutiny of the schools in the destination location? Beyond moving for career, moving home can also be for a process of financial/status advancement. At this point the home – 'homeland', the emotional ground of life, becomes a commodity insofar as the home becomes an asset for financial exchange and advancement in the adult world of self-fulfilment.[30]

A repeating motif in *Boyhood* is of the children looking back out of the car window as they leave what was their home and neighbourhood for the last time. On one occasion there is an explicit instruction from their mother that they 'don't look back', since they are, at that point, fleeing a violent stepfather. At the same time the audience understands that they are leaving step-siblings and a whole set of local relations. Yet, when the children are looking back – just what is it that they are leaving? Is it simply architecture, their own past, temporary siblings and their violent stepfather? Given that, as already set out, children learn and develop so quickly, developing fundamental capacities and characteristics in the early years of their life, it is likely that the local environment is also or perhaps even more a fundamental part of their mental/emotional ecology, whether this is the domestic home, the wider environment or their local peer group. In *Boyhood* when they move – as they inevitably do – there is nearly always a scene where they are loading up the car and leaving the house and garden (Fig 2.2). In the scenes of the first enforced move Olivia walks around the garden and porch saying 'goodbye' to many of the spaces and objects of their homeland, such as the yard, the crape myrtle and the mailbox.

FIGURE 2.2 Mason (Ellar Coltrane) in the car moving home. *Boyhood* directed by Richard Linklater © IFC Production 2014. All Rights Reserved.

Losing home

Sagas of children losing home, moving home and sometimes *finding* home in 'ordinary' (non-conflict) settings are themes in some other very striking films about childhood and family. In *Y aura-t-il de la neige à Noël /Will it Snow for Christmas?* (Sandrine Veysset, 1996), the home is 'lost' due to domestic sexual abuse. Other films such as *Le Havre* (Aki Kaurismäki, 2011), *In this World*, (Michael Winterbottom, 2002), *The Night of the Hunter* (Charles Laughton, 1955), along with *Turtles Can Fly* (Bahman Ghobadi, 2004) and *Grave of the Fireflies* (Isao Takahata, 1988) illustrate the harrowing disruption for children forced to move by conflict and abuse. Other films show children trying to maintain home in the face of both family and environmental challenges as in the *Beasts of the Southern Wild* (Benh Zeitlin, 2012). What is at stake and shown in these films is home and place as the ground of the child self, which in turn, becomes the adult self. In *Boyhood* each 'home' is only a place to be for a few years, enough to become embedded before being moved on again by adult agendas. Roots are put down – then pulled up – repeatedly. The destruction of home and place and the children's relationship with them is, I suggest, a key part of what Guattari calls the 'ecocide' of the three ecologies[31] – biological diversity, cultural diversity and individual psychic diversity.

The film *Home* (Ursula Meier, 2008) offers an interestingly provocative account of the disruption of home and its impact on children and family. It is very much a mundane story in terms of modernity, as it is about the building, and subsequent delayed opening, of a trunk road through some open agricultural land. Here home is lost not by enforced displacement of the family but by modernity crowding around the house and home. Husband and wife Michel and Marthe live with their three children in a house next to an uncompleted highway. The deserted road is a playground for cycling, inflatable pools and games in the sun. The road seems to be part of some forgotten development scheme, and the house has a feeling of tranquillity and privacy. The older teenage daughter is a fan of sunbathing and listening to music. One day, construction workers in high-visibility jackets appear out of the blue and move about the road, and it becomes obvious that the road is finally going to open. The home is much loved and the family feel that moving is not an option. The children are in the local school and the father has a job nearby. But the school and the father's employment are now on the other side of the very busy high-speed dual carriageway – with no crossing. The house, once a haven, is now permeated with traffic noise and vibrations, and the constant sense of strangers glancing through the windows and into the garden. The youngest daughter, Marion, becomes concerned about and then obsessed with the environmental consequences of the traffic pollution, monitoring the grass as it exhibits evidence of the effects of carbon monoxide emission. She becomes worried that the family will become ill, or even die from the pollution. The older daughter, Judith, continues to lead her life of sunbathing out on the front lawn in her bikini, despite attracting unwanted attention from passing motorists. One day she disappears – apparently picked up by one of the regular commuters. The remaining family members descend deeper into obsession and paranoia and the father bricks up the windows and seeks to soundproof the entire house. What the film demonstrates is the gradual unpicking of family cohesion and well-being for both the adults and the children who are under siege from the architecture of mobility and capitalism.[32]

Conclusions: children's right to place and home?

If you Google 'children's right to place' or similar phrases (with quotation marks), *you get no meaningful results*. That is how obscure this idea currently is. There are quite active 'rights to stay put' movements in the developing and developed world, for example, in relation to communities being evicted directly, or pushed out more insidiously, by planning and gentrification, in the face of regeneration, redevelopment in relation to large-scale sports events such as the Olympics, Commonwealth Games or the Football World Cup, but these are not particularly 'child focused'.[33] The trouble with 'human rights' and within them 'children's rights', as currently articulated, is that they are *nation-state* based. This is not surprising as they emanate from the United Nations in the first place. It is the nation-state we supposedly have rights to in terms of our security and in terms of belonging and identity. Yet there is often a great distance in scale, culture and politics between the nation-state, home and local territory. And, of course, the modern nation-state is a relatively recent, highly problematic, internally and externally violent spatio-political unit, built upon the destruction of local places. The nation-state-based rights of children suffer most badly when states become contested and or highly dysfunctional, as is only too obvious today.

In this context, Porteous and Smith assert the significance of 'domicide' – the 'destruction of home' – stating that 'the meaningfulness of domicide resides in the probability that home is central to our lives and the likelihood that the forcible destruction of it by powerful authorities will result in suffering on the part of the home dweller'.[34]

Therefore, rather than focusing on its temporal ingenuity, from a materialist and spatial perspective in which children's right to place is foregrounded, *Boyhood* can be seen to be about the children's efforts to develop their socio-geographical life in a series of new 'homes'.

Notes

1. See Helen Brocklehurst, 'Kids "R" us? Children as political bodies', *International Journal of Politics and Ethics*, vol. 3, no. 1 (2003), pp. 79–92.
2. See, for example, 'Play Wales' in 2015.
3. See Penelope Leach, *Children First: What Society Must Do – and Is not Doing – For Children Today* (London: Random House, 1994).
4. See Brocklehurst, 'Kids "R" us?', p. 1.
5. See Nicola Perugini and Neve Gordon, *The Human Right to Dominate* (Oxford: Oxford University Press, 2015).
6. See Owain Jones and Joanne Garde-Hansen (eds), *Geography and Memory: Explorations in Identity, Place and Becoming* (Basingstoke: Palgrave Macmillan, 2012).
7. Cited in Suzy Smith (ed.), *Country Living: My Country Childhood* (London: Coronet Books, 1999) p. 137.
8. J. Douglas Porteous and Sandra E. Smith, *Domicide: The Global Destruction of Home* (Montreal: McGill-Queen's Press, 2001) p. 63.
9. Mike Pearson and Michael Shanks, *Theatre/Archaeology: Disciplinary Dialogues* (New York: Routledge, 2005) pp. 138–9.
10. William Maxwell, *So Long, See You Tomorrow* (London: Vintage Books, 1996) p. 113.
11. Kathleen Jamie, speaking on *The Echo Chamber*, BBC Radio 4, 3 January 2016.
12. See Paul Cloke and Owain Jones, 'Unclaimed territory: childhood and disordered space(s)', *Social & Cultural Geography*, vol. 6, no. 3 (2005), pp. 311–31.
13. See Owain Jones, '"True geography [] quickly forgotten, giving away to an adult-imagined universe". Approaching the otherness of childhood', *Children's Geographies*, vol. 8, no. 2 (2008), pp. 195–212.
14. See Melissa Gregg and Gregory J. Seigworth, *The Affect Theory Reader* (Durham, NC: Duke University Press, 2010).
15. See Nigel Thrift, *Non-representational Theory: Space, Politics, Affect* (London: Routledge, 2007).
16. Gregg and Seigworth, *The Affect Theory Reader*, p. 4.
17. See Karen Lury, 'The involuntary dance: child actors, fidgeting and authenticity', in B. Henzler and W. Pauleit (eds), *Childhood, Cinema and Film Aesthetics* (Berlin: Bertz + Fischer, 2018), pp. 85–100.

18 Gilles Deleuze and Felix Guattari, *A Thousand Plateaus: Capitalism and Schizophrenia*, trans. B. Massumi (London: Athlone Press, 1988) p. 256, as quoted in Anna Catherine Hickey-Moody, 'Deleuze's children', *Educational Philosophy and Theory*, vol. 45, no. 3 (2013), p. 272 (emphasis added).
19 Julie Henry, 'The philosophical figure of the child. Descartes, Spinoza', 1. Paper presented to Lors du Scottish Seminar of Early Modern Philosophy, https://www.academia.edu/5526936/The_philosophical_Figure_of_the_Child._Descartes_Spinoza (accessed 7 October 2016).
20 Gilles Deleuze 'What children say' in D. Smith and M.A. Greco, (trans.), *Essays Critical and Clinical* (Minneapolis, MN: University of Minnesota Press, 1997), p. 61.
21 It is harder for children to express their affective becoming if home and place are lost to them, or hostile to them. A striking feature of the film *The Other Bank* (George Ovashvili, 2009) is that the child protagonist, Tedo, is often portrayed sitting still, staring. In this instance, the mobile, affective bodily becoming is curtailed by the trauma of conflict and displacement.
22 Sarah Scott, *Architecture for Children* (Camberwell, Vic. Australia: ACER Press, 2010), p. 191.
23 Colin Ward, *The Child in the City* (London: Pantheon Books, 1978); Robin C. Moore, *Childhood's Domain: Play and Place in Child Development* (Beckenham: Croom Helm, 1986).
24 See Cloke and Jones, 'Unclaimed territory' for a wider discussion on children and disordered space.
25 John Holt, *Escape From Childhood: The Needs and Rights of Children* (New York: E.P. Dutton, 1974).
26 Ivan Illich, *Deschooling Society* (New York: Harper & Row, 1971), p. 77.
27 Felix Guattari, *Soft Subversions* (New York: Semiotext(e), 1996), p. 29.
28 See Edward S. Casey, *Getting Back into Place: Towards a Renewed Understanding of the Place-World* (Bloomington, IN: Indiana University Press, 1993), and *The Fate of Place: A Philosophical History* (London: University of California Press, 1998); J. Douglas Porteous, 'Topocide: the annihilation of place', in John Eyles and David M. Smith (eds), *Qualitative Methods in Human Geography* (Cambridge: Polity Press, 1988), pp. 75–93; as well as Porteous and Smith, *Domicide*.
29 Leslie Van Gelder, *Weaving a Way Home: A Personal Journey Exploring Place and Story* (Ann Arbor, MI: University of Michigan Press, 2008), p. 4.
30 Writers such as Christina Hardyment have questioned this very forthrightly in relation to the child's well-being and rights. See Christina Hardyment, *Dream Babies: Childcare Advice from John Locke to Gina Ford* (London: Frances Lincoln Publishers, 2007).
31 See Felix Guattari, *The Three Ecologies* (New York: Semiotext(e), 2000).
32 I should add that I grew up on a farm: a family house that was compulsorily purchased for the development of large housing estates. Our entire family had to move, but we lived in the farmhouse while the farmstead, fields and what was a rural landscape were bulldozed and replaced by a suburban landscape. I was in my teenage years when that happened. I know what it is like to lose one's home forcibly. I suppose that memory informs this chapter.
33 See http://www.gamesmonitor.org.uk/ (accessed 28 July 2020).
34 Porteous and Smith, *Domicide*.

3 SYNCHRONY IN THE WORK OF HAYAO MIYAZAKI

Robert Maslen

Adults and children live in different time zones, their internal watches set by different clocks, their days constructed around alternative timetables. The question of how to communicate across the temporal divide is confronted daily by parents and offspring, teachers and pupils, at school and in the home, and is intensified in a work of art made for children. Such works are usually created by adults, whose principal challenge – how to imagine themselves into a frame of mind they inhabited years beforehand – is complicated by the problem of keeping track of the rapidly shifting cultural reference points among young people. Living in a household with children may help the would-be creator tune in to the latest developments in social media, music, gadgetry and fashion, but it is likely too to reinforce the conviction that adults can never *really* understand what makes youngsters tick. In the struggle to communicate despite this lack of understanding, artists fall back on imaginative reconstructions of their own childhoods in the vain hope that the radical changes of the intervening decades have not rendered them wholly redundant, or distorted them beyond redemption with overlays of sentiment and cliché. Such reconstructions invariably emphasize the chronological gap even as they seek to bridge it. And they often take as their subject – as the driving motor of their narratives, so to speak – the complex interplay between time zones that constitutes any given cultural or social environment in each successive generation.

The filmmaker Hayao Miyazaki is particularly concerned with this interplay of time zones, both within the communities he represents on film and among the projected audiences for his movies. Miyazaki has often stressed his belief that animated movies were originally 'created for children',[1] and he often identifies, in his interviews and writings, the precise age of the children each of his films is primarily intended to address. He is also interested in the question of how targeting a particular age group will affect other potential viewers. His original pitch for the 1986 movie *Laputa: Castle in the Sky* goes into detail on this point:

> By focusing mainly on fourth graders (the year when the number of cells in a child's brain reaches that of an adult), it will reach an audience of even younger children, and expand even further its age appeal. I am certain that hundreds

of thousands of older anime fans will come to see this film no matter what, so there is no need to overtly cater to their tastes. There is also a large, latent audience of older viewers who yearn for a film to enjoy with a more naïve, childlike spirit. The future of animation is threatened by the fact that for most films being planned today the target age is gradually creeping upwards … [*Laputa*] is a project to bring animation back to its roots.[2]

In this passage, the time zones of the various age groups that make up the film's audience are represented as both distinct and overlapping. The crucial age of the Japanese fourth-grader – nine or ten – is the point at which the brain has achieved its full physical development, making available a capacious internal space to be stocked with the wealth of experiences undergone by the subject as child, adolescent and adult over the course of a lifetime. The development of younger children points forward to this moment of cerebral maturity, making them eager to share as far as they can in the activities of their fourth-grade seniors. Meanwhile adults of all ages look back nostalgically on the fourth-grade moment as the point when their experiences – of film, among other things – were at their freshest and most exciting. The point here is not whether Miyazaki paints an accurate picture of his audience's encounter with his projected movie, but the impression he gives of the auditorium as a complex web of experiences governed both by the constantly shifting dynamics of biological development and by distinct but overlapping perspectives on the object of attention, variously oriented towards past, present or future. This auditorium has much in common with the social spaces and communities Miyazaki constructs in his films, except that here the presence of multiple perspectives shaped by different chronologies invariably triggers some form of crisis. The question of how different age groups can successfully live together, of how their distinct chronologies can be synchronized, is in many cases the central problem explored by his films.

My Neighbour Totoro (1988) is a case in point. Set in the 1950s Japan of Miyazaki's youth, the film recounts the adventures of two young girls and their father who have been forced to relocate to an old house in the country, near a hospital where the children's mother is being treated for a life-threatening illness.[3] The house turns out to be occupied by *kami*, spirits that can only be seen by children; yet it is the father who explains the spirits' identity, recalling his own encounters with the spirit world in his childhood, despite the fact that he is excluded from it now by the demands imposed on his time by his job as an academic.[4] Meanwhile the spirits provide a conduit between the children and the cyclical time zone of the other growing things among which the spirits live: from the gigantic camphor tree where the titular troll-spirit, Totoro, hides in daytime, to the trees the children plant at night with Totoro's help in the grounds of their new home, to the freshly-picked corncob they leave as a gift for their mother at the end of the movie, whose miraculous appearance on the hospital windowsill helps the sick woman recognize that she is on the road to recovery. Social time, spirit time and the cyclical time of the natural world operate side by side throughout the narrative, sometimes at odds, sometimes coming together; and the necessity that drives the plot is to achieve synchrony between these different time zones – to find a way for them to work together for the good of the human community and the ailing body of the children's mother.

The encounter between the three principal time zones in the movie is enriched by smaller chronological differences between the characters. The little girl Mei, for instance, experiences the passage of time quite differently from her big sister or her father. Her first encounter with the spirits takes place while her sister is at school and her father working at his desk. Mei plays outside as her father works, and her detachment from the regulated schedule of work and education is indicated by her wish to eat lunch in the middle of the morning. At this point in the movie only Mei occupies the imaginative and geographical vantage point that enables her to see the pair of tubby spirits who come trundling through the grass as she is playing, drifting between visibility and invisibility like daydreams and leading her to the giant being who lives inside the camphor tree, whom she promptly names Totoro. Her lack of a formal timetable gives her leisure to follow the spirits to Totoro's sleeping place, just as her lack of prejudice concerning Totoro's possibly threatening nature enables her to embrace his companionship, to occupy his space as if it were her own. The problem in the rest of the film for the other people who share Mei's home – in particular her elder sister Satsuki, who is growing out of the sorts of fantasies that dominate early childhood – is that they must learn how to synchronize themselves with her time zone, for a while at least, unlearning the sense of urgency that has been instilled in them by work, education and the imminence of death for long enough to share her vision.

Satsuki learns to do this as a result of a disruption to her regimented daily schedule. One evening she finds that her father left his umbrella behind when he went to work. It is raining, so she decides to go and meet him with it at the bus stop. She and Mei wait at the stop till dark, growing increasingly uneasy as the shadows lengthen and their father fails to arrive. Rain falls, night falls, and Mei falls asleep on Satsuki's back. The uneven dripping of water replaces the ticking of human clocks, signalling the girls' entry into an alternative time zone. Abruptly Satsuki notices Totoro standing beside her, sheltering from the rain under the inadequate protection of a leaf. She lends him her umbrella, which he accepts – though less for its intended function than for the pleasure of the sound of the rain drumming on the fabric. Soon afterwards a bus arrives; but it is not the petrol-driven machine the girls expect. Instead it is the celebrated cat-bus which furnishes one of the film's most famous images: a tabby twelve-legged vehicle whose ribcage opens to admit passengers into its fur-lined interior, and whose journeys display a cat's contempt for conventional roads and pathways, a preference for telegraph wires over carriageways, for fields and hedges over tarmac.[5] The cat-bus veers away into the night carrying Totoro, and soon an ordinary bus looms out of the darkness, with the father safely on board.

The fusion of cat and bus in the hybrid creature known as the cat-bus seems specifically calculated to conjure up the notion of what might be called synchrony: the fruitful combining of different time zones – different ways of measuring or experiencing time – in the household or elsewhere, to enable successful dialogue or other forms of social interaction.[6] Cats are domestic pets which notoriously ignore the rigid spatial and temporal structures of the human household. Buses knit the family home to the socially significant destinations of work and school, operating to a structured timetable and unchanging routes; they are inextricably linked with the notion of accurate timekeeping, even when they run late. Combining cats with buses gives you a form of public transport that ignores timetables, turning up when least expected and cutting across the regulated rural geography to reach not a place of work or education, but the object of its passengers' desires. And there is another fusion here too. Cats make a great show of being solitary yet inhabit human communities, while buses serve those communities unambiguously. The cat-bus, with its slightly menacing Cheshire-cat grin, is clearly singular – nothing like it has existed or been drawn before; yet it also supplies a collective need, in this case both transporting Totoro to his unknown destination and heralding the restoration of the father to his children, a return to the safe routine of family life, a timetable that has been under threat since the beginning of the film because of the mother's absence. The individual and the collective, human, animal and spirit, all are fused in this hybrid creature, whose impeccably timed appearances draw these categories together in the face of fear.

It is not surprising, then, that the cat-bus should show up again when the little family and its routine come under threat for a second time. On this occasion it is the girls' sick mother who fails to come home on a scheduled visit. She catches cold and is told to stay in hospital, an incident that conjures up the spectre of a permanent dissolution of the family unit by the mother's death. Fear for her mother makes Satsuki lose her temper with Mei, who then sets out on an unscheduled cross-country journey of her own to take her mother what she thinks of as a healing corncob. Mei's disappearance sparks off a frantic search by the whole of the local community, and drives Satsuki to ask for Totoro's help at his tree. The troll's response is to summon the cat-bus, which first takes Satsuki to Mei, then transports both girls to the hospital, where they leave the corncob on their mother's windowsill. More even than in the bus-stop incident, this journey connects all the time zones of the story – adult and child, human and spirit, urban and rural – much as a cat connects the human and natural worlds in its comings and goings, or a bus connects place to place within a city, and city to country within a nation. The cat-bus itself is part public transport vehicle, part spirit, part maternal womb, and its successful marriage of these elements anticipates the eventual reunion of parents with children, and of Satsuki's family with the rural community, both of which are celebrated in the evocative stills that accompany the film's end credits, where the human characters we have come to know are watched over by Totoro and his benevolent fellow spirits.

Part of the power of *My Neighbour Totoro* springs from its recognition that the ability to occupy any particular time zone – above all that of childhood, with its ready recognition of the interaction between seen and unseen, humans and spirits – will necessarily be a temporary one, and that its transitory quality need not be perceived as frightening or repugnant. At the end of the movie Satsuki's parents still cannot see the spirits, even though they have received material confirmation of their presence in the form of the corncob, which appears where it could not possibly be, inscribed with a message from Mei. It is clear, too, that Satsuki will soon move on to occupy her parents' time zone. Her awkward but friendly relationship with the boy next door anticipates her approaching puberty, just as the boy's grandmother, who seems to remember her childhood more vividly than most grown-ups, foreshadows the girls' old age. Even the stills of the final credits, which recall snapshots from a family album, remind an adult audience, at least, that they have been watching a historical reconstruction, a cartoon representation of the filmmaker's past, no longer accessible except through photographs, films and drawings. Owing to the pressures of twentieth-century life – above all its mobility, as embodied in the luggage-laden car that opened the film – moments of synchrony are fleeting, though their impact on those who experience them may be lifelong, as the very existence of *My Neighbour Totoro* testifies.

A few years after *Totoro*, Miyazaki explored the concept of synchrony from another angle in his script for Yoshifumi Kondo's movie *Whisper of the Heart* (1995), based on the manga by Aoi Hiiragi. Here the protagonist Shizuku at 14 or so is a few years older than Satsuki, and attending Junior High. Where Satsuki needed to achieve synchrony with her neighbours – her sister, the boy next door, the spirit Totoro – Shizuku's problem is that of finding a neighbourhood at all in a world where urban sprawl has broken up long-standing communities.

The same theme was developed by Miyazaki's colleague Isao Takahata in his immensely successful film of the previous year, *Pom Poko* (1994), which is set in the suburb of Tokyo where Shizuku lives, Tama New Town. In *Pom Poko*, raccoon dogs or *tanuki* fight against the incursions of suburban development on their territory; but their resistance is futile, and the *tanuki* end the film by using their traditional powers of metamorphosis to merge themselves with the city's population, walking among men and women in human form. For Takahata, then, Tama New Town consists of two time zones superimposed on one another: that of the old land and its animal cultures, in defence of which the *tanuki* fought, and that of the new suburbs, where human beings dwell unknowingly side by side with the region's aboriginal population. The coexistence of these two time zones in the suburbs is an example not of synchrony but colonization, even at the poignant moment towards the end of the film when the *tanuki* use their powers to give the audience a fleeting retrospective glimpse of the rural landscape that underlies the urban. By the time we get this glimpse, however, human culture has effectively supplanted *tanuki* culture, consigning it to the past like a ghost or a half-forgotten folktale; reconciliation between the time zones of people and animals may be possible, but this film does not offer a clear indication of how it might be achieved.

In *Whisper of the Heart*, Shizuku's human and animal neighbours, despite cohabiting with her and her family in the same suburban space, turn out to be separated from her by time, much as the *tanuki* are forever separated from their human colonists. Shizuku has to look for them in the spaces and times that open up in her official timetable; and for much of the time, without her being aware, she is abetted in this by her eccentric family. Their tiny apartment, squeezed into a hillside block in the new suburb, resembles a book-crammed annexe of the library where her father works. Here Shizuku's parents give her elbow-room to dream and write, while her schoolmates, such as her best friend Yuko, are sent off to the notorious Japanese cram schools to achieve the grades they need to attend the best high schools. Throughout the summer vacation Shizuku either works at home or explores her neighbourhood, scurrying up hidden alleyways and clambering over locked gates marked 'no entry' in pursuit of stories and ideas. Her wanderings are accompanied by the ceaseless buzzing of the summer cicadas, playing music from a hidden insect world ignored by the city's residents but full of emotional resonance for lovers of Miyazaki's earlier movie, *Nausicaa of the Valley of the Wind* (1984), whose protagonist communicated with the insects shunned by the rest of her community.

In *Whisper of the Heart*, the first clue to the existence of other neighbours besides the insects – neighbours of the heart, as the English title suggests[7] – occurs when Shizuku discovers, from library stamps, that someone in her school has been borrowing the same books as her, though at different times. The mysterious reader turns out to be a boy called Seiji, who is in another class and therefore separated from her geographically as well as chronologically, occupying a different section of the school building. She finds him with the help of a cat, an independent sharer of human space like the cat-bus in *Totoro*. In *Whisper*, too, the cat is linked with public transport; indeed, it is in a sense a public cat, ownerless and known by different names to different people, so that it plays a role in a range of stories throughout the city, connecting disconnected lives, as it were, with its amiable presence. Shizuku first meets the cat on a commuter train, following it on a whim when it alights at her station. The animal leads her to an old shop full of bric-a-brac from different periods and places, the 'World Emporium', a cheerful jumble of clocks and statues and furniture which has been assembled at random over the course of its owner's lifetime, making the shop an embodiment of synchrony. Here she runs into two figures who might equally be said to embody synchrony: the owner himself, an old man called Nishi who she later learns is Seiji's grandfather; and a small statue of a cat with coat-tails and a walking stick, which Nishi calls the Baron. It is in this shop, and in relation to the story of the cat statue, that Shizuku learns about the importance of synchrony in the late twentieth century.

The cat statue stands, among other things, for the arbitrary fracturing of relationships by history in the century's turbulent middle years. There was once a female counterpart for the Baron, a statue known as Louisa; and Shizuku learns that the woman Nishi loved, also called Louisa, bought the Louisa statue in Vienna on the day Nishi bought the Baron. The lovers were then driven apart by the outbreak of the Second World War – an event as calamitous for Louisa's people, the Europeans, as for Nishi's, the Japanese. Nishi and Louisa swore to reunite their statues – and each other – after the war; but the opportunity never arose, and the couple never met again. From then on the Baron has represented the brief moment of serendipity that brought two people of different cultures together for a little while at a time of chaos; a moment that may never be repeated.

Another object in the shop that catches Shizuku's eye is a clock Nishi has been working on, with the figure of an armoured prince on the clock face gazing soulfully up at a window. The person the knight longs to see at the window is his lover, a fairy princess; but the clock is so constructed that the lovers only glimpse each other twice a day, when the clock strikes twelve. In fact, when Shizuku sees the clock they have not seen each other for many years. The clock's mechanism was broken, and Nishi has just finished repairing it so that the two figures can again become a symbol for the complex workings of life and love, showing that lovers, like neighbours in a modern suburb, may only coincide at certain moments, when the pressures of work and history permit (the prince in the clock is a working man, the prince of the miner-dwarves who inhabit its belly). Nishi's labour on the clock confirms something else: that such intersections can themselves be brought about by hard work, and that waiting for synchrony to occur without labouring to fulfil one's desires may well be futile.

As the film goes on, Shizuku and Seiji – the girl and boy who read the same books at different times – are transformed into the working prince and princess, as it were, of Tama New Town, victims of the common twentieth-century condition of being out of synch, despite their mutual attraction. Seiji's ambition is to work as a violin-maker, for which he must serve a demanding apprenticeship in far-off Italy. Shizuku's dream is to work as a novelist. The young pair's aspirations are incompatible both with their budding relationship and with the rigorous demands of the Japanese school system. Seiji cannot find out if he has the talent to become an apprentice if he stays at school; Shizuku cannot try her hand at fiction if she works hard enough to get good grades. The solution, it would seem, is for them to pursue their chosen pathways simultaneously, apart from school and apart from each other, labouring to advance their artistic dreams in different locations. When they meet in Nishi's shop, Seiji is about to leave for a three-month trial period of violin-making in Italy, which if successful will be followed by a much longer apprenticeship. On hearing his plans, Shizuku decides to write her first novel while he is away, regardless of her studies and grades, aiming to complete the narrative by the day of Seiji's return. Seiji's absence is thereby transformed into a clockwork mechanism, a fragile chronometric device that counts out the hours until the moment the young people can get together to compare their experiences. Separated in time and space, the boy and girl will be united imaginatively through their work and through their awareness of the approaching moment when the cogs of the world's workings will reunite them.

This moment, when it comes, is marked both by further hard work and a scrupulous attention to good timing. Shizuku wakes before dawn one morning to find Seiji waiting below her bedroom window – the most perfect example of synchrony in the film (Seiji calls it a 'miracle'). He invites her to mount his bike behind him, then cycles up a steep hill to a nearby viewpoint from which the city of Tokyo can be seen spread out below. At one point during the climb Shizuku dismounts and helps push the bike, determined to do an equal part in the labour that will get them to the place they are aiming for. The pair arrive just as dawn is breaking, transforming the misty urban sprawl into a magical flooded world a little like the surreal landscape Shizuku has created in her novel. As the young couple journey to this place where perfect timing will bring beauty to the landscape, background music plays on strings and woodwind, invoking an earlier moment when Shizuku sang a song to Seiji's accompaniment and they were joined unexpectedly by Nishi and two elderly friends, who provided additional accompaniment on the antique instruments they happened to have with them. At the moment when Seiji shows Shizuku the vision of a transfigured Tokyo, the song they played together on that earlier occasion begins again; it is John Denver's 'Country Roads Take Me Home', itself transfigured by new lyrics written by Shizuku. All the different chronologies in the movie converge in time and space, harmonizing like the different instrumental parts in a musical performance, and the young couple are inspired to exchange a promise of marriage that will ensure similar moments of convergence take place many times in the future.

The miraculous transformation of West Tokyo in this scene, as witnessed by Shizuku and Seiji – its fusion with the fantastic landscape Shizuku invented for her novel, a novel she could only write with the support of Nishi, Seiji and her parents – extends the possibility of creativity throughout the community. The film's credit sequence underscores this extension of creative synchrony by recording the passage of many people – schoolchildren, old folk, workers, dog walkers, cyclists, joggers – along an anonymous stretch of road not far from the viewpoint. Trotting along beside the human passers-by is the mysterious cat who brought Seiji and Shizuku together. The audience knows that this cat has been endowed with different names and different imagined narratives by every individual who comes across it in its daily wanderings. It is a perfect symbol, then, of how the creative imagination draws together diversity into a dynamic, constantly changing unity. And it helps too to suggest how the relationship between the children has finally brought about a happy ending for all the interwoven stories they have encountered on the road through the movie's narrative: the stories of the older couple who met before the war, the prince and the princess on the clock, the feline statues known as Louisa and the Baron. The notion of synchrony between generations, between members of a local community, and between the imagined and the real, has never been more richly conjured up on screen than in this closing sequence.

Almost a decade after *Whisper of the Heart*, Miyazaki returned to the theme of synchrony in his second film of the new millennium, *Howl's Moving Castle* (2004). The film is based on a novel for children by the British author Diana Wynne Jones, whose concern with the complex chronology of domestic and other communities, where the time zones of the young, the middle-aged and the old converge and clash, is evident throughout her work. This concern is present from her early novels *Seven Days of Luke* (1975) and *Dogsbody* (1975), in which the lives of immortal beings (gods and stars) intersect with those of children, to *The Homeward Bounders* (1981), whose young protagonist finds himself ageing at a slower rate than his contemporaries, and *Fire and Hemlock* (1985), about the friendship between a young girl and a man, which alters little by little as the girl grows to adulthood.[8] Wynne Jones's version of *Howl* represents synchrony not merely as a prerequisite for the successful cohabitation of different generations within the same building or society, but as a psychological condition achieved with difficulty by individual men and women, aspects of whose personalities develop or mature at different rates, thus effectively establishing different time zones within a single mind and body. It is this perception, among other things, that seems to have drawn Miyazaki to the novel, as permitting a new departure in his lifelong exploration of temporal interfaces in domestic and social space.

The protagonist of Wynne Jones's novel is a teenage girl, Sophie Hatter, who lets herself be seduced by the rules of fairy tale into believing that her destiny is predetermined by her position as the eldest daughter in a family. This conviction comes easily to her because she lives in the land of Ingary, 'where such things as seven-league boots and cloaks of invisibility really exist' – a land of fairy tale in action, where witches are as common as bakers.[9] Since she is the eldest child, so the tales affirm, nothing interesting can ever happen to her: it is always the youngest child who sets off on adventures and wins all the prizes. In addition, her sole surviving parent is a stepmother, who Sophie assumes must therefore be tyrannous, if not wicked. As a result, Sophie's lifelong entrapment in the family hat-making business (which she does not enjoy) is for her as certain as if she had already lived through it, and she behaves and dresses as if she were already the elderly spinster she expects to be. Thus when she is transformed into a real old woman by a jealous witch, who has mistaken her for one of her attractive younger sisters (an early indication that order of birth need have no effect on a person's identity), Sophie embraces her new condition with enthusiasm. Before the transformation she was in effect an old woman trapped in a young girl's body, after it she is a young girl trapped in an old woman's body; since her life and story are now effectively over, she leaves the hat-making business and wanders out into the world to seek her fortune. But the world – and the old women who play their part in it – prove to be very much less predictable in their movements than her enslavement to fairy-tale convention has led her to expect; and the delightful metaphor for this unpredictability is the Moving Castle of the title.

Coming across the Castle by accident, Sophie discovers in it a peculiar all-male household quite unlike the 'conventional' nuclear family (if such a thing exists, which Wynne Jones would have us doubt). The family is composed of the teenager Michael, an apprentice wizard; Calcifer, a stubborn but friendly fire-demon, whose magic keeps the Castle moving; and the wizard Howl himself, a dashing charmer whose one aim in life is to dodge the responsibility to which Sophie has always been a willing slave – hence his possession of this unusual mobile home. Incorporating Sophie, these four housemates span a tremendous age range, from the apprentice, who is 15, to the demon, who has lived for millennia. But they are none of them restricted in their movements by their apparent or actual ages. In financial matters Michael behaves with a responsibility beyond his years, keeping some of the household money hidden from Howl to prevent him from wasting it. Calcifer is as dependent on the other members of the household as an infant, confined to the Castle's only hearth like a baby to its crib. Howl behaves like a spoiled adolescent, obsessed with his appearance and refusing to let Sophie clean his room. Sophie, who makes herself Howl's housekeeper because she cannot imagine herself capable of anything more, becomes increasingly energetic as the novel goes on, despite her extreme old age: dashing across the landscape in seven-league boots, plotting to foil Howl's various affairs, and rearranging the Castle so extensively that it eventually becomes her own home – quite literally so, in fact, since Howl moves the building into the hat-shop at one point to avoid the unwanted attentions of the Witch of the Waste. Each occupant of the Moving Castle encompasses more than one time zone in his or her personality, like a miniature model of a household, and the spell that governs Sophie is only the most obvious example in the book of the link between the individual body or mind and the multi-generational domestic space.

Age, in Wynne Jones's Moving Castle, is in part a matter of attitude. Even the physical strength of individual housemates' bodies varies as much in response to hormones, cold germs and lashings of self-pity as to the motions of the heart. The movement of time can easily have little effect on a person's character; it is not time that induces emotional or intellectual maturity, but successful interaction with other people, a capacity to adapt one's personal needs to the demands of a community (and to *resist* those demands, of course, when they become oppressive). Synchrony, then, for Wynne Jones, is a matter of careful and prolonged negotiation, enabling competing narratives and attitudes to achieve compatibility, to coexist. Frequent setbacks and digressions prevent the negotiating process from becoming either consistent or linear. Her book – like most of her books – is a celebration of domestic negotiation as a form of perpetual motion, repeatedly disrupting the pace and direction of conventional chronologies.

The identities of the Castle's four eccentric tenants are as flexible as their ages. Michael disguises himself as a red-bearded man, or as a horse, every time he leaves the building. Calcifer, in his capacity as (quite literally) the heart and hearth of the Castle, changes the building's appearance as well as its location with his demonic powers. Sophie successively takes on the roles of Howl's assistant, his aunt, his mother, and (eventually) his partner, as the book goes on. And Howl has a different name and role in each community he visits. The Castle's magical front door opens on a range of locations depending on the opener's wishes: Kingsbury, Porthaven, Market Chipping, and (oddly) modern Wales; and in each place Howl has a distinct identity: as reluctant royal wizard, well-intentioned local magician, demonized ladykiller, or idle waster, all of them with alternative costumes and reputations as well as names. These conflicting roles of Howl's converge and overlap in the interior of the Castle, so that it provides an active illustration of the sheer dynamism of the domestic space to which Sophie has willingly confined herself. All political and social action, all adventure, all identity originates in the creative melting-pot of the household, and the relationships between householders are always changing; responding to and influencing the changes that take place in the world beyond. Nobody can ever be fixed, the Castle implies, in any given role, whether by age, gender, birth or any other factor – unless the community they inhabit, the household and the society it is part of, and above all their own state of mind, exert all their energy to imprison them in a single unchanging function, like the clockwork prince and princess in *Whisper of the Heart*. No one character dominates the household; control of the Moving Castle alternates between Howl and Sophie, with Michael and Calcifer taking the reins when the need arises. And the shape of the community is always changing, as new members join the strange little family through Sophie's influence. It is a political as well as temporal interface, a functional democracy, where the needs, pleasures and pains of old and new inhabitants succeed one another as the focus of attention. The notion of domestic democracy, or democratic domesticity, is another thing that seems to have attracted Miyazaki to the novel when he chose to adapt it for what was slated – at the time – to be his final film, his swansong to the animation industry and the century in which he was born.

    Miyazaki's film has been described as less an adaptation than a reimagining, synchronizing the novelist's concerns with the director's through a series of daring shifts away from Wynne Jones's storyline towards a set of themes that have engaged Miyazaki for years. The problem of age remains at the centre of the narrative. Once again Sophie's premature old age is balanced by Howl's over-extended childhood, and the central problem is how to synchronize their ages, enabling them to cohabit in the Castle of the title. The problem could be said to represent the plight of an ageing filmmaker as he seeks to engage the attention of much younger viewers – the problem with which this essay began. But in addition, the two time zones that converge in each of Miyazaki's central characters – youth and elderliness, adolescence and maturity – become symptomatic of a pervasive dualism that extends through every aspect of their environment. Miyazaki's changes to the novel highlight the way the problem of synchronizing the household, of enabling the many chronologies and time zones that occupy domestic space to work fruitfully together, provides a miniature working model of the problem of synchrony that also confronts the millennial world.

The principal dualism in the film is a sociopolitical one, concerning the two alternative futures towards which Ingary may be moving: as a bright, colourful, mutually supportive community dedicated to the arts of peace, or a dark, war-ravaged wasteland, the energies of whose inhabitants are directed at mutual destruction. Suspended between these possible future destinies, the Ingary of the film is an in-between place, drawing on historical sources that look two ways. The setting of the movie, for instance, is an alternative turn-of-the-century Europe, where a pastoral landscape of mountains and flower-strewn valleys is at the same time overshadowed by smoke-spewing industrial chimneys and half-monstrous, half-comic flying gunships. The model for this landscape is Alsace, the disputed border territory between France and Germany that found itself caught at the epicentre of two world wars.[10] The machines that move around this landscape – from flying kayaks to steam-driven trams and the bomb-filled gunship-zeppelins that patrol the skies – derive from the work of the visionary French artist Albert Robida (1848–1926), who became famous in the 1880s for his exuberant illustrations of technology as he imagined it would evolve in the coming century.[11] Every visual detail of the film, then, looks in two directions, to war and to peace, to the past and the future, so that the competition between ages fought out within Howl and Sophie serves as a miniature enactment of the competition over alternative destinies being fought out in the world around them. And the Moving Castle becomes an embodiment of all these dualisms. Its erratic movements recall the jerky progress of a turn-of-the-century nation towards cataclysm or prosperity, towards life or death; in fact towards both, since the film's adult audience is conscious that both life and death will dominate the war-torn century they have just emerged from.

Our first view of this building comes with the opening credits, and it is a very different structure from the tall, chimney-shaped fortress of the novel. Mounted on four metal chicken-legs, Miyazaki's Castle resembles the hen-footed hut of Baba Yaga the Russian witch, an ambiguous figure who is either child-eater or magical helper, depending on the storyteller's whim. Its appearance points, then, to the centrality of ambiguous witches and other women in the narrative, whose apparent ages constantly fluctuate in response to internal or external pressures. The surface of the Castle bristles with gun turrets and rural cottages, as if to highlight the two opposite conditions towards which it may be moving, the military and the cosily domestic (Fig 3.1). The castle's internal and external appearance changes as the film goes on, much like the appearances of its various occupants, and these physical changes reflect the dominance of one or other tendency – the military or the domestic – at any given moment in Miyazaki's narrative.

The most significant change Miyazaki makes to the novel, then, is to place war at his movie's heart, and to embody its centrality in the eccentric mobile fortress. The other crucial change is to the film's antagonist, who in the novel is clearly

FIGURE 3.1 A 'mobile home'. *Howl's Moving Castle* directed by Hayao Miyazaki © Buena Vista Home Entertainment 2004. All Rights Reserved.

identified as the Witch of the Waste. The movie splits this antagonist in two, much as it splits nearly everything else into pairs of opposites. The Witch of the Waste starts out as the principal villain, as she is in the book: a towering, fleshy presence who conjures Sophie into decrepitude in a spontaneous fit of jealousy. But a third of the way through the film the Witch herself is stricken down with the curse of old age by a more powerful sorceress, Madame Suliman, and spends the rest of the film adjusting to her new position as the oldest member of the community that inhabits Miyazaki's version of the Moving Castle. The Witch's entrapment in the second childhood of senility fulfils the destiny she intended for Sophie – restricted to a time of life that renders her socially powerless – and contrasts with Sophie's refusal to be limited to a single time zone, a single understanding of her social and domestic role as an elderly woman.

The Witch's successor as the film's antagonist is the sorceress Suliman, Howl's former tutor in the magic arts. A more potent user of magic than either the Witch or Howl, Suliman deploys her formidable talents in the service of Ingary – or so she claims – in the combined roles of spymaster, bomber command and military general. She is eager to secure her most promising pupil as her servant and perhaps her successor in all these capacities. Her character, then, combines aspects of Miss Pentstemmon (Wynne Jones's benevolent version of Howl's old tutor), and the novel's Witch of the Waste, who wished to fix Howl in unchanging form as her puppet husband. Unlike Miss Pentstemmon and Wynne Jones's Witch, however, Madam Suliman wishes to fix Howl as a permanent child rather than a husband, just one among the host of identical pageboys who wait on her at the royal palace of Ingary. These boys look like younger versions of the wizard, and their unquestioning obedience and uniform prettiness makes them resemble toys;

clockwork toys, perhaps, or the sets of identical toy soldiers given to schoolboys in the nineteenth century as an encouragement to emulate a soldier's obedience, smartness and uniformity.

The threat posed by Suliman, then, is that of fixing the film's protagonists, Howl and Sophie, at a time of life and (more importantly) in a state of mind over which she can exert absolute control. She wants to arrest them, so to speak, as she arrested the Witch of the Waste, at a point in their physical and emotional development when they are utterly helpless except when acting on her orders. The playful mutability of the housemates in the Moving Castle poses a threat to Suliman's version of playfulness, which seeks to make other people her rigid playthings to be manipulated – or animated - as she wishes. From this point of view it is interesting to note that Miyazaki places her in a wheelchair, as if to highlight her own relative lack of mobility – and perhaps to suggest a motive for her desire to impose ever greater restrictions on her subjects' movements. In adopting this mindset Suliman sets herself at the opposite philosophical pole from Sophie – whose name balances hers as a synonym for wisdom (Suliman is a version of Solomon, the wisest of biblical monarchs, while Sophie's name derives from the Greek for wisdom). Where Suliman is all about constraint and imprisonment, Sophie is concerned with liberation and energetic drive, setting free the scarecrow Turnip (for instance) from the various scrapes in which he becomes caught, and working to free Howl from the calamitous military time zone in which Suliman is concerned to trap him.

It is at the precise moment when Suliman takes over from the Witch of the Waste as the *éminence grise* propelling the world towards a military destiny that Sophie finds a new role for herself as Suliman's principal opponent. She signals this transformation by posing as Howl's mother when she visits the sorceress to present the wizard's excuses for not joining her in the war she has chosen to orchestrate. By offering these excuses Sophie aims to protect the wizard's independence, which comes across as adolescent petulance and irresponsibility. Howl's other would-be mother, Suliman herself, wishes only to preserve him in pre-pubescent conformity and dependence. For the rest of the film the two women compete for possession of the wizard's heart, which is hidden in the hearth of the Castle and guarded by Calcifer (as in the book). Between them they stand for alternative versions of his destiny, either as imperialist warmonger or affectionate family member; and the richness of the film consists in its implicit acknowledgement that the historic moment at which he lives – at the turn of a new age when domesticity will need urgent and continuous protection from the threat of violence – means that he could well end up as both.

In this competition between powerful women, the imperialist war orchestrated by Suliman comes across as a children's game played by adults for the highest of stakes. At the end of the film Suliman draws attention to the unsettling childishness behind her plotting when she tells her pageboys: 'Let's put an end to this idiotic war.'[12] The statement implies that she could have ended the conflict at any point in the preceding action, and failed to do so only to forestall the ravages of boredom. By this stage, however, the movie's audience has long been aware of the 'idiotic' nature of her war game – that is, to its irrationality – thanks to the impossibility of determining which 'side' is being supported by which of its combatants, or even whether opposite sides exist at all. Just as the ages of the characters in the film exist in a constant state of flux, so too are they always changing sides in a conflict the causes of which are unknown and the objectives of which can never be guessed at. The faceless, tar-coloured 'blob men' who begin as henchmen of the Witch of the Waste seem to switch allegiance halfway through, hiring themselves out to Suliman after her defeat of their former mistress at the royal palace.[13] When the defeated Witch moves into Howl's Moving Castle – the fortress of her former enemy – so too does the asthmatic dog Heen, which started out as Suliman's spy but ends up as the cheerful playmate of Howl's apprentice Merkl (a much younger version of Wynne Jones's Michael). Meanwhile, Sophie's stepmother becomes Suliman's new spy, delivering a 'spy-worm' to the Moving Castle under pretence of a family reunion with her long-lost stepdaughter. Another member of Howl's household, the scarecrow Turnip, turns out in the end to have been an enchanted prince from the neighbouring country with which Ingary is at war – and once restored to human shape he promptly agrees to tell his compatriots to stop fighting. Howl himself at one stage states that it makes no difference whether he is attacking Ingarian or enemy gunships with his magic. The arbitrariness of these sudden shifts of allegiance transforms the war into a chaotic playground brawl, locking the entire cast – and by extension the country of Ingary – into a particularly grim variety of childishness from which they find it increasingly hard to extract themselves. Moving into the maturity of synchronized living is more challenging in *Howl's Moving Castle* than anywhere else in Miyazaki's oeuvre.

The most disturbing ambiguity of affiliation in Suliman's war is that of the blob men. The servants of Madame Suliman, they might be expected to form part of Ingary's army, and indeed when they attack the Moving Castle at a late stage in the action they are wearing Ingarian military uniforms. But at other times they wear civilian clothes – top hats or boaters, Venetian masks and elegant suits – some of which they share with the vicious winged monsters who emerge from the bellies of the flying gunships when they are bombing Ingary. Madame Suliman, then, seems to be fighting on both sides of the conflict she presides over. She is sinisterly irresponsible, indulging a second childhood in old age – like the Witch of the Waste – as she conducts the affairs of the country from her padded wheelchair in a flower-filled conservatory, surrounded by children. Her malicious variety of playfulness is encapsulated in the circle of dancing star-spirits that appears every time she casts a spell on rival magic-workers, entrapping them one by one – first the Witch, then Howl – in the shape that best suits her war game. Yet even Suliman does not come across as a mere monster; she is too humorous, too complex and too attractive to be despised or feared. Her body, like Howl's and Sophie's, or like Ingary itself, is a space where diverse elements converge, each in turn becoming dominant as she wearies of the game she has been playing and moves on to a new one.

War itself slips between identities as the film goes on, changing successively from game to nightmare, to game, in response to the changing moods of its conductors. At the beginning it is a carnival, a form of collective entertainment for the citizens of Ingary, whose lives are filled with toys: fancy hats from Sophie's hat-shop, fancy cakes from the bakery where her sister works, national flags, charmingly silly steam-driven vehicles. The fighting is conducted by dashing soldiers in colourful uniforms, post-adolescent show-offs who steer clockwork kayaks around the sky like teenagers in sports cars. At the harbour the civilians celebrate, with infantile enthusiasm, the deployment of the national fleet. Sophie's own stepmother adds to the air of flippant collusion with warfare by wearing a hat decorated with cannon in honour of the navy's dreadnoughts. At first, then, war is full of light and colour, but it soon grows dark and violent, swallowed up in the bomb-torn night whose reds and blacks threaten, by the end, to dominate the movie's palette. Lightness, then, and light are capable of giving birth to heaviness and gloom; playfulness can become cataclysmically destructive; and in this, war follows the trajectory along which Suliman is keen to steer her pupil Howl.[14]

From the beginning of the film Howl shares Suliman's moral ambiguity, though at first this comes across as an overgrown teenager's resistance to being pinned down. Rumour has it that the wizard devours the hearts of the girls he seduces; yet he makes his first appearance in a very different role, rescuing Sophie from the clutches of a pair of soldiers by leaping lightly with her into the sky, then parading through the air above her home town with the insouciant flamboyance of a born show-off. Even at this point, however, he is a source of danger as well as pleasure, since he is pursued by blob men who pose more of a threat to Sophie than the soldiers did. Not long afterwards, Sophie undergoes her transformation at the hands of the Witch and joins Howl's household. But here his moral ambiguity only becomes more obvious, along with his tendency to veer between mature competence and teenage irresponsibility. When Sophie starts to clean up after him in her capacity as his self-appointed mother, she accidentally switches the blond and black hair dyes in his bathroom; and the transformation of Howl's hair from blond to black signals his potential to transform himself from hero to villain, like a cowboy changing hats. This prospective switch of moral allegiance is foreshadowed by his reaction to the hair-dye incident. Howl goes into a titanic adolescent sulk, during which he generates both huge quantities of green slime, as in the novel, and a host of shadow-monsters closely resembling the blob men. This extravagant reaction, with its echoes of the sinister sorcery of the Witch and Suliman, is rendered more disturbing by the fact that immediately before this scene we witnessed Howl in action for the first time against the invading air force; an experience he seems to take far more lightly than Sophie's assault on his cosmetics.

Howl's adolescent lightness, then – his excessive concern for his appearance and the pleasures of flirtation – represents the flip side of his increasingly frequent forays into the darkness of Suliman's war. If young boys are the perfect recruits for a nation's armies, Howl's insistence on retaining his adolescent traits – his filthy, toy-strewn bedroom; the 'secret garden' of his childhood, which he claims to be protecting when he fights;[15] his love of fancy clothes – render him vulnerable to Suliman's efforts to draw him into her war games. The connection between his boyish lightness and his attraction to war is made most vividly when he shows Sophie the secret garden. At this point he looks much younger than he does elsewhere in the film, gesturing towards flowers and mountains with wide-eyed enthusiasm; but the appearance of a flying gunship prompts him to begin the change into a winged monster, a demon of combat which smiles as it launches a magical attack on the gunship with one claw-like hand. The monster and the boy cohabit in Howl, both of them symptoms of his heartlessness – that is, his staunch defence of his emotional secrets, his carapace of bright insouciance, from external assault. If the literally light-hearted Calcifer guards Howl's heart in the hearth of the Castle, safely hidden from intruders, it is for Sophie to lend him the weight he needs to launch into a mature relationship.

Sophie, on the other hand, needs to achieve synchrony with Howl if she is to escape the weight of self-inflicted anxiety that binds her to an aged body. Their first meeting shows her what is missing from her life as a teenaged girl: the lightness Howl possesses in abundance. Wearing her trademark sombre clothes and unflattering hat, she timidly skirts the carnival crowds as she crosses the city, dodging into shadowy back streets to avoid the limelight. It is in one of these alleys that Howl rescues her from the soldiers, before saving her a second time, this time from the blob men, by launching them both into the air without the aid of wings. The second rescue visually acts out the light-heartedness of first love in an echo of a celebrated scene from *Whisper of the Heart*.[16] It is not surprising, then, that after this Sophie continues to see Howl as the carefree young man of this first meeting, and that she works, as he grows steadily darker and more monstrous under Suliman's influence, to align the chaotic interior of his Castle with the brightness of his first appearance. In the process she discovers lightness and colour in herself, which are reflected in the light and colour she brings to Howl's shabby domicile – as well as in her increasingly frequent physical shifts between old age and youth. For a woman burdened with an overdeveloped sense of responsibility and wedded to the shadows, Sophie succeeds in bringing an abundance of brightness to the Castle's gloomy interior. She smashes a hole in the wall with a flying kayak while escaping from Suliman's troops, and inspires the wizard to shift the Castle to the many-windowed, sunlit hat-shop to keep his household safe. Her final transformation of the Castle, when she rebuilds it from scratch by removing Calcifer, with Howl's heart, from the building's hearth and carrying both outside, culminates in the reduction of the Castle to an open platform, its defences stripped away, its inhabitants exposed to the elements. And although this transformation begins at night, so that its implications are hidden by the darkness that surrounds the platform, when the dawn comes, it is clear that Sophie's housekeeping has finally exposed Howl and his remarkable family to the open scrutiny from which he has so sedulously been keeping them hidden.

The synchrony between Howl and Sophie reaches its culmination in the reconstructed Moving Castle of the final frames. Winging its way across an open sky, on flapping wings not so very dissimilar to the wings of the airborne gunships, the flying fortress is now dominated by cottages rather than gun turrets, gardens rather than protective armour. It represents, then, Howl's opening up of his childhood secret garden to a wider community, his entry into full socialization – an entry in which the rejuvenated Sophie fully participates. But the gun turrets are still there, and though the flying gunships are heading home they have not been dismantled or destroyed. The difficulty of achieving synchrony in personal relationships – between generations of a family or different people in the same generation – is clearly made equivalent here to the difficulty of achieving synchrony between rival nations: a harmonizing of different interests to the mutual advantage of both parties. Flight has been rendered joyful rather than threatening in the final frames of *Howl's Moving Castle* (Fig 3.2). Howl and Sophie face forward into the future from the bows of the Castle with the self-assurance of young lovers, whose relationship has been literally tested in the fire. But the future towards which they are facing – whether this is the twentieth century, when the film is set, or the beginning of the new millennium, when the film was made – will surely share the synchronies of their relationship. It will contain darkness as well as light, war as well as peace, the premature ageing brought on by anxiety as well as the exuberance of childhood prolonged into maturity. The Moving Castle remains a poignantly rickety structure in which to confront such a future.

This chapter on synchrony in the work of Hayao Miyazaki has traced the very different ways in which his films address the problem of harmonizing competing

FIGURE 3.2 In flight. *Howl's Moving Castle* directed by Hayao Miyazaki © Buena Vista Home Entertainment 2004. All Rights Reserved.

time zones in domestic, suburban and national communities. Taking as its focus three movies from three successive decades, it has discovered the presence in each of a range of overlapping chronologies governed by the different ages of family members or housemates, their staggered birth dates furnishing them with alternative histories and perspectives on the times and spaces they share. Each film charts the relationship of these household chronologies or interacting time zones to the changing dynamics of the outside world: the countryside, the suburban neighbourhood and the nation. In the process it points up the multiple chronologies, the competing ways of measuring and understanding time, that converge in these larger communities. In each film, various populations, from the domestic to the urban to the national and, by implication, the global, find themselves under threat of dissolution, of losing their capacity for collaborative coexistence in the face of the increasing mobility of populations large and small under late capitalism. And in each film the community finally succeeds in holding together against all odds, thanks to the hard work and capacious hearts of its eccentric inhabitants. In representing these different processes of achieving synchrony – of reconciling the multiple time zones their characters occupy, and of building a community from their complementary differences – Miyazaki's movies provide their intergenerational audiences with a blueprint for cohabitation. It is for those audiences to decide how far they are able or willing to follow it.

Notes

1 Hayao Miyazaki, *Starting Point 1979–1996*, trans. Beth Cary and Frederik L. Schodt (San Francisco, CA: VIZ Media, 1996), p. 49.
2 Ibid., pp. 252–3.
3 For *Totoro* as a representation of Miyazaki's childhood, see Colin Odell and Michelle le Blanc, *Studio Ghibli: The Films of Hayao Miyazaki and Isao Takahata* (Harpenden: Kamera Books, 2009), p. 79; and more expansively, Phillip E. Wegner, '"An unfinished project that was also a missed opportunity": Utopia and alternate history in Hayao Miyazaki's *My Neighbor Totoro*', *ImageText*, vol. 5, no. 2 (2010–11), http//www.english.ufl.edu/imagetext/archives/v5_2/wegner/ (accessed July 2021).
4 For an explanation of the complex term *kami*, see Michael Ashkenazi, *Handbook of Japanese Mythology* (Oxford: Oxford University Press, 2003), pp. 29–36. Miyazaki's term for Totoro and the soot-spirits is translated by Beth Cary and Frederik L. Schodt as 'goblins'; see Miyazaki, *Starting Point*, pp. 255–6.
5 Miyazaki calls it a 'mountain-lion bus', which makes it less domestic than 'cat-bus', but the vehicle's resemblance to a tabby is unmistakable; see Miyazaki, *Starting Point*, p. 257.
6 The term is widely used in the psychology of adolescence, referring to 'The carefully coordinated interaction between the parent and the child or adolescent in which, often unknowingly, they are attuned to each other's behavior'; John W. Santrock, 'Key terms: synchrony', *Adolescence*, 12th edn (New York: McGraw Hill, 2009). Some psychologists prefer the term 'alignment' to synchrony, since it implies the establishment of links between interlocutors in several domains simultaneously: timing in dialogue (e.g. speech rate), word choice, planning, memory, even posture.

See, for example, Simon Garrod and Martin J. Pickering, 'Joint action, interactive alignment, and dialog', *Topics in Cognitive Science*, vol. 1 (2009), pp. 292–304. I am grateful to Dr Kerry W. Kilborn, School of Psychology, University of Glasgow, for a discussion on this topic.

7 The Japanese title is *Mimi wo Sumaseba*, *If You Listen Closely*. This is also the title of Aoi Hiiragi's manga, on which the film is based. The emphasis on listening should encourage us to pay attention to the sound of the cicadas, as well as the movie's beautiful score by Yuji Nomi.

8 For a full account of Diana Wynne Jones's recurrent themes, see Farah Mendlesohn, *Diana Wynne Jones: The Fantastic Tradition and Children's Literature* (New York: Routledge, 2006).

9 Diana Wynne Jones, *Howl's Moving Castle* (London: HarperCollins, 2005), p. 9.

10 See Jim Hubbert, *The Art of Howl's Moving Castle* (San Francisco, CA: Viz, 2005), p. 12.

11 For Robida, see ibid., p. 49.

12 The quotation is taken from the script of the film as translated by Hubbert, *The Art of Howl's Moving Castle*, p. 252.

13 The term 'blob men' is used in ibid., p. 212, and elsewhere.

14 For an extended discussion of the concept of lightness (as against weight) in twentieth-century history, see Italo Calvino, 'Lecture 1, Lightness', in *Six Memos for the Next Millennium*, trans. Patrick Creagh (London: Penguin, 2009), pp. 3–29.

15 The term 'secret garden', with its invocation of Frances Hodgson Burnett's novel, is used in Hubbert's translation of Miyazaki's script, *The Art of Howl's Moving Castle*, p. 240.

16 The scene is a dream sequence, in which Shizuku is led through the sky by the Baron towards a city of floating towers.

PART TWO

SCREEN PERFORMANCE

4 THE ACHIEVEMENT OF JANIS WILSON, HOLLYWOOD JUVENILE SUPPORTING ACTOR

Martin Shingler

In October 1942, a 12-year-old actress by the name of Janis Wilson (1930–2003) made her screen debut in *Now, Voyager* (Irving Rapper), appearing alongside an impressive cast headed by Bette Davis. Her performance as Tina earned her a place in film history. Back in 1942, it won her a contract with Warner Bros. and a part in *Watch on the Rhine* (Herman Shumlin, 1943), supporting Bette Davis and Paul Lukas. The teenage actress subsequently made a further five films, appearing in a comedy at Columbia, two Barbara Stanwyck films and two B-movies for independent production companies, a comedy and a horror movie.[1] By the end of 1948, at the age of 18, her six-year film career was over.

When compared to MGM child star Margaret O'Brien (b. 1937), Wilson's achievement seems rather paltry. Margaret O'Brien also came to public attention at the end of 1942, at the age of five, after appearing in *Journey for Margaret* (W.S. Van Dyke). Her Hollywood profile rose significantly the following year with her supporting roles in Greer Garson's *Madame Curie* (Mervyn LeRoy, 1943) and Joan Fontaine's *Jane Eyre* (Robert Stevenson, 1943). However, her career-defining role came in 1944 when she played Tootie in Vincente Minnelli's *Meet Me in St Louis*, receiving second billing to Judy Garland.[2] By the end of the 1940s, after Wilson had retired, O'Brien's career was still going strong. In 1949, she co-starred alongside June Allyson, Elizabeth Taylor and Janet Leigh in *Little Women* (Mervyn LeRoy) and took the leading role of Mary Lennox in *The Secret Garden* (Fred M. Wilcox), supported by Herbert Marshall and Dean Stockwell. After 1950, O'Brien remained successful as an actress on television and in TV movies, her career spanning a remarkable eight decades.

While Wilson's short Hollywood career seems rather insignificant in comparison to O'Brien's, it is still noteworthy and, as I hope to demonstrate here, her screen performances reward detailed scrutiny. In particular, analysis of her work brings to light some telling insights into the role of juvenile supporting actors in studio-era Hollywood, the challenges that confronted them and the techniques used to provide effective support to adult stars. By taking a leaf out of Andrew Klevan's book *Film Performance* (2005), I intend to subject a small number of Wilson's screen performances to detailed analysis, concentrating closely on isolated sequences and attending to the moment-by-moment development of her performance as Tina in *Now, Voyager* and young Martha in *The Strange Love of Martha Ivers* (Lewis Milestone, 1946). Here I shall examine the relationship of her acting to other elements of film style (i.e. *mise en scène* and cinematography) in a bid to appreciate the way in which Wilson and her fellow actors created performances rich in meaning.[3] In order to better understand this process, I shall also employ a method advocated by Cynthia Baron and Sharon Marie Carnicke in *Reframing Screen Performance* (2008), which combines script analysis with a close reading of the film itself, subdividing the scene or sequence into separate units of action or 'beats', each with their own specific narrative objective, mood or rhythm.[4] These enable the structural dynamics of a performance to be more readily comprehended, while also providing insight into the acting choices available to and made by the actors. By subjecting Wilson's screen performances to such close and systematic analysis, I hope to demonstrate the strength, subtlety and coherence of her work as a child actor in Hollywood during the 1940s.

Now, Voyager was not only Janis Wilson's debut but also her defining role. For her first film, she performed alongside an impressive cast headed by Warners' most successful star at the time, Bette Davis. The supporting cast was just as impressive, featuring Hollywood's latest European romantic male lead, Paul Henreid, the British actors Claude Rains, Gladys Cooper and John Loder, the fine comic talents of Ilka Chase, Mary Wickes and Franklin Pangborn, and experienced juvenile, Bonita Granville. In 1942, at 19 years of age, Granville was making the transition from playing juvenile to adult roles, having made her screen debut ten years earlier in 1932, subsequently acting with Bette Davis in *It's Love I'm After* (Archie Mayo, 1936) and starring in the title role of Warners' *Nancy Drew* mysteries in 1938 and 1939. Taking on the juvenile role of Tina in *Now, Voyager* was therefore a daunting prospect for Wilson as a 12-year-old novice making her screen debut alongside such an illustrious company of actors.

Wilson was cast in the role of Tina Durrance, the daughter of Jerry (Paul Henreid), a married man who becomes the secret lover of the film's heroine, Charlotte Vale (Bette Davis). During the film's final 30 minutes, Charlotte meets and forms a close bond with Tina and, in order to preserve this relationship, she finally sacrifices her affair with Jerry. During this final half-hour of the movie, Tina is transformed from a withdrawn and miserable adolescent into a more confident and happy teenager. For much of the time, she displays a melodramatic personality and a tendency towards exaggerated reactions, such as when she frantically kisses Charlotte's fingers after she has burned them on a hot potato roasting on a camp fire. On another occasion, Tina declares that she would rather sicken and die than have anything bad happen to Charlotte. The challenge of playing such a neurotic and hysterical character was something that the Warner studio publicists highlighted in the press book for *Now, Voyager*, which contains an article on the young actress, described here as 'Janice Wilson', entitled '12 Yr. Old Tops in Screen Debut of Different Role':

> Betting on a 12-year old girl making her screen debut in a Bette Davis picture is like wagering on a filly in the Kentucky Derby. Even experienced players of the movie-acting world often get the nervous jitters at the prospect of stacking up against a lady so formidable. A little Santa Barbara, Calif., girl named Janice Wilson didn't know about this legend. She simply moved in on 'Now, Voyager' at Warner Bros. and played scene after scene with Miss Davis as sincerely as if she were make-believing in her own back yard. The result is that Janice has made a solid hit, has won a contract, and has been cast with Bette again in 'Watch on the Rhine'.
>
> Janice's part in 'Now, Voyager' called for an inhibited, affection-starved little girl, not a mischievous one, but a bewildered, neurotic juvenile headed for frustration and old-maid-dom.
>
> In getting away with that kind of part, Janice has apparently brought something new to the screen.[5]

This clearly established Wilson's difference from other Hollywood female child stars. Unlike Shirley Temple, Elizabeth Taylor and Judy Garland, she did not have Garland's voice and was neither pretty nor cute. While other child actors often achieved Hollywood stardom through a combination of tears and twee, Wilson brought a sullen and rather charmless brand of adolescent angst to the screen, hinting at something altogether more disturbed and disturbing: something that Hollywood publicists would find almost impossible to brand and package for popular consumption in the same way as they did for Margaret O'Brien, the new kid on the block in 1942.

Warner publicists did little to promote Wilson's appearance in *Now, Voyager* and there is no evidence to suggest that the studio was interested in developing her into a child star. Consequently, her name was excluded from the opening titles of the film, while her name and image were absent from film posters, which either featured Bette Davis alone or Davis with Henreid. Nor was Wilson included in the theatrical trailer, which featured only Paul Henreid, Claude Rains, Gladys Cooper and Ilka Chase, in addition to Bette Davis. It is unusual that the promotional materials made no mention of Wilson, particularly given her character's crucial role in the plot. Standard Hollywood practice was to announce important new talent with the word 'Introducing ... ' before their name, in the publicity accompanying the release of their first film. The absence of the line 'Introducing Janis Wilson' from the promotional materials for *Now, Voyager* suggests that Warners had no intention of building her up into a star in 1942, which is confirmed by their subsequent failure to cast her in more substantial roles. This, however, was certainly not for want of talent. Analysis of Wilson's screen debut reveals an intelligent and articulate performer, a child capable of holding her own against Hollywood's finest and most acclaimed star actors.

Janis Wilson makes her screen entrance in *Now, Voyager* after 86 minutes in a 3½-minute scene with Davis and Katherine Alexander. Using Baron and Carnicke's method of performance analysis, this scene can be subdivided into six units of action.[6] These might be described as the Arrival, the Approach, the Puzzle, the Interruption, the Decision and Collusion. The scene charts the first meeting of Charlotte Vale and Tina shortly after her return to Cascade, a sanatorium in New England. Arriving in the hallway, Charlotte spots Tina sitting in an adjacent room. She approaches and sits down beside her, engaging her in conversation, inquiring about her name and age, before being interrupted by the head nurse, Miss Trask (Katherine Alexander), who has come to inform the girl that she is to spend the evening playing table tennis with some young people. Mortified by having to join the others, Tina begs to be excluded and Charlotte comes to her aid by proposing that she join her on an errand in to town. Surprised and relieved, Tina accepts this invitation, dashing out of the room to fetch her coat, while the nurse informs Charlotte that she has been given the room next to Tina's and may well hear her crying during the night. Miss Trask also asks Charlotte to encourage the girl to eat something while they are out as, in addition to her bouts of nocturnal crying, she has a habit of refusing to eat. During the course of this scene, a number of basic facts about Tina are established, including several things that Charlotte and Tina have in common: most notably, their tendency towards depression and their fear of social interaction.

Analysis of Wilson's first scene reveals her competency as an actor, involving a range of actions and emotions, beginning with a very contained and subdued performance that erupts at a critical moment into a frenzy of movement, sound and emotional excess (i.e. hysteria). There is, however, only one brief moment when Wilson's performance dominates the screen, distracting attention away from the film's star player, Bette Davis. Wilson first appears in the second unit of this scene (the Approach), after Charlotte has entered the hallway of Cascade and been met by Miss Trask. While being escorted up to her room, Charlotte spies a forlorn child, sitting by herself, lost in her thoughts and visibly depressed.[7] She halts at the foot of the staircase, recognizing the girl as her lover's child, arrested by the sight of her sitting glumly at a table, pondering over a jigsaw puzzle. The girl, with spectacles and lank dark hair, rests her head in both hands, supported by her elbows on the table.[8] Though bent low, her face is still visible. Romantic music (previously heard during Charlotte and Jerry's love scenes) swells on the soundtrack, marking the significance of this moment and establishing the connection with Jerry. A puzzled and frowning Charlotte edges towards the girl, the camera moving with her as she advances hesitantly, coming to rest in the doorway.[9] Propelling herself forward, Charlotte announces her presence by asking in a cheery voice 'How's it coming?', while the camera pans to the left to reveal Wilson. By contrast, in the screenplay Charlotte purposefully disturbs a chair to alert the girl to her presence and Tina responds by looking up at her quickly with a 'suspicious look'.[10] In the film, however, Charlotte approaches unheeded and, even when addressed, Wilson does not look up. Her face remains in the grip of her hands, stretching her mouth into a false grin that emphasizes the sadness of her large eyes behind her glasses. Without raising her eyes to look at her interlocutor, she utters her first word, saying in a flat voice, 'alright'.

The third unit of action (the Puzzle) is established as Charlotte settles herself down beside the girl at the table and proceeds to help her with the jigsaw, posing a series of questions, initially about the puzzle and then about Tina herself, that are either ignored or challenged. While Davis is animated, Tina's movements are heavily restricted and slow. After asking Tina what the puzzle is about and having received the sorrowful reply, 'I don't know' from the girl, Davis bursts into motion, transferring a handbag from one hand to the other, seizing a piece of the jigsaw and fitting it into place. This brings Davis's body much closer to Wilson's. Still the child makes no response, even as she settles in beside her. Charlotte enquires about the title of the picture, removing her coat, while moving her chair in closer, prompting a cut to a medium-close shot of Wilson in the foreground to the left of the frame and Davis in the centre and middle distance, what might be called the 'star spot'. From here, Davis executes a set of small incidental actions, while Tina remains largely impassive until provoked to speak to and look at her neighbour. Taking up several pieces of the puzzle, Charlotte acknowledges that 'some people prefer to do a puzzle alone'. This final word triggers Tina's first major response. In the screenplay, it states that the 'child raises her eyes then, but not her chin, and looks at Charlotte'.[11] In the film, it is at this very moment that Wilson begins to move, slowly and deliberately turning her head to look at the woman beside her, dropping and raising her eyes as she gives Charlotte the 'once over' before declaring 'I know who you are' in an accusatory voice. According to the screenplay, her tone is 'antagonistic' but this suggests a level of animosity towards Charlotte that is not fully achieved by Wilson's performance.[12] On the contrary, the young actress presents her character here as guarded and suspicious (because she suspects that Charlotte is her new nurse) but her efforts to remain stern and stand-offish prove unsustainable. For instance, although her voice sounds hostile (such as when she declares, 'You can't fool me') her eyes are noticeably softer, being frequently cast down, appearing more submissive than offensive. Consequently, while Wilson adheres precisely to the script, her interpretation is more nuanced and ambiguous, hinting at the character's innately affectionate nature and her need for companionship and love that are being repressed at this stage.[13]

As Tina is beginning to open up to Charlotte, their intimate conversation is interrupted by Miss Trask, marking the start of a new unit of action – the Interruption. Katherine Alexander bursts into the scene, her first words heard over a medium-close-shot of Tina and Charlotte, motivating a cut to her striding across the room. Informed that a game of ping-pong has been arranged for her with a group of young people, Tina declares sorrowfully, 'They don't want me.' Charlotte now detaches herself, rising from her seat and walking towards the camera, while Tina (in the background of the shot) expresses mortification at having to join the other children.[14] Alarmed at the prospect of being the worst player, she declares to the nurse, 'I'll die, I'll just die', light glinting off the braces on her teeth as she speaks (Fig 4.1). Told not to dramatize, Wilson gasps, jumping up from the table and swiftly executing her first major dramatic movement, seizing hold of the nurse and pleading, 'Please, please, please ... don't make me, don't make me!' Her voice is loud and desperate, becoming increasingly choked with emotion.[15] 'Oh don't make me!' she pleads more loudly, dramatically, even melodramatically, before burying herself into the nurse's body. While Tina sobs, Charlotte intervenes, persuading Miss Trask to let Tina accompany her to town. Having cried quietly into the body of Katherine Alexander throughout this exchange (her sobbing being conveniently muffled so as not to distract from the dialogue), Wilson raises her head slowly, her sobs subsiding. This initiates the fifth unit of action - the Decision - which includes Wilson's big moment.

At first, only the back of her head is seen, her long dark hair concealing her face, until she turns towards the camera to fix Charlotte with an intense gaze of wonder. Without a word, she drops her eyes and turns slowly and methodically from one woman to the other and back again before pausing, nodding gently

FIGURE 4.1 Janis Wilson distraught as 'Tina' in *Now, Voyager* directed by Irving Rapper © Warner Bros. 1942. All Rights Reserved.

and whispering 'yes' by way of accepting Charlotte's invitation to accompany her. This is a critical point in the drama, Tina deciding between remaining at Cascade or going with Charlotte. To mark the significance of this, Wilson takes her time (about twelve seconds), performing in the star spot by occupying the centre and middle ground, flanked by Alexander facing forward in the distance on the left and Davis in the foreground with her back to the camera on the right. The young unknown actress is the focus of attention: of the two women in the scene, of the camera, the crew in the studio and the audience in the movie theatre. She takes her time to turn from Alexander to Davis and from Davis to Alexander and, finally, back to Davis, pauses, gazing up at Charlotte, motivating a cut to a close-shot of Charlotte's expectant face, followed by the reverse shot. Only then does she speak, slowly, softly, with a slight bow of her head and a drop of her eyes. 'Yes.' With all eyes still upon her, Wilson spins rapidly round and takes hold of Alexander again to deliver her longest line, 'Oh please let me go with this lady, I promise to drink all my cocoa tonight if you will.'[16] Wilson imparts considerable energy into her final line of the scene, speaking quickly in a voice full of emotion, of desperation. Although Miss Trask tells her not to 'carry on', she is persuaded, telling the girl to go and get her coat. Wilson makes her exit by spinning round and trotting quickly out of the room.[17]

What stands out about Wilson's first scene in *Now, Voyager* is her high level of concentration and her deliberateness, using minimal gestures that are purposeful and measured. Moreover, there is a striking contrast between the start and end of the scene, from her initial fixed position with all energy removed from her words and gestures to her swift and dramatic speech and movements provoked by Miss Trask. During this scene, the young actress demonstrates her control, on the one hand, and her ability to explode in an excess of movement, sound and emotion, on the other. The first part of this scene is all about containment, Wilson holding her face between her hands for a long period of time, stretching her mouth into a fixed, artificial grin that makes her seem both unnatural and ugly. When she says her second line, 'I don't know', her voice lacks energy and the pitch descends, making her sound dejected. The words drop lifelessly from her lips. It is noticeable that in a rare departure from the screenplay, Wilson does not move at all when Davis invades her space, coming to sit very close to her. This absolute stillness seems remarkable for a young person, yet it enables Davis to dominate the scene, maintaining the attention of the viewer. It is her movements that capture the audience's attention, such as when she wriggles out of her coat or moves her hands and arms about, transferring her bag or picking up pieces of the jigsaw puzzle. It is several minutes before Wilson moves and when she does she is slow and deliberate, turning to look at Davis, directing the audience's gaze back towards the star. Rarely does she retain Charlotte's and the audience's gaze for long: most notably, when she does so it is when she makes her decision to accept the invitation to accompany the unknown woman in to town, sealing her fate by choosing Charlotte's guardianship over that of the staff at Cascade.

Janis Wilson appears opposite Bette Davis in a further eight scenes in *Now, Voyager*, charting their growing intimacy and Tina's evolution into a more confident and happy adolescent. Having won the girl's trust on their trip in to town and by comforting her at night, Charlotte is granted permission by Dr Jacquith to take Tina camping. After informing her father of this by telephone (disclosing the fact that Charlotte is Tina's new companion), there follows a montage sequence of their trip (fishing, running through woods, boating and sleeping under the stars), before a scene in the woods beside a camp fire, in which Tina expresses her wish that Charlotte was her mother and is given permission to call her Camille (Jerry's pet name for her) rather than Miss Vale. Here, Charlotte tells the girl that she has asked Jacquith to be allowed to take her home with her to Boston. In the screenplay, the camping sequence is followed by a scene in Tina's studio at the Vale mansion on Marlborough Street in which she is happily working on a picture of Charlotte's cocker spaniel, until told that her father and Dr Jacquith are about to visit. Thinking that she is to be taken away, she bursts into tears and is comforted by Charlotte, who reassures her that she loves her as much as her father does.[18] This scene, however, was cut from the film, effecting a direct transition from the campsite in the woods to Tina's party at the Vale mansion. On entering the house, Jacquith is surprised by its makeover and congenial atmosphere, while Jerry is amazed by the sight of his daughter, who appears to him at the top of the stairs dressed in an elegant party dress, her hair in ringlets and her face free of braces and spectacles. After she has thrown herself into his arms, he tells her how lovely she looks and that he loves her. She then takes him to see her room while, in the next scene, Charlotte and Jacquith discuss the construction of a new children's building at Cascade due to her beneficence. Janis Wilson makes her final appearance at this point, informing Charlotte that her father has gone in to the library. Charlotte tells Tina to take care of Jacquith while she goes to see Jerry, the girl being delighted by the irony of having to take care of a doctor, so that the last image of her (pretty, confident and smiling, Fig 4.2) stands in marked contrast to the first image of her gazing listlessly at the jigsaw puzzle at Cascade.

Janis Wilson's performances in *Now, Voyager* reveal a child actor with a remarkable degree of control, able to produce contained actions with confidence against more powerful and seasoned performers. She ably fills out the screen (occupying the spaces adjacent to the star) providing a focus for the star's attention, being someone she can play off and against without losing the attention of the audience. It is also clear that Wilson is effective when either under-playing (e.g. subdued or sulky) or over-playing (i.e. when dramatizing, such as when she declares 'I'll die, I'll just die!'). She is less effective, however, when trying to be sweet. Alarm bells start to ring in the nocturnal crying scene when Charlotte tells Tina that she thinks she is pretty and Wilson responds by batting her eyelashes several times à la 'Bette Davis'. Things get much worse, however, on the staircase at the Vale mansion when Tina asks Charlotte, 'Would it sound too funny if Daddy should call you my name for you, Camille?' Here the problem lies in the way she

FIGURE 4.2 The 'make over' of Janis Wilson as 'Tina' in Now, Voyager directed by Irving Rapper © Warner Bros. 1942. All Rights Reserved.

says the word 'you', stressing it by elongating the word and puckering her lips. It is not just the emphasis she gives to it that registers as phoney but also a degree of elegance to the voice, being both posh and romanticized. While Davis replies (in a voice choked with emotion), 'I think it would sound very nice indeed', it actually sounds ridiculous.

When *Variety* reviewed the film on 19 August 1942, following its trade showing, Janis Wilson was said to have contributed 'a moving characterisation as Henreid's young, neurotic daughter'.[19] When the film was released two months later, the New York critics concentrated on the performances of Davis, Henreid, Rains and Cooper, few noting Wilson's contribution, although Archer Winsten, in the *New York Post*, noted that 'Little Miss Janice Wilson deserves praise for her work.'[20] Clearly, Warner executives were sufficiently impressed to put her under contract and cast her alongside Bette Davis again in *Watch on the Rhine* (1943). However, the studio did not grant her star status nor give her a leading role, making no use of her at all in 1944. In fact, Warners only cast her on one more occasion, in a very minor role in the Barbara Stanwyck vehicle *My Reputation* in 1946. However, when *Now, Voyager*'s producer, Hal B. Wallis made *The Strange Love of Martha Ivers* at Paramount Studios in 1946, he chose Wilson for the role of young Martha, the adult Martha being played by Stanwyck. The challenge here was less to impersonate the adult star than to portray young Martha as a troubled teenager, deeply unhappy since the death of her parents, which has forced her to live with her wealthy widowed aunt, Mrs Ivers. A further challenge was to perform opposite Judith Anderson (as Mrs Ivers), an actress most famous for her Oscar-winning performance as Mrs Danvers in Rebecca (Alfred Hitchcock, 1940). This did not, however, entail Wilson reprising her performance of Tina for *The Strange Love of Martha Ivers* since Martha is a different type of personality, being stronger, more resilient and feisty, making her much more defiant, wilful and confrontational. Consequently, Wilson's performance required a very different set of articulations in order to bring the character of young Martha Ivers to life.

Wilson is introduced in the film's opening scene, discovered by her friend Sam (Darryl Hickman) hiding in a railway truck, having fled from her aunt's house. Their attempt to run away is thwarted by the police, who escort Martha home. There she confronts her aunt in a scene that exposes the hostility and resentment at the heart of their relationship. When her aunt commands her to step closer, she looks down before taking two small steps forward, her head bowed. When further commanded to look at her, Wilson slowly raises her head and then, and only then, lifts her eyes to look into the woman's face. Her lips are tightly closed, her jaw tense, while light reflects off her high forehead as she stares intently and with hatred at the older woman. Through a tense mouth, the girl declares that she is sorry, sorry for being caught, which earns her a slap across the face. In response, her eyes flare with shock and fury while the rest of her body remains rigid. Refusing to cry, she tenses her forehead, the veins above her eyebrows visibly pulsing, her shoulders rising and falling slightly with the effort of suppressing her emotions. Her aunt warns her that no matter how many times she runs away she will always be brought back. 'You don't own the whole world,' Martha declares loudly, in a voice noticeably deeper than in *Now, Voyager*. 'Enough of it to make sure you'll always be brought back here,' Anderson replies, as the young woman fixes her gaze to the floor, refusing to speak further until finally provoked by her aunt's vicious comments about her deceased parents. Here she fires the words 'shut up' four times into Anderson's face and, after being called a nobody, she shouts 'I'll kill you!' moving forward to attack until restrained by her tutor, Mr O'Neil (Roman Bohnen), who grabs her by the shoulders. Held back, her hands flare out, making ineffectual stabbing motions as she gasps and squeals with frustration. Catching her breath, Martha controls herself, confronting her aunt face to face. Told to go to her room, she turns and slowly walks away, her head held high, signalling her pride, although as she passes through the doorway it drops so that she crosses the hall with her head bowed, looking defeated.

This scene is a prelude to one of the most dramatic moments of the film, when Martha attacks her aunt on the staircase during a thunderstorm. As lightning flashes, a hand seizes the cane that Mrs Ivers is using to beat Martha's pet kitten to death. The cane is quickly wrestled out of the woman's grasp and is then seen raised above Wilson's head. A reverse shot of Judith Anderson follows, her eyes closed and her right hand raised protectively before her face as she begins to tumble backwards on the stairs, motivating a wavering point-of-view shot of the ceiling as she loses her balance. Wilson's face looks aghast, the cane held above and behind her head, as the woman falls down the stairs. Wilson's face becomes more composed moments later when, standing over the dead body, she invents a story of seeing a man assaulting her aunt and then fleeing from the house. Mr O'Neil is incredulous but decides to go along with this tale. Wilson's slow deliberate movements convey her character's sense of purpose and her implacable spirit. Later, in her bedroom, the tutor tells Martha that now that she is alone in the world, he and his son Walter (Mickey Kuhn) will always stand by her. A pact is made, the truth of the aunt's death being concealed so long as Mr O'Neil and his son are able to profit from Martha's inheritance. The girl complies with an act of deferential gratitude. Here Wilson makes it clear that she is acting, playing along. She gazes at her tutor passively, her head slightly to one side, an image of gentle compliance. While closing her eyes she says in a soft voice, with mock gratitude, 'Thank you, Mr O'Neil', speaking slowly, as though in a dream, although instantly the sound of a distant train whistle disturbs her composure, initiating a cut to her friend Sam on board a train heading out of town, the image fading and bringing this opening section of the film to a close.

There is no doubt that the performances of Janis Wilson dominate the opening sixteen minutes of *The Strange Love of Martha Ivers* and, moreover, that her two confrontation scenes with Anderson are among the film's most dramatic moments. Wilson's appearances throughout this section are entirely effective, largely on account of the fact that she is required to be sulky, stern and deliberate rather than sweet, pretty or cute. Studio publicists described Wilson as a '15-year-old emotional actress' in the press book for *The Strange Love of Martha Ivers*, stating that she plays 'no ordinary part' in this film. In a short article entitled 'Fifteen-year-old in "Martha Ivers"', Wilson is referred to as a 'talented youngster' who, having previously been cast in Stanwyck's *My Reputation* and Davis's *Now, Voyager* and *Watch on the Rhine*, now appears 'in excellent acting company'. As before, the New York critics ignored Wilson's performance in favour of those of the adult stars, although Kate Cameron of the *Daily News* did note that all the child stars were fine, while *Variety* observed that the opening sequences were 'dominated by young Janis Wilson, playing Miss Stanwyck as a girl'.

Analysis of Wilson's performance in the opening section of *The Strange Love of Martha Ivers* confirms that she was a fine screen performer: intelligent and articulate, well suited to playing complex juvenile roles such as moody teenagers and psychologically troubled adolescents. Nevertheless, her track record in terms of casting suggests that she lacked star quality, that ineffable quality often referred to as 'charisma' or 'It'. Karen Lury has discussed the importance of 'It' for child stars in *The Child in Film*, writing that, '[w]hilst the child actor's skill and acting style need to be contextualised within the film text and the historical period of production, it does seem to be evident that success is based on possession of an idiosyncratic quality that makes the child, perhaps, "abnormally interesting"'.[21] If success and stardom for child actors depended on them being abnormally interesting, then Janis Wilson's lack of success and stardom can probably be ascribed to an absence of this quality. Nevertheless, it may well have been this very lack that made her such an effective supporting actor for the likes of Bette Davis. For, as Karen Lury has also written, '[i]f the successful child actor is often blessed (or cursed) with It, then another risk accrues to their presence beside the adult actors – that they will upstage these actors and draw the audience's attention and admiration towards them unfairly'.[22] As analysis of her first scene in *Now, Voyager* has revealed, Janis Wilson seldom drew attention away from the adult stars she performed with, making her particularly well suited to supporting roles in star vehicles.

Being the star of a film is clearly no easy task and relatively few child actors attain stardom and even fewer sustain star status for long. However, being a juvenile supporting actor is also a challenge. For a child actor to effectively play against and support an adult star they require skill, an intelligent grasp of the dynamics of human interaction, concentration and physical control. Janis Wilson had these abilities. Although she may have lacked the star quality of Shirley Temple, Elizabeth Taylor, Judy Garland or Margaret O'Brien, she was nevertheless an accomplished juvenile supporting actor who deserves her place in film history.

Notes

1. Janis Wilson's filmography is as follows: *Now, Voyager* (Irving Rapper, 1942), *Watch on the Rhine* (Herman Shumlin, 1943), *Welcome Home* (Jack Moss, 1945), *My Reputation* (Curtis Bernhardt, 1946), *The Strange Love of Martha Ivers* (Lewis Milestone, 1946), *Heading for Heaven* (Lewis D. Collins, 1947) and *The Creeper* (Jean Yarbrough, 1948).
2. Karen Lury, *The Child in Film: Tears, Fears and Fairy Tales* (London: I.B. Tauris, 2010), pp. 151–3.
3. Andrew Klevan, *Film Performance: From Achievement to Appreciation* (London: Wallflower, 2005), p. 103.
4. Cynthia Baron and Sharon Marie Carnicke, *Reframing Screen Performance* (Ann Arbor, MI: University of Michigan Press, 2008), p. 210.
5. Warner Bros. press book for *Now, Voyager* (1942), p. 5. A copy is available at the library of the British Film Institute.
6. Baron and Carnicke, *Reframing Screen Performance*, p. 210.
7. In the screenplay, she is described as a 'most piteously unattractive child'. Jeanne Allen (ed.), *Now, Voyager*, Wisconsin/Warner Bros. Screenplay Series (Madison, WI: The University of Wisconsin Press, 1984), p. 188.
8. The screenplay notes that she is 'just sitting there, staring down, not moving a muscle', which is precisely what Wilson does. Ibid.
9. The screenplay notes that Charlotte 'still can't believe that this is Jerry's child – and yet – there can't be any mistake'. Ibid.
10. Ibid.
11. Ibid., p. 189.
12. Ibid.
13. While Wilson sticks to the script, Davis makes a series of minor departures. For instance, when Tina asserts 'You know my name, that's why you stood there and

stared at me,' Davis replies 'Oh, that was very rude of me!' casting her eyes down in order to add (slowly and hesitatingly) 'but, you see, you reminded me of somebody.' Davis has changed this line from the screenplay, which states, 'How rude of me. But it was only because you reminded me of somebody', which seems more confident. When Tina asks who she reminds her of, Davis hesitates, her eyelashes flickering, almost mechanically and so very 'Bette Davis'. She drops her head and, gazing down at the puzzle so that her face falls into shadow, she laughs nervously as she begins to answer, 'Well, if you must know...'. Here, she turns slowly to look into the girl's eyes, the camera reframing to a medium-close shot with Wilson on the left in the foreground and Davis in the star spot (i.e. the centre and middle ground). Only then does Davis complete her line with the word 'myself', quickly adding in a much lighter tone, 'of course, at your age'. In so doing, Davis leaves out the words 'in lots of ways of' from the screenplay. Allen (ed.), *Now, Voyager*, p. 190.

14 Davis's empathy for the girl is telegraphed via a tense mouth and a hand that presses against her stomach, suggesting a feeling a nausea deep down inside.
15 The screenplay states here she 'beseeches with a terror-stricken expression'. Allen (ed.), *Now, Voyager*, p. 191.
16 In the screenplay, Tina also says 'Upon my word of honor' but this is omitted from the film. Ibid.
17 In the screenplay, it states: 'Tina shoots out of the room like a bird let out of a cage'. Ibid., p. 192.
18 Ibid., pp. 210–12.
19 Anon., Review of *Now, Voyager*, *Variety*, 19 August 1942.
20 Archer Winsten, Review of *Now, Voyager*, *The New York Post*, 23 October 1942.
21 Lury, *The Child in Film*, p. 147.
22 Ibid., p. 148.

5 PERFORMING BLACK BOYHOOD, QUIET AND *MOONLIGHT*

Karen Lury

This chapter focuses on the performance of child actors: while this is a topic I have approached before, the purpose of my argument here is to extend and revisit these discussions and to think carefully and critically about the significance of race. It is based, in part, on the discussion I had with students from a class on screen performance in which I had wanted to introduce and expand on notions of subjectivity and performance and on the significance of race, including exploring racist caricatures in the history of cinema, using work by Donald Bogle and other writers.[1] For the seminar, I had asked the class to view Barry Jenkins's 2016 film *Moonlight* (2016). Opening the discussion, I expressed my anxiety that the film perhaps took us back too neatly and unnervingly to discussions we had at the beginning of the course concerning the Kuleshov effect. This 'effect', associated with the Soviet filmmaker Lev Kuleshov, is related to his famous experiment, in which the same static shot of a man's expressionless face is intercut with different images; in most reports of the experiment this is a bowl of soup, a woman and a coffin.[2] When viewed alongside one another, audiences apparently read into the man's expressionless face appropriate emotions that refer to associations prompted by the secondary images. So, respectively, they saw, or believed they saw, that the man was expressing hunger in relation to the picture of the soup, desire in relation to the woman, and sorrow in relation to the picture of the coffin. This effect poses a particular challenge for the analysis of screen performance – if the audience is so ready or so willing to read the appropriate emotion from an expressionless face, then what agency can the film actor really have? What more, really, can the actor add when the audience and the context of the film as a collaborative production (incorporating narrative, editing, cinematography, music, sound) and the context of the film's exhibition and reception (the audience's desire to attribute meaning) already do so much of the work? And since the young actors playing the main character in *Moonlight* (known as 'Little' when a boy, by his name Chiron as a teenager and 'Black' as a man) appear to say and do very little in terms of their performance, what could be said about their expressions and performance that would not fall into the kind of speculation and easy attribution that the Kuleshov effect exposes? Was the impact of their presence and performance little more than a trick of the light, and the careful and artful composition of their bodies, skin and faces?

In seeking to award agency and authorship to the screen performer, the class and I had previously discussed the technique and popular reputation of the 'method', which seemingly allows actors to claim some authorship of their performance. The discourse (both critical and popular) surrounding the method, while not always coherent, generally suggests that actors who are believed to employ this technique to produce specific actions and expressions that are informed by their idiosyncratic psychology, suggesting that a successful performance depends upon the engagement by the actor with an interior self that can be mined to provoke a repertoire of appropriate, naturalistic gestures.[3] Certainly, the performances of the *adult* actors in *Moonlight* (notably Mahershala Ali and Naomie Harris) were naturalistic and expressive. But they and the child actors weren't described as 'method'. As I have noted elsewhere, children also pose a particular issue in relation to the dominance of the 'method' in contemporary discourses of acting, because they are not usually understood to have (indeed are often defined by their lack of) agency and interiority. They may have presence, be compelling or beautiful, but they don't act in the same way that adults do. They can't be or do 'method'.[4]

This is further problematized in relation to *Moonlight* because we are discussing black children and black teenage actors. The method, and its success in terms of its association with wide critical acclaim for particular performances, is almost exclusively associated and celebrated as a consequence of the apparent labour, dedication and complex subjectivity of white, male, adult actors. This means that the method and the contemporary discourse surrounding successful acting is a racialized, if not explicitly racist, discourse since it is rare or exceptional to suggest that black actors employ the 'method'. Further, it is also problematic because as a technique the method is related to the belief that interiority and agency are, in the contemporary and liberal conception of the self, integral or even the essence of subjecthood, and as a consequence, with the current conception of human-ness itself. Simply put, therefore, the contemporary and dominant models of good acting and subjecthood and agency are aligned. This isn't surprising – how could they not be? However, the alliance of these discourses – of acting and subjecthood – are unfortunately established and dependent upon their exclusion of women, queer individuals, people of colour and children, or in other words, those individuals who are other to the adult, heterosexual, white male.

I am not suggesting that actors of colour, queer individuals, women and children don't act – of course they do – but rather that their performance is often 'too little' or 'too much' and within the context of Western mainstream cinema, their acting is rarely evaluated or celebrated in the same way that white, adult, male actors' performances are (as Martin Shingler's previous chapter goes some way to illustrating). For instance, children can often seem to do too little in terms of their performance – they are perceived to be stilted or awkward – or alternatively they do too much – seemingly hysterical, melodramatic and precocious. Frequently children and these 'other' performers are perceived as being primarily body (their external qualities) and lacking agency (a force determined in part by an assumed interiority). Their presence is at once hyper-visible, yet at the same time, their actions, gestures, expressions and narrative status are often less important than the other actors they appear alongside. As performers, it is difficult to attribute agency to their appearance or performance, as this appears to be over-determined either by the constraints of the film's narrative, or by conventions of editing and cinematography.

The students and I had discussed all these issues over the weeks of the class – questions of agency, authorship and evaluation had emerged in the discussion of different adult stars' performance as well as the behaviour on screen of non-human beings such as animals. We discussed, in detail, aspects of the three actors who played Little/Chiron/Black, especially Little and Chiron, since our focus was on the child and young person as screen performer. The students commented on the immersive aspects of the *mise en scène*, in particular highlighting the key scene in which Little (Alex L. Hibbert) is taught to swim by Juan (Mahershala Ali.) Overall, we observed that Hibbert's performance (and that of Ashton Sanders who plays Chiron) were marked by the fact that they were mostly silent and that our understanding of character was driven, primarily, by our proximity to both the actors and to the events in the film – encouraged by that sense of an immersion within the *mise en scène*. Throughout the film, there is recurrent proximity and attention paid to the actors' faces and skin. In addition to numerous close-ups of their faces, this was also evident in the way in which the hand-held camera repeatedly follows Little, and later Chiron, as he makes his way through school corridors and along the streets and backyards to and from his home.

The relative silence of the characters further pushes our attention to what we can see of the character rather than what we hear. I suggested to the class that his silence might be attributed to the traumatic context in which Little (and later as Chiron) finds himself: living in poverty, bullied in school, Little's situation worsens as we observe his mother becoming addicted to crack. In that sense, his character might have chosen to be selectively mute; just as, for instance, the traumatized little girl, Johanna, played by Helena Zengel, in the recent Western *News of the World* (Paul Greengrass, 2020) chooses not to speak. Other traumatized boy characters in films have also been frequently characterized by their inability or unwillingness to speak: for instance, two Scottish, white, working-class boys, Jamie (Stephen Archibald) in Bill Douglas's *My Childhood* (1972), or James (William Eadie) in *Ratcatcher* (Lynne Ramsay, 1999) are also reticent and rarely speak. An exception to this (perhaps not coincidentally) is the cheerfully verbose adolescent Ricky Baker (Julian Dennison) in Taikia Waititi's film the *Hunt for the Wilderpeople* (2016). Yet Hibbert's and Sanders's performances suggest not so much that Little/Chiron is silent but more that he is *quiet* – a subtle difference which would mean that the character is not being prevented or inhibited from speaking but is choosing not to. As Jenkins observed of himself as a child: 'The way I grew up, I was kind of a quiet kid. I ended up watching people a lot, more than interacting, in a certain way.'[5] The likelihood that Little and Chiron's behaviour and the actors' performances owed something to the distinct qualities of 'quiet-ness' was inspired by a short essay/interview with Barry Jenkins by Michael Boyce Gillespie, in which he draws specifically on Kevin Quashie's conception of 'quiet' as an under-valued, under-remarked way of being for Black masculinity.[6] Crucially, Quashie does not suggest that quiet is the same as silence, or a result of being silenced; it is not acquiescence or repression. Instead, he suggests, 'The distinction between quiet and silence is more clear: silence, in a purely denotative sense, implies something that is suppressed or repressed, an interiority that is about withholding, something hidden or absent; quiet, more simply, is presence.'[7]

In terms of what the youngest child actor, Hibbert (as Little) does or doesn't do, the concept of quiet can offer a way into a more compelling reading of his performance than simply suggesting that he doesn't *do* anything – it ascribes meaning, for example, to the way that his face fills the screen, with his head tilted down, or to one side, to his slow, careful blinking and the sense of his waiting for and engaging with the look of others. Our proximity to his quiet makes him both present and a presence. In that sense, his presence and quiet is akin to the description that Quashie offers of the athletes Tommie Smith and John Carlos and their black power salute at the 1968 Olympics, which he uses as his model example of quiet.[8] Like these sportsmen, Hibbert's performance (and later, Ashton Sanders's as the teenage Chiron) could be described as 'vulnerable as they are aggressive, as pensive as they are solidly righteous'.[9] Interestingly, in relation to techniques of performance, however, the depiction of the interior that is inhabited (expressed?) through quiet is not simply an evocation of the interior as imagined through a psychoanalytic model of consciousness: 'It is not to be confused with interiority or consciousness, since it is something more chaotic than that; it is more akin to hunger, memory, forgetting, the edges of all the humanity one has.'[10]

Quashie is radical here in his refusal to suggest that quiet is akin to our existing or dominant conception of interiority – rather than an internal conversation, he is suggesting that it is more like an overwhelming tide of bodily sensation and feelings (hunger, memory, forgetting). He also describes this inchoate assemblage as encompassing 'wild motion'. As an affective quality, this might be associated with an experience similar to yearning, which refers to the constant pull and ache of desire and melancholy. The quality of yearning could be said to inform much of Jenkins's work, and is evident in his debut film, *Medicine for Melancholy* (2008), in which a young black couple have a desultory but nevertheless highly charged encounter. One reviewer suggested that it was 'both sad and vibrant, meandering and formally sure-footed',[11] something that also resonates with *Moonlight*'s distinctive combination of a loose narrative structure and strict formal composition.

Within the context of black culture, 'quiet' challenges the way in which black expression is commonly and reductively limited to a contrarian or resistant position in which the expression of black subjectivity is primarily defined by its expressiveness (Quashie calls this 'public-ness'), whether this is manifest in speech, song or prayer. This does not mean that the power of the black voice and the demand for agency (to be heard, to be seen and to act) are not important, and Quashie is insistent that quiet is not a substitute for these activities and ways of being. Quiet is rather an expansion of how it is to be and to be seen. It is sensitive to and disrupts the contemporary expectation that individuals must be articulate to give voice to their demands – instead, as Quashie suggests, of Smith and Carlos, that quiet is evident in the way in which 'though they do not speak, their language is a generous vocabulary of humanity'.[12] It is an instance, perhaps, where the hyper-visibility of the performer is turned around. If the black athlete or black child is to be 'stared at' (as exceptional) then their quiet is less a withdrawal, and more a demand for reciprocity from the spectator and for the spectator to do the work of interpretation – to do, in effect, 'face work'. As Rosemarie Garland-Thomson suggests: 'Staring is a sensory sorting process of determining an interpretive foreground and background, of formulating an ocular hermeneutics. Face work is a constantly dynamic, delicate dance of mutual scrutiny, adjustment, call, and response.'[13]

As she goes on to argue, staring can be an ethical and productive encounter – but to be so the starer needs to be willing to be arrested, held and encouraged into a position of 'attentive identification'. The subject of the stare – the staree – also has agency, however, and must be able to negotiate, manage and choreograph the way in which they are stared at. Consider for example the way she describes the work of the staree as they are being stared at:

The staree must assess the precise attitude of the starer, measuring intentions and attitudes so as to respond in the most effective way. Facilitating your starers' maintenance of face means relieving them of anxiety, understanding their motivations, and working with them to overcome their limited understanding of human variation and their social awkwardness at facing it.[14]

In many instances, Hibbert as Little does just this – in his encounters with adults and in a sense, with the camera (and the anticipated audience.) Hibbert does not flinch; while he may look down, away or up and to one side, he is negotiating rather than refusing the gaze – or indeed the stare – of the on-screen adult and the film's audience. A key example occurs during his first encounter with Teresa (Janelle Monae), Juan's girlfriend. Little is bought to their shared house by Juan; Teresa gets in the driver's seat of the car to sit next to him, ostensibly to get some kind of verbal response (Juan has thus far been unable to get Little to talk.) Like many of the sequences in the film it is brief and inconclusive – Teresa looks at Little, he looks down and then without turning his head he looks sideways at her. The scene then immediately cuts to inside the house, at dinner, where Little is eating, watched by Juan and Teresa (Fig 5.1). Intriguingly, in this sequence he does

FIGURE 5.1 Alex Hibbert as 'Little' in *Moonlight* directed by Barry Jenkins © A24 2016. All Rights Reserved.

speak (not a great deal, revealing not much more than his name and nickname) but in fact the audience don't *see* him speaking very much – most of his dialogue is heard when we are looking instead at Teresa and Juan's reactions to him. When we return to looking/staring at Little, he is quiet again, looking down, nodding and only registering visible discomfort (after a question asked about his absent father) by moving his arms into a defensive position and moving his fingers slowly on the table. When asked by Teresa whether he wants to stay the night, he simply looks up without moving his head (so in a gesture that is at once flirtatious and cautious) and nods. On the one hand, therefore, Hibbert is not doing very much, he's barely speaking, and any physical movements he makes are small and restrained. On the other hand, it feels like a master class in terms of the way in which he demonstrates how Little acknowledges and then manipulates the gaze and reactions of the adults on screen and, in turn, it is evidently Hibbert who is directing the reactions and emotions of the film audience who, like Teresa and Juan, are staring at him.

In Quashie's discussion of quiet, the focus is on adult expression and adult interiority. However, in the context of this discussion of the black child's expressiveness and subjectivity I am drawn to this conception of quiet because it unravels the way in which voice and agency are equally and continually championed and expected of the child. Or, at least, the way in which our conception of what it *means* to have agency has often demanded that the child has to speak and to act in a specific way, in order to be recognized and heard by adults. Often this requires that the child's voice be articulate, that their behaviour is civilized and their emotions legible. While many authors have reflected on the importance of voice and agency with respect to the child and noted its problematic qualities, in a thoughtful essay, Michael Wyness makes a key contribution by noting that this kind of agency is unequally distributed, with working-class children and children from poor families often unable to participate in the discursive and institutional frameworks set up to award an agency that is dependent on a particular performance by the child of their voice (or their ability to 'tell their story' often again and again for different gatekeepers and service providers.)[15] The restrictive or alienating aspect of what Wyness calls 'institutional agency' is reflected in *Moonlight*, in a scene occurring immediately after an encounter in which Chiron has been beaten up by his friend (and love interest) Kevin (as a teenager, Kevin is played by Jaden Pinner). Having received first aid, this scene involves the principal of his school asking Chiron to name the boys involved. In response, Chiron declines, saying, 'You don't even know.' The principal – played by a young black woman (Tanisha Cidel) – says sarcastically, 'Oh, I don't?' but Chiron makes it clear that he can't and won't name names, as 'speaking up' is not something he is able or wants to do. Instead, as the sound in the scene is distorted and ultimately fades out, Sanders flinches and turns away from the principal as she steps over to offer comfort. The camera is set low, looking up; as Sanders turns his face to the camera he briefly looks straight into the lens, breaking the 'fourth wall' in an instance of direct address (Fig 5.2). Although his face does not completely occupy the screen (the principal remains visible but out of focus) there is no question that Chiron/Sanders' face dominates the screen and that he is looking back at the (anticipated) audience. Nothing is said and in terms of his performative intention, we cannot be certain whether this brief glance through the lens was wholly instigated by direction from Jenkins or whether it was Sanders's own decision.

Either way, it is a key example of the significance of quiet, and the use of close-up in Sanders' portrayal of Chiron. The impact of this brief moment of direct address is to reverse what might otherwise be the overpowering affect of the scene. Instead of amplifying a sentimental sympathy for his character, Sanders' ability to stall his apparent distress and then implicitly challenge the audience effectively throws back pity in the spectator's face. If we were to apply James Naremore's terms in relation to the modes of acting here, it is perhaps the point at which Sanders' performance moves from expressive (naturalistic) to rhetorical (demonstrative or didactic.)[16] As Jenkins himself suggested, 'Ashton would explain what his approach was, from moment to moment. It's a very intellectual approach to the

FIGURE 5.2 Ashton Sanders as teen Chiron looking back through the camera in *Moonlight* directed by Barry Jenkins © A24 2016. All Rights Reserved.

performance, but then what you see on the screen is very raw.'[17] It also aligns with the previous instances of direct address by black actors. In her essay focusing on the performance of black actors in a series of independent films from the 1960s, Katherine Kinney suggests that direct address is the moment when the actor, in close-up, engages the anticipated audience:

> These brief moments contextualize the film's compositional pattern by acknowledging the camera's intimate proximity, the dramatic space it defines, and the black actors' claim to that space. That acknowledgment refashions scrutiny as reciprocity, the dramatic exchange between actor and camera.[18]

What is interesting about this glance by Sanders is that although there are numerous instances where the actors in *Moonlight* look directly into the camera lens, it is usually clear what (or who) they are looking at and this is always within the world of the film itself. As previously noted, *Moonlight* is full (one might almost say defined by) the exchange of looks between the actors and depictions of Little/Chiron/Black watching, looking and returning the gaze of others or themselves. For instance, there are several, carefully choreographed scenes in which Little/Chiron/Black look at their reflections in a mirror. Chiron's (Sanders') glance is, however, the one of the few instances in which it is the film's audience rather than another object or subject in the world of the film that is being engaged by the actor's/character's gaze. In that sense, it meets with Kinney's examples of how instances of direct address by black actors claim the space between performer and audience and how this challenges the restrictions of film technology and narrative commonly encountered by the black actor. As Jenkins observed, it also relates to the kind of interaction associated with live theatre, in which the audience is directly engaged: 'We wanted to find a few little moments to use the idea of the actors looking right at the camera. And that goes back to theater.'[19]

Although this brief instance of direct address illustrates the actor's (Sanders') potential for agency, in doing so it perversely reveals how the character (Chiron) cannot participate or be supported via an institutionalized agency. Chiron's unwillingness or inability to speak here chimes with the character's employment elsewhere of an 'embedded' agency, which Wyness presents as an alternative to the socially legitimate institutional model which prioritizes the voice of the child. In contrast, in Wyness's model of embedded agency, it is the material and routine activities that the child carries out – such as taking responsibility in the home, caring for family members, self care – that provide him (or her) with agency and serve as an alternative to his (in)ability to 'speak up'. In that sense, instances where we see Little, for example, prepare and take a bath on his own (carefully heating water on the stove) and other moments where Chiron covers his mother with a blanket as she sleeps off a drug binge, can be understood as embedded agency even though these same events may also be recognized as a consequence of parental neglect.[20] Wyness notes that this embedded form of agency emerges because 'At another level, children in poverty draw on their agency in mitigating a lack of social and political participation, which directly confronts more discursive forms of agency. Thus, agency can operate in the absence of participation.'[21]

What Wyness is suggesting is that the refusal or inability of the child to speak up, or to vocalize their situation does not mean that the child cannot or does not express their agency in other ways. For Little (and later Chiron) participation within an institutionally determined model of agency is clearly demonstrated to be inadequate and irrelevant. As actors, therefore, Hibbert and Sanders are portraying characters in which agency is embodied by routine actions, and they are required to express a non-verbal model of agency that is, as Wyness suggests, 'embedded and relational' rather than discursive and vocally expressive. The embodied and embedded character of their agency is exemplified by the many sequences in which we simply observe Little watching others, taking care of himself, or when we follow Chiron walking from school to his house, or along the school's corridors or in the extended sequence where he takes a trip on public transport ending up on the beach, where he meets Kevin.

In terms of performance, it is not just that the actors do these actions, but how they are done. How to describe this? I have already noted, for example, the way that Hibbert holds his head, how he takes his time to look, often moving his face first and then his eyes, or looking up without moving his head, in a manner that might almost be comic if it weren't also touching. Similarly, the awkward gait of Sanders in jeans that are at once too narrow, too straight and too short, with his arms held slightly too stiffly at his side, amplifies the sense that his body is being stretched by puberty (a period of awkward and ridiculous grace) whilst simultaneously exposing how Chiron is constantly on edge, or on high alert, ready to defend himself or run.

While Jenkins's direction undoubtedly encourages the audience's fascination and attention to Hibbert, as he is frequently centred in the frame and we have numerous close-ups of his face, it is Hibbert's ability to hold that attention that is key to the sense of quiet in his performance. Another particularly effective scene in which Hibbert claims our attention is when Little comes to Juan's house and asks some questions: what 'faggot' means and whether he is one, and secondly, whether Juan has supplied drugs to his mother (Fig 5.3). Seated and centred in the frame between Juan and Teresa he speaks quietly, and his head hangs forward, seemingly heavy, as he looks up and turns his face from side to side, looking alternately at the two adults, leaving significant pauses between the few sentences he does say. The maturity and surprising control Hibbert as Little demonstrates here makes the way in which he is called 'little man' by both Juan and his mother's boyfriend resonate over and above its appropriate familiarity as a common nickname for young black boys by older black men.[22] The quality of Hibbert's mature and perhaps world-weary performance in this scene can be detected by reflecting how differently he appears in one of the few instances in the film where he is more playful, less measured and less watchful. After he has been

FIGURE 5.3 'What's a faggot?' Little's question in *Moonlight* directed by Barry Jenkins © A24 2016. All Rights Reserved.

taught to swim by Juan and is playing with the waves at the beach, Hibbert can be seen in long shot, running back and forwards as the waves approach and retreat, neither looking at nor responding to the gaze of others (Juan may be watching but we do not have confirmation of his point of view). Hibbert's running to and from the waves as they come into the shore, his (just audible) laughter, the evident relaxation in his shoulders and apparent lack of self-consciousness evoke a lighter, more 'childlike' and apparently spontaneous aspect to Little, revealing how careful, constrained and controlled most of his other interactions and activities are. Another scene, in which Little is filmed (again from a distance) dancing with his classmates, in a free for all, shows Hibbert presenting Little as focused and quietly exuberant, dancing as much, if not more, with his reflection than with his peers. These instances serve to remind the audience that Little is a child, after all, and not a 'little man'.

Hibbert's and Sanders' performances make an impression, in part, because they are awarded the screen time and focus rarely accorded to other black child actors. In numerous sequences, their heads, shoulders and bodies are set within frames within the frame of the film image itself – in hallways, mirror frames and doorways. In many of these scenes the camera's focus is on their faces and since many of these encounters are without dialogue, it would seem that we are encouraged to concentrate on tiny movements in and across their face, such as the flicker and shine of light and shadow as well as minute gestures such as blinking, looking and breathing. In relation to the child actor and child performance many spectators will be familiar with the camera's seeming fascination with the child's face, as it expresses fear, love and perhaps most often wonder. Indeed many of Stephen Spielberg's child-centred films are driven by this passion; see for instance, the child's face expressing fear, wonder and love in *War of the Worlds* (2005), *Close Encounters of the Third Kind* (1977), *E.T.* (1982) and *A.I.: Artificial Intelligence* (2001).[23]

Within the class we had spent some time considering the significance of the close-up in adult actors and as a key aspect of cinematic performance – looking at, amongst others, the work of actors such as Lillian Gish, Al Pacino, Tom Hardy and Nicole Kidman, we had learned to value and scrutinize the performance of the actor in close-up, where the smallest tremors of the face might reveal their agency as actors and award complexity to the character they were playing. The details – rapid movements of the eyes, blinking, a tear, a slight smile or frown - might be small but they could be found, identified, evaluated. But despite the focus on the performer's faces *Moonlight* didn't sit easily alongside these examples. Yes, there were close-ups but as black faces could they, should they, be read in the way that white faces are? It is the white face, after all, that has dominated the discussion of the significance of the close-up. In her important essay on the close-up in cinema, Mary Ann Doane makes us aware of this, as she carefully, if not unequivocally, cites Deleuze and Guattari, who suggest that the semiotics of the face, is not only – or coincidentally – based on the white face, but that:

> the face is determined by a white wall/black hole system—the white wall of significance or the field of play of the signifier and the black hole of subjectivity, of passion, consciousness, the illusion of a depth. In such a system, the face becomes the screen upon which the signifier is inscribed, reaffirming the role of the face as text, accessible to a reading that fixes meaning. Simultaneously, the 'black hole' allows access to an assumed interiority where passions and affects reside.[24]

This face, which Doane suggests may be aligned with the impact or meaning of the cinematic close-up, is understood as operating within 'faciality' – a racist system that oppresses and restricts subjectivity, attributing subjecthood only to those with a 'face' (the 'White Man') and dehumanizing those without such faces – Deleuze and Guattari suggest such individuals are from 'primitive societies'.

Whether or not this abstract conception of the face and the system of faciality is accepted (and certainly Doane treats it with some caution), it resonates with the way in which the close-up of faces in Western cinema have previously been read, understood, critiqued, admired and celebrated. The white wall/black holes of the magnified face have been the focus of key writings on the close-up and its erotic power, whether this is Roland Barthes' limpid prose reflecting on the face of Garbo (whose eyes, he suggests are not simply holes, but wounds), or the many critiques of the angelic yet potentially monstrous close-up of Grace Kelly's white face in the opening sequence of Hitchcock's *Rear Window* (1954).[25] And in relation to the face of the child actor, as I have indicated, the absence or elision of the black child in Western cinema for much of the twentieth century has meant that it is white children's faces in close-up that are read again and again. Even child actors' faces from outside Hollywood – such as Ana Torrent's piquant close-ups in the Spanish film, *Spirit of the Beehive* (*El Espiritu de la colemena,* Victor Erice, 1973) or the soft, enduring close-up of a young child's face in the extraordinary Latvian film *10 minutes older* (Herz Frank, 1978) (in which the child's face and his reactions to the unseen theatre production are the sole content of the film), all replicate the way in which the close-up of the face as a familiar text is constituted of pale skin and dark eyes.[26] Interiority, in these readings, as Doane reminds us, is situated, or believed to reside in the 'black holes' (the eyes, the mouth) in the 'white face'. The question is, therefore, whether *Moonlight* asks us to read the black child's face in the same way or does it ask us to do something different?

One way in which *Moonlight* challenged the close-up's exclusive relation to the 'white face' and instead invited the scrutiny of the spectator was through the care in which the characters and their faces were lit and filmed. While it might seem self-evident, the care taken in shooting and presenting the black skin of Little and Chiron's faces is crucial. As Richard Dyer and others have noted, the history of lighting in Western cinema has continuously privileged white skin, establishing it as the 'norm' and further amplifying its metaphorical value by establishing numerous techniques (such as backlighting to create a halo effect, and the use of key lighting to eliminate shadows) that underpin the way in which whiteness and 'light' itself are understood to be metaphorically virtuous and epistemologically rigorous.[27] As Racquel Gates also suggests, 'film and television industries have typically prioritized the beautification of white skin on screen, with lighting and colour schemas designed to optimize every nuanced detail of white skin and white performance'.[28]

In *Moonlight*, however, it is black faces such as Little's that are prioritized; they glisten – an effect apparently desired by Jenkins and facilitated by *Moonlight*'s make-up artist, Doniella Davy, and her careful application of rosehip, grape seed or baby oil onto the actors' faces and skin to ensure that they took up and held the light.[29] The title of the film, after all, refers precisely to the way in which black skin holds and transforms light ('in moonlight black boys look blue'). As Gates suggests, we need to be careful here, as 'the celebration of *Moonlight*'s cinematography veers into the territory of fetishization',[30] but my point is that the attention paid to lighting, colour saturation (even to the extent of mimicking specific film stocks) and framing in the film does not simply replicate the way in which the close-up and lighting works for white performers. Although as Gates suggests, there is merit in the way that the images in *Moonlight* are 'beautiful precisely in the way that white images have traditionally been beautiful and black ones have not'[31] there is, I would suggest, something else – in part related to the question of interiority and childhood – at work. While, as Dyer has suggested, conventional lighting in Western cinema often confers a luminous, translucent quality to white faces in close-up (particularly for white women and I would argue for white children too)[32] in *Moonlight*, Little and Chiron's faces refuse transparency: they are beautiful but solid, the light does not (mythically) come 'from within' but bounces off. In his comments as to how casting decisions were made in relation to the three actors chosen to play the character of Little/Chiron/Black, Jenkins has noted that he was not so much concerned that the actors looked (or even acted) like one another but more that they were 'iceberg actors'.

> I wasn't worried about whether they all looked and sounded the same. What I was concerned about was, when the camera's on them and they're not speaking, how's this person going to emote? Are they going to try and externalize their emotions, or are we going to just feel the pain beneath the surface? The iceberg theory. They're all iceberg actors, man.[33]

The 'iceberg theory' commonly refers to a sense in which much is buried beneath the surface since it is only the tip of the iceberg that is usually seen above sea level. As a metaphor it is intriguing in this context, as it is not simply about 'hidden depths' but about an interiority that is implacable and potentially destructive. It is a force – an energy or agency – representing the quiet nature of the characters in which their reticence does not reflect a lack of interiority.

I began this chapter by seeking to discover how we might evaluate children's acting in cinema and specifically to think about a black child's performance. In *Moonlight*, Hibbert and Sanders do not sing or rap and they rarely shout. Their facial expressions are predominantly low key, characterized by small movements of their eyes and when they move their hands they do so carefully and cautiously. Their lack of exhibition is in counterpoint to the elaborate and heightened formal qualities of the film in terms of its use of sound, colour and composition and our attention is often simply drawn to the way the light plays over the skin of these children. In terms of physical exuberance there are only two instances where we see Hibbert as Little playing or dancing in a relatively carefree manner; and when Sanders depicts the same character he too has only one scene of extraordinary physicality and violence (where he crashes a school chair over the head of his chief tormentor.) Chiron's intimate encounter with Kevin on the beach is also expressed quietly - primarily through the way his hands grasp at grains of sand on the beach. While I have presented this as a problem in relation to the analysis of performance (what can be seen?) I have also chosen to do so because the performances here resist the kind of 'public-ness' that Quashie suggests is too often demanded or expected of black masculinity. In accordance with this, I have resisted another narrative, which might have focused on the very few, but nonetheless well-known, black child performers, whose expressive and visible skills in terms of their comic timing, dancing and singing were exceptional. For example, I could have examined the performances of the young black boys who played 'Buckwheat' in versions of the comic series, *The Little Rascals*, including William Thomas Jr. in the MGM film series (1934–44), or as played by Ross Bagley in 1994 in a feature film outing, or again – in yet another 'sequel' – this time featuring Isaiah Fredericks (made in 2014). I could have examined the rich repertoire of gestures and exclamations of Gary Coleman, perhaps the most famous child actor on American television in the twentieth century, on which the success of the sitcom *Diff'rnt Strokes* (NBC, 1978–84) almost entirely depended, and noted his superb control of exaggerated facial expressions, vocal dexterity and comic timing. I have also ignored the most famous young black performer of the last fifty years, Michael Jackson, whose professional abilities in terms of his uncanny mimicry, vocal and dancing skills were exceptional. I did not include them because they were not excellent but because as performers and in their various performances, they seemed to me to be overlaid, or perhaps haunted, with the various kinds of masks and performative expressiveness that black performers have been obliged to reproduce over the history of theatre, cinema and in popular entertainment. These young boys were fast-talking and better, bigger, dumber, cuter, sweeter and more intelligent in terms of their knowingness and delivery than the many white children they frequently acted and performed alongside. It is beyond the scope of this chapter to go in to the various ways in which black performance – and specifically the performance of the black child – is over-determined; however, it would seem fair to suggest that all of these performers had to manage the racist expectations of white audiences whilst using their extraordinary skills and talent to express their own subjectivity and to create believable characters and credible performances. In *Moonlight*, however, this overt expressiveness was largely absent. The direction of Jenkins and the skills of his young actors allowed for a characterization of a black boyhood that creates presence and is equally remarkable in its affective qualities. At the same time, it escapes definition through conventional modes of evaluation, asking us to think about the history of cinema and within this the importance of looking, of staring and about the micro-expressions of blinking and breathing; the weight of the glance as well as the ambiguity of the sigh.

Notes

1. Donald Bogle, *Toms, Coons, Mulattoes, Mammies & Bucks: An Interpretative History of Blacks in American Films* (New York: Continuum, 1989 [first pub. 1973]) and Carole E. Henderson, '"King Kong Ain't Got Sh** On Me": Allegories, Anxieties, and the Performance of Race in Mass Media', *Journal of Popular Culture*, vol. 43, no. 6 (2010), pp. 1207–21. The Screen Performance class was taught at the University of Glasgow (online due to the pandemic) between January and March 2021 and I want to thank the students for their commitment and enthusiasm in the session on *Moonlight* and many others. I would also like to acknowledge that inspiration for the essay is partly due to my second marking of another student's audiovisual essay that was submitted as part of the assessment for a course taught by my colleague Ian Garwood. The essay was by Veronika Radman, called: 'Eye/contact: acts of looking in *Moonlight* and *Medicine for Melancholy*'.
2. See Stephen Prince and Wayne E. Hensley 'The Kuleshov Effect: recreating the Classic Experiment', *Cinema Journal*, vol. 31, no. 2 (Winter 1992), pp. 59–75.
3. See Cynthia Baron, Diane Carson and Frank P. Tomasulo (eds), *More than a Method: Trends and Traditions in Contemporary Film Performance* (Detroit, MI: Wayne State University Press, 2004) and Sharon Carnicke, 'Lee Strasberg's Paradox of the Actor',

in Peter Kramer and Alan Lovell (eds), *Screen Acting* (London: Routledge, 1999) pp. 75–88.
4   Karen Lury, 'The involuntary dance: child actors, fidgeting and authenticity', in B. Henzler and W. Pauleit (eds.), *Childhood, Cinema and Film Aesthetics* (Berlin: Bertz + Fischer, 2018), pp. 85–100.
5   Nicolas Rapold, Interview with Barry Jenkins, *Film Comment* vol. 52, no. 5 (Sep/Oct 2016), p. 45.
6   Michael Boyce Gillespie, 'One step ahead: a conversation with Barry Jenkins', *Film Quarterly*, vol. 70, no. 3 (Spring 2017), pp. 52–62.
7   Kevin Everod Quashie, 'The trouble with publicness: toward a theory of black quiet', *African-American Review*, vol. 43, no. 2–3 (2009), pp. 329–43, p. 334.
8   It is inevitable that many readers might also think of the 'quietness' of 'taking the knee' in relation to recent sporting events, where sportsmen and women (black and white), bend on one knee to align themselves in protest against the treatment of African Americans, a gesture that is now increasingly understood as a shared symbolic act against racism in many countries. While this performative gesture is no doubt related, I suspect 'quiet-ness' in Quashie's work is significantly and specifically linked to the performing bodies of individual African Americans. It is notable, for instance, that in Quashie's example in the 1968 Olympics, the White sportsman, the Australian Peter Norman, who shared the plinth with Tommie Smith and John Carlos, was an ally (signalled by a pin he was wearing) but he did not make the salute.
9   Ibid., p. 329.
10 Ibid., p. 334.
11 A.O. Scott, 'A short-term affair leads to Big Questions', *New York Times*, 29 January 2009.
12 Quashie, 'The Trouble with Publicness', p. 337.
13 Rosemarie Garland-Thomson, 'Ways of staring', *Journal of Visual Culture*, vol. 5, no. 2 (2006), pp. 173–92, pp. 176–7.
14 Ibid., p. 180.
15 Michael Wyness, 'The Recognition and Distribution of Children's Agency in the UK', in Sandra Dinter and Ralf Schneider (eds), *Transdisciplinary Perspectives on Childhood in Contemporary Britain: Literature, Media and Society* (London: Routledge, 2018) pp. 230–47.
16 See James Naremore, *Acting in the Cinema* (Berkeley, CA: University of California Press, 1988).
17 Rapold, Interview with Barry Jenkins, p. 44.
18 Katherine Kinney, 'Facing the camera: black actors and direct address in independent films of the 1960s', *JCMS: Journal of Cinema and Media Studies*, vol. 59, no. 1 (Fall 2019), pp. 66–88, p. 78.
19 Rapold, Interview with Barry Jenkins, p. 45.
20 The recent British film *Rocks* (Sarah Gavron, 2019) demonstrates how this material, embedded agency operates and how (unlike for Little) its practices can be spread across a number of children. Bukky Bakray as the eponymous 'Rocks' may not operate within institutional agency (she does her best to avoid the well-intentioned care of adults or to 'tell' anyone about her family difficulties) but is in other areas more typically verbose, outspoken, performative and expressive.
21 Wyness, 'Children's Agency in the UK', p. 241.
22 Circulating around this nickname, of course, is the loaded distinction between 'boy' and man in relation to black men, as 'boy' is a historically racist appellation for black men, and while it is still a potentially patronizing tern, 'little man' as applied from an older black man to the black boy child implies at least some measure of respect.

23 See the audiovisual essay by Kevin B. Lee, 'The Spielberg face' originally published 13 December 2011 on Fandor, available at https://vimeo.com/199572277 (accessed July 2021).
24 Mary Ann Doane, 'The Close-Up, Scale and Detail in the Cinema', *differences: A Journal of Feminist Cultural Studies*, vol. 14, no. 3 (2005), pp. 89–111, p. 105.
25 See Roland Barthes, 'The Face of Garbo' in Annette Lavers (trans.), *Mythologies* (New York: Hill and Wang, 1972). In relation to Grace Kelly's entrance/initial close-up in *Rear Window* there are many commentaries, but a useful and perceptive analysis (and summary of other readings) is provided by Douglas Pye, 'Enter Lisa: *Rear Window* (1954)', in Tom Brown and James Walters (eds), *Film Moments: Criticism, Theory, History* (London: British Film Institute, 2010), pp. 45–9.
26 Problematically, one of the few image genres in which the black child's face is often seen in close-up is in charity appeals, where the intent is clearly to provoke pity and is often at the expense of the child's individuality.
27 See Richard Dyer, *White: Essays on Race and Culture* (London: Routledge, 1997), specifically the chapter/essay 'The Light of the World' (pp. 82–144).
28 Racquel Gates, 'The last shall be first: aesthetics and politics in black film and media', *Film Quarterly*, vol. 71, no. 2 (2017), pp. 38–45, p. 40.
29 See Elle Silver, '*Moonlight* make up artist: Doniella Davy', FRNDY LMRN, 24 February 2018, available at https://www.frndylmrn.com/blog/2018/2/24/moonlight-make-up-artist-doniella-davy (accessed July 2021).
30 Gates, 'The last shall be first', p. 40.
31 Gates, 'The last shall be first', p. 44.
32 See 'The Light of the World', in Dyer, *White*.
33 Rapold, Interview with Barry Jenkins, p. 44.

6 CHILDREN IN DOCUMENTARIES: OR, THE CAMERA NEVER LIES

Stella Bruzzi

Children in front of the camera in nonfictional situations are fascinating and often unusually affecting. Their appearances commonly seem spontaneous and uncontrolled and convey an authenticity that the 'performances' by adults in similar situations appear to lack. Each week in London Weekend Television's popular series *Child's Play,* which was hosted by Michael Aspel and ran from 1984 to 1988, two pairs of contestants (a member of the general public and a celebrity) watched video footage of primary-school children describing and defining something; the television audience was told what that something was, whilst the contestants had to work it out. The results were frequently hilarious as many of the children saw the mundane, supposedly familiar things they were being asked to describe in totally unexpected and idiosyncratic ways, the implication being that the state of childhood dictates that children see and interact with the world differently from adults. So what happens when the 'adult' genre of documentary looks at and engages with children? In this essay I will examine several examples of documentaries that feature children being and 'acting up' in front of the camera, comparing the relatively ingenuous appearances in *Seven Up* (Paul Almond, 1964) and *Être et avoir* (Nicolas Philibert, 2002) to the more disingenuous ones in *Capturing the Friedmans* (Andrew Jarecki, 2003) and *Tarnation* (Jonathan Caouette, 2003). In each of these examples there is an explicit sense of the differences between childhood and adulthood (between 'innocence' and 'experience') and there is an concomitantly implicit sense of how, taking account of this difference, children might be expected to act in front of the documentary camera – a camera that conventionally is allied with the adult point of view (although not in *Capturing the Friedmans* and *Tarnation*, which is one reason why these documentaries make for uncomfortable viewing).

But first I will turn briefly to the final reel of John Huston's *San Pietro* (1945), the middle part of his wartime documentary trilogy, which shows the American army's arrival (at the very end of 1943) into the liberated but virtually destroyed Italian hilltop town of San Pietro Infine, a town that was never rebuilt and now only exists as ruins in the Liri Valley between Rome and Naples. *San Pietro* is, until the last ten minutes, extremely gritty, realistic and adult. Based on reconstructions, Huston and his crew filmed alongside the infantrymen and, until the last reel, its brutal images are accompanied by Walter Huston's booming, insistent voice-over, describing the advances of the US Army's 143rd regiment through the Liri Valley. The entry of some of the US forces into San Pietro (two battalions continued on towards Rome) marks a moment of significant transition as the documentary's style alters completely. In the last ten minutes, instead of Walter Huston's relentless narration, there is music, and rather than each shot being filled with the frantic, dangerous action of combat, each image now focuses on civilians, often children, returning to their ruined lives (many had been living in caves nearby as the battles for liberation raged around them). The images underline the starkly divergent perspectives on the experience of war between adults and children: weeping mothers breastfeed their suckling babies; women carry their life's belongings on their heads – one carries baskets, others a suitcase or a sideboard, and one, with equal poise and purposefulness, balances aloft a small-sized coffin; a man, distraught with grief, turns to the camera after unearthing a body in the rubble. As the children emerge from hiding, they have an entirely different rapport with the camera: they run towards it, they grin into it, they are stopped in their carefree tracks by it; some of them point at it, some walk in front of it, others run past it and one little boy, walking thoughtfully up a steep, rubbly path, eyes the camera with deep suspicion and stops, as if it is in his way and will not let him pass.

Intermittently the narration does return, to remind us that 'living has resumed in San Pietro' or that 'children are able to forget quickly. Yesterday they wept, today there are smiles and even laughter. Tomorrow it will be as if the bad things had never happened.' However, rather like the remainder of the film (which was accused by the US Army at the time of being both too graphic and anti-war in its sentiments) this final reel is tonally ambiguous: children, we are told authoritatively, forget the horrors of war, they symbolize regeneration, life and the future, and yet, even as they beam unselfconsciously into the lens, Huston's camera dwells on some of the realities of the children's present existence, which we as spectators cannot help but project into the future: their wild, matted hair and dirty faces, their ramshackle get-ups of filthy trousers and makeshift belts, threadbare sweaters and grubby socks, crude handmade shirts and the battered adult shoes one child wears as he traipses through a muddy field. These children have a simple and straightforward relationship to the camera, but they also do not yet understand how it is representing them nor what messages – about class, poverty, war – are conveyed through the compelling images of them. The sparse use of voice-over for this reel in an otherwise narration-heavy documentary is highly suggestive of a certain adult guilt (or at the very least self-consciousness) to do with recognizing the grimness of these children's lives whilst wanting to disavow the hardships probably still to come and the pressure to give the documentary an uplifting ending. The tensions between the adults' and the children's perspectives are silent, eloquent reminders that children find themselves caught up in events that circumscribe and damage their lives forever, but over which they have little or no control. One of the most beautiful moments in Huston's powerful documentary is a close-up shot, held for a couple of seconds longer than most, of a dishevelled, carefree girl smiling into the camera, breathing in an excessively heavy manner as if self-conscious or nervous of the scrutiny. This moment is sweet though heavily poignant, and carries several inferences: the girl has most likely been surviving in a cave alongside her family to escape the battle over her town; she has never seen anything as sophisticated as a movie camera before and is fascinated by it; she has been singled out and feels special, wanted, as a result. This is the uncomplicated version of the relationship between apparatus and subject – but this is a documentary about war, in which context is all, so the girl's innocence is entirely circumscribed and compromised by the brutality it disavows.

The nonfictional camera is, as a rule, and as it appears in both *San Pietro* and *Child's Play*, discernibly adult, as a result of which the relationship between who is *doing* the looking and who is being *looked at* becomes an unequal one. This imbalance inevitably recalls the early psychoanalytic film studies debates around the look, voyeurism and objectification. However cute the children are in the impressionistic final reel of *San Pietro*, they are nevertheless the vulnerable objects of a sophisticated subjective gaze, not yet equipped with the tools to comprehend – or challenge – the ways in which their images are framed. This lack of knowledge is rendered in *San Pietro* as innocence by Huston, who has so emotively and provocatively juxtaposed the images of children with the violence and loss of life that has preceded this final reel. If we contrast for a moment the hyperventilating girl's excited look to camera with the distraught man's anguished gaze into the same lens a few minutes previously, then it becomes evident that part of what these final minutes of *San Pietro* illustrate is that the art of being 'looked at' is something that is learnt, that falls within the realm of adulthood and experience, manifest only once innocence has been lost.

In an article principally about the torture of Iraqi prisoners in Abu Ghraib, Susan Sontag wrote:

> To live is to be photographed, to have a record of one's life, and therefore to go on with one's life oblivious, or claiming to be oblivious, to the camera's nonstop attentions. But to live is also to pose. The act is to share in the community of actions recorded as images.[1]

For Sontag this postmodern definition of living as having one's life recorded in images is, within the parameters of this chapter, allied to adulthood in the sense that it is related to a time when one realizes some of the potential connotations of the photograph and the pose. The symbiosis between life and record argued by Sontag in relation to the photographs taken in Abu Ghraib is central to documentary (or 'art of record')[2] more broadly, and is reminiscent of Judith Butler's definition of gender as imitative and performative, while also recalling early writings on the gaze in art and cinema.[3] I would like to propose that we use these ideas, alongside Sontag's belief in life's innate performativity, as tools through which to begin to articulate the collision and friction as opposed to the similarity between the child's look and the adult's perspective in documentaries. Children in documentaries – in a state of being 'looked at' – are usually unaware of the connotations their images carry, even in the most desperate and brutal situations. Vicky Lebeau, in her discussion of images of children argues: 'It is often enough, the photographic image of a child – whether still or moving – that comes both to render our hostility and to rend the visual field', before listing some of these pregnant, eloquent images:

> the small boy, wearing a cap and a yellow star, raising his hands at gunpoint, during the Nazis' destruction of the Warsaw ghetto in 1943… a young girl, Elizabeth Eckford, surrounded by a white mob, as she walks to school in Little Rock, Arkansas in 1957; a naked young girl, nine-year-old Phan Thi Kim Phuc, fleeing her village in South Vietnam after being doused with napalm… the photograph of a newborn baby, buried in the rubble of a Beirut suburb… towards the beginning of 2006.[4]

Abused, distraught, murdered children speak so eloquently of the horrors of war because the child's very innocence and lack of awareness exists in contradistinction to and highlights, for the adult audience, the violence of such images and situations. Echoing Sontag's post-9/11 imperative 'Let the atrocious images haunt us',[5] Lebeau goes on to remark that 'such images may well have a unique capacity to haunt us' as 'they haunt the visual iconography of childhood' and function as 'evidence of the destruction of children and childhoods, cultures and communities'.[6] These are documentary examples of the image of a child articulating the violation and destruction of childish innocence.

As further demonstration of the differences between the documentary performances by children or adults, it needs to be recognized that adulthood and adult performances are performative in ways that childhood and children's performances seldom are. The children in *San Pietro* lack guile and self-awareness and they have not yet learnt that identity is imitative, that, as Judith Butler articulates in *Gender Trouble*,

> acts, gestures, and desire produce the effect of an internal core or substance, but produce this *on the surface* of the body… Such acts, gestures, enactments, generally construed, are *performative* in the sense that the essence or identity that they otherwise purport to express are *fabrications* manufactured and sustained through corporeal signs and other discursive means.[7]

Nor do the children in Huston's documentary think that to 'live is to pose'. Similarly, the terrified girl fleeing her napalmed village is confronted with the extreme cruelties of the adult world, but she is also not aware – until later – of the broader, transformative connotations of her image. Kim Phuc at first (in 1972) hated the photograph and 'struggled' with the publicity that surrounded it. Eventually, she 'came to realise', as two journalists phrased it, 'that if her pain and terror had not been captured on film that day, the bombing – like so many other wartime terrors – might have been lost to history'. Kim Phuc concluded forty-three years later: 'I realized that if I couldn't escape that picture, I wanted to go back to work with that picture for peace. And that is my choice.'[8] Nick Ut's 'Napalm Girl' was one of the most iconic, resonant and enduring images of the Vietnam War; it was also, as Kim Phuc's ambivalence articulates here, an equally forceful example of the child's powerlessness in front of the adult camera. As a war photograph Ut's image is exemplary; alongside news footage of US soldiers in body bags, for instance, it brought 'home' – into living rooms, onto kitchen tables – the brutality of war. Ut (just 15 years old himself in 1972) did not just take the photograph, he also accepted some responsibility for it, taking Kim Phuc to hospital to receive treatment for her burns. And yet Ut's photo ultimately also resonates with the child's vulnerability and lack of control over her or his image and how it might be used. The photograph but not the child is in this instance performative.

In *Documentary: Witness and Self-revelation*, John Ellis frames similar discussions of documentary performance slightly differently, through engaging with sociologist Erving Goffman's ideas of the presentation of the self in everyday life. Ellis argues that 'Unlike the actor in a play, our everyday encounters involve performances of self, a display that involves identity and biography, mediated by the kind of "face" that we have developed in our dealings with different social situations.'[9] Children, as in *San Pietro*, pose, yes, and acquire a self-consciousness understandably lacking when they were babies or toddlers, but this is not quite the same as having acquired an understanding of 'performances of self' as they have yet to acquire a sense of themselves as social constructs or that their 'faces' represent 'the expression(s) of biography and experience' as Ellis goes on to assert.[10] Children necessarily complicate or invalidate the rules of the conventional documentary encounter; they can – as Kim Phuc does in Ut's still image – affirm the idea that 'there are moments when every person can choose to be sincere',[11] not because they have yet learnt that to look or to be looked at are such loaded actions, but because they are not necessarily conscious of the choices they could make. Having said this, both *Capturing the Friedmans* and *Tarnation* offer potent examples in which the childhood home movie footage that dominates both documentaries suggests that their protagonists understand – only too well – the implications of the camera's gaze. However, before discussing those films in more detail, I turn to the other end of the spectrum and focus on two more conventional examples of child-centred documentaries, namely *Seven Up!* and *Être et avoir*.

Although it has since become the first in a longitudinal documentary series, *Seven Up!* – one of the most instantly recognizable child-centred documentaries – was originally conceived as a one-off film for Granada Television's current affairs *World in Action* strand. Paul Almond, a Canadian, and *World in Action*'s first series editor Tim Hewat, an Australian, were fascinated and horrified by the rigidity of the British class system and set about making a documentary through which to explore it. The starting premise for *Seven Up!* was the Jesuit, Francis Xavier's, maxim 'Give me a child until he is seven, and I will give you the man.' Through interviewing and observing 7-year-old children, Almond and Hewat wanted to test the theory that it is a child's social background that determines his/her adult future and their social positioning, so their two researchers, Michael Apted and Gordon McDougall, were tasked with finding twenty children in three weeks. *Seven Up!* is heavily didactic; it counterbalances Douglas Keay's authoritative 'Voice of God'[12] narration with the interviews with the children and footage of them being brought together for one day in London, which is when they go to the zoo, play in an adventure playground and have a party.

The interactive,[13] interview-based form *Seven Up!* takes formalizes the relationship between the adults behind the camera and the children in front of it, unlike the less intrusive observational style adopted by either *San Pietro* or *Être et avoir*. The question and answer format leads to the clear demarcation of adult and child domains and roles, and imposes an adult perspective onto the children's responses (reinforced by the fact that consent for the children's participation in the documentary was granted not by them, but by their parents or guardians). Much of the narration and many of the prompting questions relate to social concerns (what are the children's views of racial difference, what do they think of children from different social backgrounds to theirs) and to the issue of growing up (which schools and universities the children think they will attend; what they want to become). Many of the children already, aged 7, appear to have an adult perspective on their own futures, especially the more socially privileged ones. The trio of prep-school boys interviewed together on a sofa (John, Andrew and Charles), for example, cheerily rattle off the list of independent schools they will attend prior to going up to either Cambridge or Oxford while fidgeting about, talking over each other and fiddling with their regulation knee-high woollen socks. At the other end of *Seven Up!*'s social spectrum, a wary Paul asks 'What does university mean?', Sue says she is 'going to work in Woolworth's', and Tony almost sings with excitement when he reveals that he wants to become a jockey when he grows up.

Although the only faces featured are those of the twenty children and their classmates, they are fitted into an adult-determined documentary. However likeable the grinning Neil is when explaining that he wants to 'be an astronaut, but if I can't be an astronaut, I think I'll be a coach driver' or however socially aware Jackie shows herself to be, despite being framed by the film as one of the less privileged East End girls, when she says that, if she had £2.00, she would help the poor, 'because the poor, if you don't help them they'd sort of die', *Seven Up!* is prescriptive and the children's performances defined by the documentary's ideological parameters. It is the adult voices – Keay's avuncular narration or the occasional questions from behind the camera – that usually come first in a sequence and thereby dictate what ensues. *Seven Up!* is obsessed with class and although it sets out to subject the British class system to scrutiny, it comes nowhere near subverting it, but rather confirms its resilience and rigidity, through its script, its questions and also the hierarchical filmmaking techniques it adopts, notably the interview. The film ends with Keay suggesting it has given a glimpse of Britain's future, but what *Seven Up!* rarely gives a glimpse into is the children in situations not directed by adults. The moments when the child subjects do arguably manage to shuffle off the shackles of the film's didactic format are when they are captured doing other things besides being interviewed for *Seven Up!* – jostling in the queue for the pictures on Saturday morning (Fig 6.1), playing in the playground or visiting London Zoo. Despite the persistence of the nullifying and oppressive 'voice of God', these sequences are permitted to live and breathe in ways the interviews rarely do. The energetic hand-held camera mucking in with the children queuing for 'the flicks', observing their expectant faces and their lively exchanges, is fleetingly reminiscent of the puppet show in Truffaut's *Les 400 Coups* and how that documentary-esque sequence momentarily leaves behind the fiction film that surrounds it. It's a great pity that even here Keay feels the need to tell us what to think.

For all its fascination as a longitudinal study (and here I have consciously talked only about the first, stand-alone documentary), *Seven Up!* does not grant the children much freedom to exist beyond the social archetypes its script requires

FIGURE 6.1 In the queue for the cinema. *Seven Up!* © Granada Television 1964.

CHILDREN IN DOCUMENTARIES 107

them to conform to, so the children's performances are circumscribed and the interviews very seldom elicit spontaneous responses or the sort of engagingly absurd answers *Child's Play* recorded on a weekly basis. In the concluding playground sequence, for example, as the children interact with each other the narration draws our attention to the fact that the boys from the children's home are building a house. As Symon rather half-heartedly takes a pickaxe to a mound of hard earth, the sequence's contrivances seem to seep out, and one cannot help but wonder if these children were directed to build a house. The children in *Seven Up!* are representative figures as well as individuals; their social role as important as their personal performances. In *Taking the Long View: A Study of Longitudinal Documentary* Richard Kilborn observes that 'One of the several consequences of the longevity of long docs is that viewers are, in many cases, able to follow subjects whom they first encounter as children through to the phase in their lives where they are bringing up children of their own.'[14] From a performative perspective, what occurs as the series goes along in terms of the cumulative relationships between the children and the adults they become is that, whereas in *Seven Up!*, the adult point of view was imposed onto or dictated the child's, later on in the series viewers are repeatedly invited to see the child in every adult (a process aided by the editing in of the childhood footage into each set of adult interviews), so that the child defines the adult in a way that becomes unusual (usually, as in *Seven Up!*, it is the other way round). This becomes the case especially with Neil, whose appearances at seven are the most overwhelmingly engaging and all-defining, and who later becomes so heavily defined by his psychological and nervous collapse. Through the painful later interviews our primary impulse whilst viewing them is probably to want to recall the happy child who grimaces at the thought of 'coloured people' because the term makes 'you think of a purple person with red eyes and yellow feet'. The adult Neil – sitting in front of dirty net curtains in his London squat at 21, admitting at 28, as he walks along the side of a breathtakingly beautiful loch in the Western Highlands of Scotland, that he's known locally 'as an eccentric', or painfully eloquent at 35 and in Shetland about how viewers 'flooded me with letters and thought I could solve their problems'. Neil seemed to lose his childish unselfconsciousness earlier than the other Seven Uppers (maybe with the exception of Suzy), but our awareness of Neil's painful loss of innocence cannot be the only reason for our powerful responses (and the collectivity of the *Seven Up!* series viewing experience over the decades is exemplified by the regular outpouring of emotion over Neil). Childhood, Neil's passage through life seems to suggest, offers no preparation for, no protection against adulthood. He remains powerfully, movingly eloquent about both life and himself; his alienation from society as an adult being felt all the more keenly as, with each episode, Michael Apted reminds us of his engaged and engaging self. We probably look for clues in the ultra-serious, chess-playing boy of 14 for what was to come, but by and large the clips from the earlier *Seven Up!* provide seductive and nostalgic relief.

The generational narrative dynamics of *Être et avoir* are not the same as those of *Seven Up!* in that the differences between childhood and adulthood are acted out on the screen as opposed to from one side of the camera to the other. Philibert's documentary follows a tiny rural French primary school in the Puy-de-Dôme region (comprising a single class for children of all ages through to secondary school) through the seasons and from the start to the end of a scholastic year. The focal point of the interaction between children and adults is the pupils' engagement with their teacher, Georges Lopez, and as Phil Powrie observes, 'we rarely see the families of the children, as if the school, which has children of all ages in a single class, provides a surrogate family closer to what Roudinesco calls the "tribe" than the bourgeois family of modern times'.[15] Lopez, who is in virtually every sequence of *Être et avoir,* is also, for his pupils, in omnipresent *loco parentis*, functioning as their teacher, mentor, counsellor and nanny. He is an idealized surrogate father, most effectively with Natalie, one of his older pupils about to depart for middle school. Natalie is an elective virtual mute, and one especially moving sequence occurs towards the end of the film as Lopez questions her about her extreme taciturnity and talks to her about the potential difficulties of transferring schools. The primary school classroom is portrayed as a cocoon for the children in *Être et avoir*, who are not ready yet for the adult world and who are here tenderly protected and looked after by Lopez, even when being reprimanded.

Philibert's documentary, considering how recently it was made, is notably old-fashioned. In its *cinéma verité* languidness it seems blissfully unaware of docusoaps, reality television and all the other recent transmutations of the observational documentary mode, and the film's depiction of children, school and life in rural France is similarly nostalgic and backwards glancing. Shari Kizirian considers the timing of Philibert's seventh feature-length documentary as historically important – that *Être et avoir* premiered at Cannes in May 2002, some nine months after the attacks on the World Trade Center, 11 September 2001, and less than a year before the USA's 'misdirected fury was unleashed on the Iraqis'.[16] Although in this turbulent political context it 'provided a brief respite of calm', the film also, for me, functions as an act of nostalgic disavowal, intent on harking back to a different era of observational, people-centred and non-interventionist documentary filmmaking and is reluctant to confront or reinvoke the brutalities of the world around it. The much-cited sequence of Lopez asking Jo-Jo to wash his paint-encrusted hands is cute and moving, Philibert having captured the sort of privileged exchange of trusting, loving looks between teacher and pupil that only comes to a director and crew who have filmed with their subjects for almost 600 hours. However, its historical proximity to 9/11 notwithstanding, the children in *Être et avoir* are exaggeratedly far removed from the images of children being liberated from the concentration camps, for example, or Kim Phuc running naked down a South Vietnamese road, which Butler argued 'disrupted the visual field and the entire sense of public identity that was built upon that field'.[17]

The non-intrusive observation in *Être et avoir* of children learning how to read and write or spending time on non- and pre-word-based activities such as colouring in, hark back to an earlier, more innocent mode of documentary filmmaking and how to use the child on film, and point to the fact that the younger ones are only just beginning to learn the language that, in Lacanian terms, will mark them out as social entities equipped to engage with an adult-defined world. The children's innocence and the film's clearly demarcated distinction between the domains of childhood and adulthood are emphasized in the sequence only a few minutes in when Jo-Jo and some of the other smaller children are being taught to write through being asked to form the word 'maman'. Moments later, a group of smaller children again are mixing the ingredients for pancakes that, in a while, the older pupils will toss, making a dreadful mess. The idyllic nature of this school experience is emphasized by the fact that so much of what we see being learnt in *Être et avoir* is being learnt for the first time. Conversely, the older children are overtly preoccupied at the prospect of having to leave this idyll behind. Natalie's trauma at her imminent separation from Lopez – the surrogate parent who understands and is sympathetic to her pathological silence – or the pre-adolescent tensions between Olivier and Julien are framed negatively in *Être et avoir* as being part of growing up: the children's necessary but painful transition to middle school, adolescence and experience. The sentimental attachment to the innocence of childhood harks back to *Child's Play* and the amusement that series derived from looking at children through jaded adult spectacles as they strive to define things they only partially understand. An equivalent moment in *Être et avoir* is Jo-Jo and Marie performing the mundane task of trying to photocopy some pages from a book. Jo-Jo teeters on a chair and discards the many miscopied reproductions, clumsily moving the oversize book around the glass in the vain hope of positioning it correctly (Fig 6.2). We – as adult viewers – would be able to help, but in fact simply relish the spectacle of him getting it wrong and learning.

As he walks away (having been shoved off the chair by Marie who wants to try her luck at photocopying) Jo-Jo glances briefly into the camera, peripherally or fleetingly aware of its attentions, but not destabilized by it. The one in *Être et avoir* who is manifestly destabilized by the camera's presence is the adult Lopez. There is, of course, Lopez's only interview in the documentary (for the remainder of it, he is shown in action as it were – performing his job, being a teacher) which is especially stilted, but there are also less formal points at which he signals an awareness of the camera's presence and implicitly responds to its gaze. A few minutes before the photocopying sequence, Lopez is in the classroom with his pupils and begins to ruminate aloud about how he has been giving dictations for thirty-five years, an observation that is surely as much for our benefit as it is for theirs (that Lopez is on the verge of retirement is significant in terms of his deep bond with the cheeky but lovable Jo-Jo, a pupil he would not have guided through to middle school). Lopez conforms squarely to Ellis's notion of the 'performances of self' in 'our everyday encounters'[18] – doubly so, for in his everyday encounters

FIGURE 6.2 At the photocopier. *Être et avoir* directed by Nicolas Philibert © Maïa Films 2002. All Rights Reserved.

with his pupils as their teacher he is necessarily performing (even without the cameras being present), and in *Être et avoir* he is being asked to go about this everyday role for the benefit of the cameras whilst making out for the vast majority of the film that the camera is not there. The performative complexity of Lopez's situation relative to the children's is yet another way in which *Être et avoir* has to differentiate between the worlds of adult and child.

Two very different documentaries in which the distinction between child and adult perspectives is blurred if not altogether erased are *Capturing the Friedmans* and *Tarnation*, both documentaries that use a large amount of childhood home movie material juxtaposed with footage of the far more recent past, and which are also structured around personal testimony and memory. Through the course of both films, one comes as a spectator to appreciate that personal testimony and 'truth' are neither consistently, nor reliably, related.[19] This is especially the case with *Capturing the Friedmans*, a documentary that opens to the strains of the 1963 pop hit 'Act Naturally', an ostensibly facile song that equates the ability to act naturally with becoming a big movie star, used here to faux naive effect as a commentary on both the Friedman's own ostensible naivety (in letting Jarecki in to film them) and their abilities to 'act naturally' for the home movie camera – even after Arnold's trial has begun.[20] As the opening to a film about charges of paedophilia (brought against father and son, Arnold and Jesse Friedman) the glibness of this opening is unsettling, especially set against the home movie archive, which, by its very nature, is footage – like the interviews in *Seven Up!* – framed by an adult perspective where family members perform for a sophisticated, knowing and adult onlooker.

This would not seem so uncomfortably ambiguous if it were not for the fact that Andrew Jarecki, the documentary's director, is never explicit about his views on the case, namely that he thinks Jesse is innocent, and indeed, alongside his producer Marc Smerling, took an active role in the appeal and in attempting to get Jesse's conviction quashed.[21] Though compelling, *Capturing the Friedmans* makes me uneasy because of, as Xan Brooks put it in his review of the film, 'its teasing lack of judgement',[22] which, in a film about alleged child abuse, is manifestly problematic.

As details of the case emerge, as the family falls apart and finally as Arnold dies in prison, the discordance between reality and happy memories (the joshing around in the home movies) becomes irreversible and it becomes traumatic to look at images of the Friedman children playing against the backdrop of this story of child abuse, especially as so many of the home movie sequences are prefaced by or juxtaposed with the words of mother Elaine Friedman, the one family member who, from the outset, believes her husband – at least – to be guilty. This proximity between adult testimony or commentary and childhood home movie footage makes for extremely disturbing viewing throughout. Home movies are artless, responsive, observational, spontaneous; they are not generally highly wrought or heavily constructed. Home movies offer access to events, although they are usually too close to those events to explain or comment upon them. They are fragments as opposed to complete actions or narratives. A quintessential example of this is Abraham Zapruder's footage of the death of President Kennedy: the most infamous home movie as well as the most infamous snuff movie of all time. The family home movie is especially evocative, it both captures largely inconsequential action on film, while remaining emphatically performative.[23] It is rare – except, as happens with Zapruder's or the Friedman's footage, when it becomes part of an alternative narrative – for other families' home movies to be interesting to a wider audience. There are two layers of home movie in *Capturing the Friedmans:* there is the 'authentic' childhood footage, and there is the material David Friedman films around the time of his father's and brother's arrest. The juxtaposition of the two means that even the childhood footage has lost its innocence and no longer conforms to the ideal of 'conscripted "togetherness"' the family home movie putatively represents.[24] When Jesse's lawyer, Peter Panaro recollects, for example, that his client told him he had been abused by Arnold as a child, this revelation is juxtaposed with pictures of Jesse *as* a child. Elaine repeatedly asserts that the Friedmans were 'a family' (with all the suggestions of 'conscripted "togetherness"' that term implies) and home movie material to support her case – birthdays, holidays and the like – is edited in, only to be disavowed or contradicted by events and by Elaine herself. The apparent 'truth' in this case does not reside in these images of happy children smiling at and playing up for the camera, but in the shocking collision between these and the allegations of paedophilia. Both *Seven Up!* and *Être et avoir* are motivated by understanding the dialogue between the adult camera and the child subject and the more complex accompanying dialogue between childhood and adulthood – but also clearly demarcating these domains as separate. *Capturing the Friedmans*, like *Tarnation* (which I will discuss in more detail in a moment) is a documentary about huge and tragic subjects (allegations of child abuse and a mother's schizophrenia), which share and express a sense of the loss of that distinction between the generations. The separation and distance between the generations compels us as viewers to reconsider the status of the performances for and in front of the adult camera and to fret about the differences between the potential fakery of the performances of excessive 'innocence', 'naturalness' and 'happiness' captured in *Capturing the Friedmans* and the apparent honest naivety of the childish performances in *Être et avoir* or *Seven Up!*. Although *Capturing the Friedmans* definitely encapsulates our shared understanding of the home movie as the family at its most 'authentic', it also carries more ambiguous notions of the family playing at being a family – the home movie as uncanny repetition of innocent domesticity. Again, the lyrics of 'Act Naturally' are relevant here: the idea that 'they' (adults) are going to 'make a big star out of me' if I – in this instance the child – 'act naturally' could be either facile or *faux* facile, carrying equal connotations of both welcomed fame and cynical exploitation.

Jonathan Caouette's *Tarnation* offers a very different and morally unambiguous image of traumatic childhood. Released the same year as *Capturing the Friedmans* and only a year after *Être et avoir*, it is so vastly different that it could be from another era entirely. In *Documentary: Witness and Self-revelation* Ellis discusses 'slow film' and how shooting and editing have both 'undergone radical changes since the 1980s under the impact of successive forms of digital technology'.[25] Ellis is principally interested in the impact of these developments on working practices – noting that documentary filmmaking is now 'more accessible beyond the confines of the broadcast and cinema industries' and that 'it has become easier to edit, and easier to construct complex combinations of sounds and images'.[26] He then goes on to cite Geoff King on the increase in the rapidity of particularly Hollywood editing and shot length, but Ellis's distinction between slow and fast film accurately reflects the differences between *Être et avoir*, an ostentatiously 'slow' documentary, and *Tarnation*, with its use of short shots, split screens and complex soundtrack as, at times, a parodically 'fast' one.

Caouette's working methods and techniques have been well documented in virtually every article written about the film: that he shot the adult portions of it on a Sony Handycam and the childhood sections on Hi-8, that he edited over 160 hours of footage using free iMovie software and that it cost a mere $218.32 to make, excluding distribution costs. As Caouette describes it, *Tarnation* is 'an amalgam of everything: excerpts from my own CD collection; grabbing pieces from VHS and going to my Hi-8 camera. Then uploading that into the movie.'[27] It borrows its style from the traditions of non-narrative avant-garde film and music video, despite the imposition of a very clear narrative arc, namely the story to date of Caouette's turbulent life. As Caouette mentions in the same interview when asked about how he has been 'compiling everything, grabbing everything starting at the age of ten and half or eleven': 'It is odd, isn't it? It's as if I've been inadvertently making this film all my life',[28] a filmed life that continues into *Walk Away Renee*, the follow up feature which premiered at Cannes 2011.[29]

If we remind ourselves of Sontag's assertion that 'to live is to be photographed' and that to be photographed or 'to pose' offers the subject 'deep satisfaction', *Tarnation* moves us as spectators precisely because it suggests that, throughout Caouette's life, living and posing have been interchangeable facets of the same experience, which for a child (as he is in the earliest home movie footage extracts) is atypical and destabilizing. The definition of 'tarnation' is the act of damning or the condition of being damned,[30] and instead of signalling a distinction between childhood and adulthood, *Tarnation* suggests that they are points on the same continuum – that childhood is 'damned' by segueing all too smoothly into adulthood, a psychological and intellectual premise emphasized by its frenetic visual style and, most specifically, Caouette's rapport with and use of the camera. Unlike the Friedmans, for whom filming was a communal, familial activity, for Jonathan Caouette it is solitary and solipsistic, and the camera's gaze is ambivalently voyeuristic: it intrudes on and makes us uncomfortable viewers of the mental illness of Jonathan's mother Renee, his grandmother Rosemary and his grandfather Adolph; it also captures the equally traumatic spectacle of Jonathan's exhibitionist performances into it.

The most affecting and troubling of these is Caouette aged 11 filming himself, using his tripod-mounted camera in the hallway, as the fictional character Hilary Chapman, an abused wife, testifying in court and explaining why she murdered her violent husband. Quarter of an hour into *Tarnation*, this is its first extended sequence in close-up. Speaking directly into the static camera, 'Hilary' gives a painful, agitated account of her marriage to 'Jimmy', her 'little baby Caroline' and the repeated acts of domestic violence that culminated in 'Jimmy' pointing a gun to her head shouting 'I'll kill you, bitch, I'll kill you' before 'Hilary' 'blew his ass away'. The image is of imperfect quality, but the sickly tungsten yellow hue is morbidly appropriate, while the close-up image framed by the fixed camera is oppressive and claustrophobic. This image of an 11-year-old boy giving a moving, hysterical performance of an abused wife is, to borrow from Sontag, atrocious and haunting, because it suggests that Caouette both knows and does not fully comprehend the implications of his performance and, as a result, it blows apart securely held beliefs about documentary's inherent performativity: the surety of Ellis's idea that 'Face is, in many ways, the expression of biography and experience';[31] Thomas Waugh's notion of 'the right to play oneself';[32] or my own borrowings from Butler in formulating my definition of all documentary as performative. In one interview Caouette gives this elliptical account of Hilary:

> It wasn't a character that I developed prior to [filming]. It was actually inspired by two compelling things that I saw on television that day, and I just turned the camera on and just kind of went to town ... acting was the only out that I had. Definitely looking back, there was in Hilary an emulation of my mother ... It

was a very abusive marriage she went through … Some of the story, specifically the gun held up to her head, being kicked in the stomach, all that stuff my mom has gone through, that she told me about, I believe.[33]

Caouette's multiple performances and the fictional characters he constructs, especially within the context of his explosively fragmented documentary, enact the early loss and destruction of childish innocence. *Tarnation* is, ostensibly at least, a documentary about adult lives from a child's point of view but, within this framework, presents the generational world turned upside down: its adults are so needy, so unstable that certainty, solidity and awareness reside more with the child – a child, though, who has never experienced the normative transition from childhood to adulthood. However, inasmuch as 'in the ranking of suffering, children become substitutable and no longer recognisable as individual humans',[34] Caouette's uprooting and deeply unsettling 'performances of self' (and multiple others), become representative of childhood suffering and neglect more pervasively.

Children's performances in documentaries problematize so many received ideas about documentary and how nonfictional images function. They are also full of contradictions: whereas for Caouette 'to live' may be 'to be photographed' as Sontag surmises, the children in *San Pietro*, *Seven Up!* and *Être et avoir* have not yet learnt the rules of that particular game. And although the whole film is concerned with the mutuality of photography and living, neither have the sons in *Capturing the Friedmans*. Life, like documentary, is inherently performative for adults, but such an assumption is necessarily more contentious when applied to children, for performativity implies social and self-awareness, which are often still forming in children. Children's 'performances of self' are typically either representative, as Butler argues: that is, they are placed in the position – as the children are in *Seven Up!*, of standing for, representing a social group. Or, within the adult parameters of documentary film, mediated through adult eyes. 'Be yourself' is an oddly impossible instruction to an adult, but it is a more realizable proposition to a child because, as we see in the photocopier scene in *Être et avoir*, there is a greater chance that for children, what they are experiencing in their here and now is of more interest than the camera, or the performative layers of filming and how they might come across on film. Although not all children lack guile, the intellectual and psychological complexities of the gaze and the camera's objectifying potential have not, by most children, been fully negotiated. Through discussing contrasting examples of the child in documentary I have sought to explore how they are all, in diverse ways, expressive of generational tensions between adult and child, between the adult looking at children and children returning that look. When, in a documentary such as *Tarnation*, in which its autobiographical status also serves to destabilize notions of separation between adult and childhood experiences, generational differences are subverted and childishness is in danger of being engulfed by the implied guile and disingenuousness of performances that we are aware have been constructed specifically for the camera. Conversely, in documentaries such as *Être et avoir*, the children are fascinating because they are so different from us as adults, so unaware – in most cases – of the perils of growing up. One of the most frequently viewed and cited sequences from *Spellbound*, Jeffrey Blitz's spelling bee documentary (2002) is the boy Harry misspelling 'banns'. Harry squirms and grimaces as he circles round the possibilities of this short but tricky word, unself-conscious – or so it seems – of the 'performance of self' he is giving for the camera. But what is the pleasure in watching this? It is not seeing a child fail, but rather having him confirm that he is still different from us and has not yet learnt either 'to-be-looked-at-ness' or the perils and powers of documentary performance. Children are perhaps at their most beguiling when they appear to be without guile, as they are in *Être et avoir*, when they are in the moment, responsive and unpremeditated. While we are fascinated with Caouette, his multiple performances of self exemplify adult audiences' unhealthy predilection for freak show documentaries (to cite Jon Dovey's book of that title) in which the children at least seem half-aware of the adult's performative game.

Notes

1. Susan Sontag, 'Regarding the torture of others', *New York Times Magazine*, 23 May 2004, p. 28.
2. See John Corner, *The Art of Record: A Critical Introduction to Documentary* (Manchester: Manchester University Press, 1996).
3. See, for example, John Berger's description of gendered difference: 'One might simplify this by saying: men act and women appear. Men look at women. Women watch themselves being looked at. This determines not only most relations between men and women but also the relation of women to themselves. The surveyor of woman in herself is male: the surveyed female. Thus she turns herself into an object – and most particularly an object of vision: a sight.' John Berger, *Ways of Seeing* (London: Penguin, 1972), p. 45; also Laura Mulvey, 'Visual pleasure and narrative cinema', *Screen*, vol. 16, no. 3 (1975), pp. 6–18.
4. Vicky Lebeau, *Childhood and Cinema* (London: Reaktion, 2008), p. 138.
5. Susan Sontag, *Regarding the Pain of Others* (London: Penguin, 2003), p. 102.
6. Lebeau, *Childhood and Cinema*, pp. 138–9.
7. Judith Butler, *Gender Trouble: Feminism and the Subversion of Identity* (London: Routledge, 1990), p. 136.
8. Paula Newton and Thom Patterson, 'The girl in the picture: Kim Phuc's journey from war to forgiveness', *CNN*, 20 August 2015, http://edition.cnn.com/2015/06/22/world/kim-phuc-where-is-she-now/index.html (accessed July 2021).
9. John Ellis, *Documentary: Witness and Self-revelation* (London: Routledge, 2012), p. 50.
10. Ibid.
11. Ibid., p. 51.
12. 'Voice of God' narration is generally understood to be an authoritative, male voice-over, such as Laurence Olivier's in *The World at War*. For a full discussion of narration in non-fiction film, see Stella Bruzzi, *New Documentary* (London: Routledge, 2006), ch. 2.
13. For a full discussion of the 'interactive mode', see Bill Nichols, *Representing Reality: Issues and Concepts in Documentary* (Bloomington, IN: Indiana University Press, 1992), pp. 44–56.

14 Richard Kilborn, *Taking the Long View: A Study of Longitudinal Documentary* (Manchester: Manchester University Press, 2010), p. 89.
15 Phil Powrie, 'Unfamilar places: "heterospection" and recent French films on children', *Screen*, vol. 46, no. 3 (2005), p. 345.
16 Shail Kizirian, '*Être et avoir:* the medium and the moment', *Senses of Cinema*, no. 60 (2011).
17 Butler, *Gender Trouble*, p. 150.
18 Ellis, *Documentary*, p. 50.
19 See my discussion of *Capturing the Friedmans* in Bruzzi, *New Documentary* (2nd edn), pp. 238–45.
20 Lyrics quoted in *Capturing the Friedmans* include, 'They're gonna put me in the movies, They're gonna make a big star out of me.'
21 For example, Jarecki and Smerling 'spent the years since the documentary's release traveling the world at their expense to interview some of the 14 former students whose testimony contributed to Jesse Friedman's conviction'. Tracey Levy, 'Exonerating the Friedmans', *Tablet*, 21 November 2012, http://www.tabletmag.com/jewish-arts-and-culture/117317/exonerating-the-friedmans (accessed July 2021).
22 Xan Brooks, 'Family viewing' (review of *Capturing the Friedmans*), *Sight and Sound*, April 2004, pp. 40–1.
23 Although it's been subsumed for ever more into a different narrative, Zapruder's twenty-six seconds of film was, abutting as it did conventional family home movie images, intended simply as a family memento of the president's visit to Dallas.
24 Marsha Orgeron and Devin Orgeron, 'Familial pursuits, editorial acts: documentaries after the age of home video', *The Velvet Light Trap*, no. 60 (2007), p. 49.
25 Ellis, *Documentary*, p. 84.
26 Ibid.
27 Laurence Hegarty, 'An interview with Jonathan Caouette', *Projections*, vol. 1, no. 2 (2007), p. 28.
28 Ibid.
29 However, the two features fulfil markedly different personal functions for their director: *Tarnation* 'was made with a sense of urgency, and there was a heavy sense of catharsis connected to it', while conversely *Walk Away Renee* was made 'a lot more out of happenstance and circumstance … it was more about the idea that I had a lot of B-roll from *Tarnation* just residing on external hard drives, and I had the need to do something with it.' Kurt Osenlund, 'Interview: Jonathan Caouette', 20 July 2012, www.slantmagazine.com/film/feature/interview-jonathan-caouette/319 (accessed July 2021).
30 Cf. http://www.thefreedictionary.com/tarnation (accessed July 2021), which also indicates that the term is specific to New England and the Southern USA.
31 Ellis, *Documentary*, p. 50.
32 Thomas Waugh, *The Right to Play Oneself: Looking Back on Documentary Film* (Minneapolis, MN: University of Minnesota Press, 2011), p. xv.
33 Hegarty, 'An interview with Jonathan Caouette', p. 21.
34 Butler, *Gender Trouble*, p. 29.

PART THREE

HISTORIES

7 KUSTURICA'S CHILDREN: THE BUBBLE THAT BURSTS HISTORY

Dimitris Eleftheriotis

This chapter will examine the relationship between the cohesion and robust nature of grand historical narratives and the fragile but durable chaotic agencies of children. I will explore the centrality of children in Emir Kusturica's 'Yugoslavian' films in order to demonstrate how, amongst the messy aesthetics of the films and the messy lives of the characters that inhabit them, children possess a remarkable resilience that undermines and ultimately shatters the monolithic 'hardness' of historical discourse.

Underground (Emir Kusturica, 1995), which won the director the Palme d'Or for a record second time, has forced an intense scrutiny of the interface between art and history. Released when the Bosnian phase of the Yugoslav wars was moving to its final and most tragic chapter, *Underground*'s epic narrative expands over fifty-five years of the region's history, starting with the German invasion of 1941 and ending in a loosely defined present. At a moment when political and moral clarity were in demand and calls for military intervention were appearing from several quarters – not only from the combatants but also an ever increasing number of Western politicians and intellectuals (Susan Sontag famously staged a performance of *Waiting for Godot* in Sarajevo in 1993) – the film was criticized for being too messy, further muddying the waters of an already complex historical and political situation and contributing to confusion and apathy. Historical and critical clarity were demanded and the film's 'messiness' had to be purified and fixed into an unambiguous statement on the conflict. Alain Finkielkraut denounced *Underground* from the pages of *Le Monde*; and, when it was revealed that he had not even watched the film, he defended himself in *Libération* by claiming that the urgency of the situation meant that the film had to be denounced immediately, branding Kusturica a 'collaborator'.[1] Slavoj Žižek castigated the film's apparent unwillingness to take sides by classifying it as a typical case of a 'neo-fascism' that 'is more and more "postmodern", civilized, playful, involving ironic self-distance, yet for all that no less fascist'.[2]

In its absolutism what such critical condemnation indicates is that 'messiness' threatens clear, unambiguous and orderly historical accounts, which in their mastery of the past become elevated to official history. The multiple connotations of 'messiness' as a negative category in relation to, inter alia: the disciplinary upbringing of children; the political clarity of history; and cinematic style provide the focus of my essay. It is, however, important to address briefly how *Underground* functioned as a text that in its political 'messiness' retroactively influenced Kusturica's overall career, including the pre-1990 films that I address here, both altering and redefining their significance.[3] Dina Iordanova's comprehensive study of Kusturica's films up to 2001 opens its considerations with the question 'Who is Kusturica?', which is answered in the first instance in relation to his ethnic 'roots' and 'allegiances', a rather insensitive line of enquiry given the historical context.[4] What compounds the irony is that the pro ex-Yugoslavia stand that is attributed to *Underground* is then deployed as an interpretative framework for the pre-1990 films, which earlier critical reception had actually praised for their 'messing-up' of the officially sanctioned and sanitized history of Yugoslavia as a socialist paradise. Viewed from the perspective of the 'betrayal' of *Underground* these earlier films are now either ignored or cited as manifestations of Kusturica's alleged neo-fascist representation of the history of the Balkans as an 'eternal orgy of drinking, singing and copulating'.[5]

I too was an actor on this stage – I could move, speak, react on my own volition. The inevitable counterforce would just have to wait.[6]

(p. 265)

Focusing on *Do You Remember Dolly Bell?* (Yug, 1981; henceforth *Dolly*), *When Father Was Away On Business* (Yug, 1985; henceforth *When*) and *Time of the Gypsies* (Yug, 1989; henceforth *Time*) this chapter will consider some of the ways in which Kusturica's messing-up of official history is carried out during the volatile period following Tito's death in 1980 and the disintegration of Yugoslavia that started in 1990, challenging any black and white binary accounts of the now extinct state's history. The films are set in a clear historical context but one that cannot be defined as either an ever-improving socialist paradise, or a totalitarian communist hell. Rather they expose the naivety and reductive qualities of both official, state-sanctioned versions of Yugoslavian history, and Western Cold War aphorisms, by constructing rich and chaotic narratives of everyday life. In Kusturica's films, communities and extended families are employed as mediating structures between the forces and processes of history and the complex, infinite microcosms of individual lives with their often conflicting anxieties and desires. More specifically, this chapter will argue that the children,[7] who are central in the three films, are potent agents in the interrogation and the process of 'messing-up' official history. Furthermore, the 'child' as a discursive category abounds with tensions between order, tidiness, cleanliness and messiness: since hygienic practices, well-organized and clean living space, neatness of presentation, to mention but a few, are all values held as essential for the 'proper' development of children, with messiness signifying a deep-rooted sign of immaturity that has to be ironed out through the deployment of a panoply of disciplinary and regulatory processes. The incessant pursuit or demand for order and tidiness identifies messiness as the natural mode of the child's existence and the child itself as an agent of disorder. In addition, there is also discursive messiness around childhood as a category, with the child held as the ultimate explanatory framework (most obviously demonstrated in psychoanalysis) of what an adult becomes. Yet the child is always a 'work in progress', unstable at his or her core, an entity that requires adult attention and care in order to be fully formed.[8] This leaves conceptualizations of the child's subjectivity and agency suspended between past, present and future (what one is, was, will become); simultaneously the lynchpin of identity and its most volatile component.

In relation to children's fiction, Jacqueline Rose sees, in the spinning of narratives about or for children, the desire to impose order: not only on the messiness of personal accounts of identity formation but also on the threatening mess of symbolic systems:

> What we constantly see in discussion of children's fiction is how the child can be used to hold off a panic, a threat to our assumption that language is something which can simply be organised and cohered, and that sexuality, while it cannot be removed, will eventually take the forms in which we prefer to recognise and acknowledge each other. Childhood also serves as a term of universal reference which conceals all the historical divisions and difficulties of which children, no less than ourselves, form a part.[9]

Order and messiness also enter the discourse through the construction of a protective 'bubble' of childhood created by adults, which seeks to isolate and sanitize the child from the 'dirt' of the real world of the adults: for instance, through careful use of language or the systematic classification of the suitability of cultural material. A whole set of discourses, practices, aspirations and values are in place in order to construct and secure that such 'bubbles' are indeed possible and functional. The clearest manifestations of such discourses are articles of legislation such as the various Children's Acts in the UK and the controversial guidelines articulated by the United Nations Convention on the Rights of the Child (1989), the latter underpinned by the promise to 'help meet every child's right to be healthy, to be educated, to be treated fairly, to be listened to, and to have a childhood protected from violence, abuse and exploitation'.[10] Key institutions (legal, medical, educational, cultural, sociopolitical) are enlisted in the discursive production of such bubbles, but its primary location, the space within which it is created, respected and protected, is the family.

Through their dramaturgic and representational practices, Kusturica's films also construct bubbles of childhood. Yet in his films, these bubbles are inhabited by children who are not protected, sanitized or isolated from the broad historical processes that surround them. Unlike the anxious discursive production of sterile, utterly protected bubbles imagined by legislation and policy, Kusturica's bubbles are porous and permeable, fragile to historical forces but also hard enough to mess up the linearity and to confuse the rigidity of history. The children do not simplistically function as sentimental representational shorthand for the harshness and oppression of the political situation. Instead, they are involved in a dynamic relationship with historical reality by asserting and celebrating their existence in the micro-histories that run parallel to and interrogate such reality. The personal narratives of Kusturica's children construct a type of agency and subjectivity that is in stark contrast with the anonymous subjects of the grand socialist meta-narratives and grants them a critical edge that ultimately explodes these narratives' apparent legitimacy and historical accuracy. The films enable and foreground the incessant activities of the children, a 'bubbling-up' of agency that disturbs the powerful, linear surface of dominant history's symbolic violence.

The 'bubble of childhood' in Kusturica's films plays overlapping roles in the critical reception and political evaluation of his work. Firstly, it emerges as part of the accusation of 'Yugo-nostalgia' frequently levelled at him (which he mischievously accepts) and these bubbles are possibly an expression of the sentimental investment in childhood that his films can, in a certain reductive manner, evoke and which may then be conflated as an expression of nostalgia for the political regime. Secondly, Kusturica himself delves into mischief and chaos, creating an atmosphere which he often describes as 'childlike' – this refers not only formally to the construction of his films, through the chaotic planes of shot composition, movement of and in the frame and overall *mise en scène*, but also to the content; his deliberate 'messing up' of historical narratives and orders.

Life was too busy to dwell on things like age

(p. 26)

As I will demonstrate in my analysis, children in the early Kusturica films, at least partially because the treatment of gender operates in the most patriarchal and orderly manner imaginable, complicate and in effect mess up the politics of bio-power and the universality, coherence and manageability of other historical accounts and grand narratives. All three films place boys at the centre of their narratives but remain, one suspects deliberately, ambiguous about the precise age of the protagonists.

Dolly is set in the early 1960s in Sarajevo and revolves around a typical family with four children with a particular focus on Dino, an active, if 'inclined to delinquency' member of the Youth Club run by the Communist Party. Dino is a teenager but played by Slavko Stimic (a regular in Kusturica's films) who at the time of the film's production was 20. During the course of the film Dino becomes the lead singer of a popular music quartet, falls in love with 'Dolly Bell' (Liliana Blagojevic) – a sex-worker placed under Dino's protection by her pimp Pog (Mirsad Zulic). Dino's father Maho (Slobodan Aligrudic) dies following a brief but serious illness and at the end of the film and after a successful performance by Dino's band, the family leave their neighbourhood as their long-expected relocation is finally authorized.

The protagonist of *When* is Malik, a 6-year-old boy played by Moreno D'E Bartolli, who was 10 years old at the time of production (and looking every bit his real age). The film's story is focalized around two years of Malik's life, the 1950–52 period, when his father Mesa (Miki Manolovic, another of Kusturica's regular leads) is sent first to prison and then to exile for making inappropriate political comments. The family moves from Sarajevo to Zvornik, Mesa's place of exile, where Malik falls in love with Masa (Silvija Puharic) who suffers from a mysterious disease and eventually dies. Mesa's political rehabilitation is completed and the family return to Sarajevo as the film ends with a chaotic wedding party.

Defining the age of Perhan, the protagonist of *Time of the Gypsies* is even more challenging. He is played by Davor Dujnovic who was 20 at the time of production. More confusingly, the film is playful and inconsistent with his appearance, employing costume, props and make-up to construct him initially as a very young teenager but later as significantly older, as he becomes more and more involved in the world of adults. Perhan lives in a Romany community with his grandmother, uncle and poliomyelitis-inflicted younger sister Dzamila (Suada Karisik). Perhan falls in love with his neighbour, Azra (Sinolicka Trpkova). In order to cure his sister and raise money to marry Azra, Perhan joins the gang of the 'gypsy king' Ahmed (Bora Todorovic) who operates a criminal business between Yugoslavia and Italy. Azra dies while giving birth and when Perhan discovers that Ahmed has been lying to him and using Dzamila in his gang of child-beggars, he kills him but is then shot and dies.

The three films are very uneven in their treatment of children, centralizing their narratives on one particular child but downplaying or even completely marginalizing others. Dino's sister and two brothers are inconsequential to the story, contributing to the *mise en scène* of the family set-up but not endowed with narrative agency. Similarly, Mirza (Malik's older brother played by Davoue Dujnovic) is primarily used for his accordion playing, providing diegetic iterations of the film's main musical theme, Iosif Ivanici's classic Balkan waltz 'The Waves of the Danube'. In *Time* Dzamila's main function seems to be her illness, which is used as a causal narrative force, ultimately only 'meaningful' in terms of her sentimental value for Perhan, since she says very little and has no influence on the future for herself or for her family. Justifying the feminist critique often levelled at Kusturica, the characters with narrative agency are therefore exclusively boys or men, with girls and women functioning as an affective and symbolic *mise en scène*, often reduced to iconographic clichés that draw on a repertoire of dubious stereotypes: the mother, the whore or the helpless little sister.

The ambiguity around the precise age of the young protagonists – and their status as children (of whatever age) – does not undermine the key place that Dino, Malik and Perhan occupy. Given the historical nature of the films it is important to recognize the specific significance that childhood holds in the context of the communist mode of governance that underpinned former Yugoslavia. Children had always been an important target group in communist societies in general, with a number of youth organizations playing a key role in the ideological and political control of society. Organizations such as the Soviet Komsomol or the Yugoslavian Pioneers provided a protective and controlled environment, which sanitized or protected children from what was perceived to be the contaminating, harmful influences of capitalist values and culture. One of these groups' functions was the filtering of international cultural influences. The only works approved by the State were those produced in other countries of 'existing socialism', in the context of the international communist fraternity or representing the struggles of the oppressed around the world. Yet Yugoslavia's case is peculiar, in that after the 1948 break with USSR and Stalin, it became considerably more open to Western influence, allowing greater mobility to and from its national territory. Another crucial function of youth organizations was to cultivate the kinds of values that were believed to be appropriate to inspire the generations of future communists who would build the socialist utopia. The specific qualities of such modes of communist appropriations of childhood are explored in both *Dolly* and *When*, the former scrutinizing the Sarajevo Youth Club to which Dino belongs, the latter referring extensively to Malik's experience of communist youth groups.

Every room has a room-feeling.

(p. 14)

I will now examine how the three films construct childhood through the use of setting and *mise en scène* and identify the ways in which they open that space to broader sociopolitical discourses and historical processes, creating a bubble that is well defined but also extremely porous. Two configurations surface with regularity in the films: a domestic space, usually identified as the family's home, and a more public space where children enjoy a degree of autonomy with minimal adult presence and control. While I refer to the latter in passing as a significant arena where key aspects of the children's agency and subjectivity unfold and where the intervention of state ideological control is most evident, my primary focus is on the domestic context and the family as a spatial articulation of the protective bubble of childhood.

The ambiguity with which Kusturica imbues his films is very evident in the treatment of domestic familial space. On one level, the families of his films are dysfunctional, teeming with dark secrets, with betrayals lurking at each turn of the narrative. Maho is an alcoholic, Mesa has an affair with physical education teacher Ankica (Mira Furlan), who eventually marries his brother-in-law and Perhan suspects that the father of his child is his uncle (Husnija Hasimovic). At the same time, however, the families share moments of intimacy, tenderness and companionship often expressed as a *mise en scène* of bodies bundled together on a shared bed or around a dinner table. Dialogue fades out in these instances with only music accompanying the *tableaux vivants* of familial togetherness. These moments are signalled by a slowing-down of the pace to a complete stillness, providing utopian pauses within the otherwise exuberant, fast and chaotic Kusturica style. They are rare and short-lived moments that become affective counterpoints to a familial space that is continuously invaded by the menacing presence of the state and its politics, or which, otherwise, implodes because of its own failings.

> **Even when we said a room was silent… there were still the tiny sounds of floor-board warping, or clocks ticking, or the rattling of stray water droplets in the radiators, the velveteen brush of cars outside.**
>
> (p. 309)

In *Dolly* the family dreams of larger and 'proper' accommodation as they scrape by daily in their current accommodation, a house that constantly leaks when it rains. With basins hastily commandeered to gather the rain, the ability of the house-as-home to act as an effective protective shell is graphically undermined. In *Time* Merdzan takes revenge on his family by mechanically lifting up the frame of the house, exposing Perhan, Dzamila and their grandmother to the rain, thereby leaving them – literally – without a roof over their heads. In *When,* Malik and his mother Sena (Miriana Karanovic) visit Mesa in his place of exile where they all share a tiny room. Here a blanket is employed as a partition between the adults who are trying to make love and their son. Malik feels left out and does everything he can to abolish this flimsy boundary. He succeeds and, perhaps ironically, the image of Malik in the bed squeezed between his parents becomes yet another instance of familial togetherness.

But such moments offer a flawed and short-lived togetherness in that they negate the desires of Malik's parents and otherwise point to the very failure of the communist governance to provide adequate accommodation for its citizens. As Michel Foucault has noted, a key aspect of spatial distribution of sexual roles in the modern family household is the creation of private space, especially in the form of separate bedrooms for children and adults.[11] The inadequate accommodation of the families, which is evident in all three films and most eloquently presented in *When*'s makeshift bedroom, therefore has a double effect: it enforces utopian moments of intimacy but also underlines the power of the political (in its systemic failures or oppressive control) to penetrate familial privacy.

The significance of the image of the 'leaky home' is a clear sign of the material collapse of the protected space of the family and a manifestation of the family sphere's infiltration by the broader historical and social context that stealthily 'leaks' into the bubble of childhood. This is a theme (the family at the mercy of historical forces, history experienced through the lens of the family) that Kusturica, in several interviews, has declared as underpinning the construction of his cinematic tales.[12] These authorial 'declarations of intent' are supported by the remarkable inventiveness and variation with which his films express this visually. In *Time* children try to conceal themselves under boxes but as they move their presence becomes entertainingly obvious – the same comic visual trick is repeated in his later *Black Cat, White Cat*. Through this particular convention, the 'child in the box', the desire for privacy and cover is ridiculed as impossible, an ostrich-like act of self-deception which in its expression of an impossible desire for privacy taints the comedic mood with a bitter aftertaste. It is precisely the desire for a proper and functional 'bubble', a modern house, which becomes the main motivational force behind Perhan's adventures, leading to his demise – the comedic visualization of the moving box therefore becomes tragic within the film's narrative context.[13]

In the opening post-credit scene of *When*, as Malik's voice-over begins to tell his story, a medium shot places him in the centre and foreground of the frame (Fig 7.1). The boy is on a moving cart with his best friend Joza (Slobodan Aligrudic). The intimacy of the shots of the boys is further emphasized by the out of focus background while the voice-over helps establish the cart and the boys' passage as a self-contained autonomous space, an audiovisual manifestation of the bubble of childhood. However, the blurry figures of farm workers are recognizable in the background and their 'Come on comrades' chants are audible, infiltrating the space of the boys.

In Dino's leaky home the family is not simply exposed to or infiltrated by the elements. Important family discussions are seen to be conducted in the same manner as Communist Party meetings, with Maho chairing the sessions and setting the agenda, with minutes taken and the sons addressed as 'comrades'. In this particular case the presence of the state is felt as a force that is simultaneously 'soft' (as an ideological influence on family relationships) and 'hard' (through the domination of the everyday familial proceedings).

FIGURE 7.1 On the trailer in *When Father Was Away on Business* directed by Emir Kusturica © Centar Film 1985. All Rights Reserved.

Another and more complex exploration of the interplay between the private and personal and the contextual and political takes place in a scene where Malik is accompanying his father on a business visit to a town near Zvornik. It is clear that this 'business' is just an excuse for Mesa and his friends to indulge in what Sena describes as 'whore mongering'. The scene unfolds in a music hall decorated by an enormous banner that reads 'Culture, Art, Entertainment' – the official slogan of the cultural policy of the party. Three local women join the men at their table and Mesa begins his sexual advances to one of them, covertly using his feet. Malik slides under the table, thereby spying on his father's activities and when things seem to go beyond his approval, he sets the tablecloth on fire. In this way, the film creates two concentric spaces: the space of the music hall whose walls are lined with the official 'Party line' on the event it apparently stages but which, in reality, facilitates Mesa's 'whore mongering' and another space: the table under which the transgression is monitored and disrupted by Malik. It is Malik's action that comes to the rescue of familial unity whilst simultaneously foregrounding the hypocrisy of the official narrative and its irrelevance to the most valued aspects of Malik's life. In the close-ups of Malik's pensive and observant face under the table we can perceive a spatial and more literal configuration of a 'bubble' that has a more private, personal and individualized character. There are two important aspects in these shots of Malik. While on a representational level the *mise en scène* of a self-contained bubble created under the table is disturbed by Mesa's searching, desiring feet, Malik's intervention temporarily interrupts his father's sexual advances (Fig 7.2). Whilst the protection and care of the state and the family fail Malik, it is precisely their failure that enables and inspires his narrative agency. Furthermore, the shots under the table are similar in their construction – the framed face, the fascination and engagement with an object, the facial expression, the closed-form composition – with a series of images of other children across all three films. The shot of Dino's fascination with the colourful light bulbs and the loudspeakers playing music in the opening of *Dolly*, that of Perhan's absorption as he hypnotizes his pet turkey, and the concluding shot of *When*, with Malik flying over the land, carry a utopian affect in their self-sufficiency and completeness that is comparable to the images of the bundled family, however much they are short-lived and fragile.

> **I suppose children are particularly susceptible to such irrational connections: with so much unknown, they are less concerned with the sticky details than with trying to create a working map of the world.**
>
> (p. 143)

A specific quality exclusive to children in these films[14] is the possession of or obsession with a 'paranormal' ability of sorts, which informs the discursive and affective constructions of their 'bubble' and operates in a similarly complex and multidirectional manner: Dino practices hypnosis, Malik sleepwalks and Perhan has telekinetic powers. The presence of the paranormal in these films might

FIGURE 7.2 The disruptive 'bubble' of childhood in *When Father Was Away on Business* directed by Emir Kusturica © Centar Film 1985. All Rights Reserved.

be attributed to the discursive affinity that Adam Phillips identifies between childhood and insanity:

> Our earliest lives are lived in a state of sane madness – of intense feelings and fearfully acute sensations. We grow up to protect ourselves from these feelings: and then as adults we call this defence 'sanity'. Looked at this way, sanity begins to sound like a word we might use for all adult states of mind in which we are not children, in which we do not experience things intensely.[15]

While practice of the paranormal does not necessarily entail an insane subject, it does fall on the other side of rational discourse. And the paranormal activities of these children have important critical functions. Read as political allegories, hypnosis, sleepwalking and telekinesis can be seen as fundamental ideological representations of the way in which a totalitarian state relates to and controls its citizens: projecting and enforcing sets of beliefs and ideas as reality, compelling them into mindless actions, exercising remote regulation of their movements and desires. In Kusturica's films the embodiment of the ideological apparatus of the state in the paranormal activities of the young protagonists is deeply ambiguous. Malik's sleepwalking is not necessarily involuntary and the boy uses it tactically, such as in one particular escapade, which takes him from his home through the night streets of Zvornik and ultimately, into the bed of Masa. This raises interesting questions around agency, as here the apparent passivity of sleepwalking (citizenship under communism?) is used as a pretext for the covert but active pursuit of personal objectives. Similarly, Dino's technique of hypnosis and the repetition of the phrase 'every day in every way, I'm getting a little better', is resonant of the grand narrative of progress and of the idealized figure of the communist as the supremely evolved hero of humankind. And while Dino has long debates with his father about the similarities between personal improvement through self-hypnosis and communist character-building, he mainly uses the technique in order to achieve mundane and practical goals such as the sexual conquest of Dolly Belle. The irrelevance of the grand narrative of progress (that underpins the all-conquering communist subject) is also comically exposed when Dino advises his friend Marbles (who plans on making an advance to a girl at the Youth Club) to 'take control of his destiny' by repeating the 'every day in every way, I'm getting a little better' mantra. Unimpressed by the promise of self-perfection Marbles's response is poignant: 'that's all right but what will I do tomorrow?' In this way, the belief in the paranormal – or irrational powers – that is characteristic of childhood is employed in a way that bursts the supposedly watertight construction of official history, reclaiming the primacy of mundane needs and desires over supposedly more significant teleological trajectories. The acceptance of the paranormal here also exposes the fundamental insanity of beliefs and ideas as articulated by the communist state, which claim to be materialist, rational, even scientific in nature, but are revealed here as little more than childlike flights of fancy that also verge on the paranormal and/or irrational.

These moments happened, perhaps, but they were not happening, they no longer existed, and so to collect them together seemed a bit false.

(p. 203)

Children in these films are also pivotal in their systematic undermining of neat binaries and as they frustrate attempts to impose clear either/or versions of Cold War history. This is reinforced by Kusturica's proliferation of possibilities not only in relation to the young protagonists' subjectivity and agency (hovering between activity and passivity, self-determination and subjugation, happiness and unhappiness) but through his busy, chaotic and ultimately 'messy' style of filmmaking that refuses to establish a hierarchical organization of events and objects. A comparable messiness informs Reif Larsen's 2009 novel *The Selected Works of T. S. Spivet* – quotations from which frame this chapter. The novel itself consists of a dense and often confusing conglomeration of maps, notes, first-person narratives, diary entries and drawings, all created by the titular boy who obsessively records almost everything that attracts his attention. The layout of the book is such that a lot of material appears in the margins of the pages, often in the form of notes related to the main text. The following note that the boy provides as he reads a discovered journal is particularly insightful:

I wanted to see Emma's childhood sketchbook! I wanted to hold it up against my own notebooks and see if we were sketching the same things. What had happened to that sketchbook? What happened to all the historical detritus in the world? Some of it made it into drawers of museums, okay, but what about all those postcards, the photoplates, the maps on napkins, the private journals with little latches on them? Did they burn in house fires? Were they sold at yard sales for 75¢? Or did they all just crumble into themselves like everything else in this world, the secret little stories contained within their pages disappearing, disappearing, and now gone forever.[16]

This is an eloquent commentary on the reduction necessarily involved in the construction of any grand history and, in its evocation of a subjectivity fascinated with 'historical detritus', the book presents a literary parallel to the way in which children function in the pre-1990 Kusturica films; for what Dino and Malik primarily and, to a lesser extent Perhan, bring about in the films is a retrieval of detritus from the 'dustbins of history'. The proliferation of the complex yet small stories that emerge, which bubble up and disrupt the smoothness of master or meta-narratives constitute a mighty centrifugal force that confuses simplistic and reductive versions of Yugoslavian history.

Post-1945 Yugoslavian history is messy: a country both communist and anti-Soviet, consisting of several semi-independent republics but somehow holding together,[17] exercising oppressive control over its citizens but also, uniquely for a communist state at the time, open to foreign visitors.[18] Judith Keane outlines the critical role that a clear and orderly official history played in holding the country together, a role carried out through the subordination of difference and fragmentation:

> A carefully contrived national history and collective memory provided the glue of Tito's Yugoslav state. The foundation myths which nourished the over-arching official story emphasized the experiences which citizens shared across the six constituents republics. By contrast, the personal stories of ordinary citizens were framed by their particular experiences of work and region and, most importantly of all, by the web of family networks in which their lives were embedded.[19]

Kusturica's films therefore operate on a personal level but the private sphere of the protagonists is permeated with the political and historical context, so that ultimately we are standing neither with post-Tito officialdom nor, as Keene explains, 'with the Cold War warriors of the West'.[20] In part, this is achieved through the particular historical moments that are chosen to provide the setting of the films.

In *Dolly*, Dino's pop band is set up by the party as a way to 'combat delinquency'. In the opening of the film, and in a manner that reveals the communist obsession with order and uniformity, the Secretary of the Sarajevo branch stands in front of a map and comically declares:

> The situation today is very complex. In recent times the number of juvenile and adult delinquency in our vicinity has been on the rise… Look. One

sociopolitical cell in our community has a band. Another hasn't. That can't go on, comrades.

However, Dino's experiences in the Youth Club are not necessarily orderly and suggest a confusion of national origins, amorality and cultural influences. Aside from the impropriety of meeting Dolly Bell through her pimp – who is a prominent member of the Club – Dino's cultural curiosities and interests are fuelled by a very mixed menu that consists of a hodgepodge of international trends. While folk nationalist music is performed in the Club, the young members mainly enjoy films like the Italian exploitation documentary *Europa di notte* (Alessandro Blasetti, 1959), which features night life in the European capitals with the young spectators swaying to the rhythm of Colin Hicks (an 'English rock-n-roller') performing in London[21] and admiring the act of striptease artist Dolly Bell[22] in a night club in Paris. The Youth Club also hosts Dino's band performance of Adriano Celentano's 1962 hit 'Ventriquattro mila baci' (24,000 kisses)[23] which features prominently in the film's soundtrack: here then, the cultural influences come from an eclectic engagement with what the state has allowed, through international distribution and in national versions of current and international popular music genres. The celebration of such an arbitrary mix not only messes up any sense of national cultural hegemony but also foregrounds the incoherence of official cultural policy.

While in many ways *Time* appears to be the least historically explicit of the three films, its use of setting creates counterpoints that similarly complicate any official history. The story is clearly informed by widely reported child-trafficking stories at the time[24] and was made just before the outbreak of the Yugoslav wars, taking the marginalized Roma community as its focus. Perhan and Djamilla's first journey to Italy takes them through the length of Yugoslavia and most of its republics, travelling on the 'Brotherhood and Unity' Highway, opened by Tito in 1950, that runs from Belgrade to Zagreb. As its name (an official party slogan) indicates, it was a key symbol of the post-war nation-building Titoist project. That the motorway was used for illegal trafficking and is traversed by the Roma children of the film (unwelcome outsiders to any of the nation's republics), a year before the outbreak of the Yugoslav wars – a conflict that shattered any illusions of brotherhood and unity – is a perceptive anticipation of the country's messy future. Also affectively undermining the official account of fraternity is Djamilla's reception in the hostile and inhospitable hospital in Ljubljana, where the terrified girl is greeted by a doctor with the 'reassuring' statement that 'Comrade Tito had his operation here'.

In *When,* Malik follows the Yugoslavian football team as they progress towards the final of the 1952 Olympic Games, with the radio coverage of the game against USSR dominating the soundtrack in the final scene of the film. This is a sporting expression of the open political hostility between the two countries that erupted in 1948 and provides the historical context of the film.[25] Mesa expresses the view that

Tito's break with Stalin is 'a step too far' and is persecuted for his beliefs.[26] However, this is an opinion complicated by the film, as it is clear that the persecution is very much orchestrated by his brother-in-law, the local party strongman, who is jealous of Mesa's affair with Ankica. Thus Mesa, a Stalinist, becomes a victim of the pogrom that the anti-Stalinist policy of Tito instigated; and in any case, this apparent political motive is just a cover for the real reason, which is the personal antagonism between the two men.

The title of the film also captures some of the complexities of life as experienced by Malik. The excuse that 'father is away on business' is used to conceal the harsh political truth to his young son. On the other hand, it is what Mesa does when he is away (the affair with Ankica, the 'whore mongering' that Malik witnesses) that puts both himself and his family into trouble and arguably affects Malik in a more direct manner. 'Being away' in this context is therefore both a political punishment and the opportunity for personal betrayal. Malik, however, is not just a helpless victim of his father and the political system: he is also capable of wreaking havoc and disrupting the attempts at order that are thrown at him. Chosen to deliver a speech at a communist pageant, Malik messes up his concluding lines, pledging to 'keep walking on the path followed by Tito led by the Party', landing his father in trouble with the hierarchy, since this construction presents a deviation from the official line that suggests that it is the *Party being led* by Tito and not the other way around. Malik's 'error' foregrounds the contradiction of the Yugoslavian ideology which criticized Stalinism but which, at the same time, built a personality cult around Tito. It encapsulates, like the semi-deliberate sleepwalking elsewhere in the film, the fluctuating agency that Kusturica's films construct for his child protagonists. Hovering between activity and passivity, intentionality and error, knowledge and ignorance, neither Dionysian nor Apollonian,[27] the children of Kusturica's films are able to move freely between polar opposites, demolishing simplistic, politically purposeful, orderly accounts of history.

In Kusturica's chaotic films the bubble of childhood that renders the children 'special' is permeated by the familial and historical context. However, Dino, Malik and Perhan, in turn, 'bubble up' disruptively and make obvious the complexity of history as it is lived, thereby exposing the naivety of ideologues and historians from either side of the Cold War divide, who seek to identify clear and uncomplicated positions and a coherent teleological narrative. Of these children, perhaps Malik provides the best example of an agency capable of negotiating the most difficult situations that arise within the family, community and national historical context. After attending the funeral of Joza's father (who is in fact not dead – his wife has provocatively requested a burial in order to expose the state's silence on his disappearance) Malik delivers a particularly insightful interior monologue that concludes: 'Is there anyone in the coffin? I know that when someone dies, he is no more but he can't just vanish – when Mama told me to shut up I understood everything.' The silence imposed by the state and demanded by his mother is only superficially upheld, his voice-over signalling both Malik's understanding of its political significance and at the same time, revealing the key role that the film allows him to play in exposing the 'messy reality' of life in Yugoslavia.

> **The boundedness of a comic frame was satisfying, as nothing could penetrate the insularity of that world. Except the boundedness was what always left me feeling a little hollow.**[28]
>
> (p. 319)

The attention to 'detritus' facilitated by Dino, Malik and Perhan works in tandem with the films' aesthetics of disorder. It is beyond the scope of the present chapter to fully explore Kusturica's style but I will briefly point out just two of the ways in which he systematically undermines order and simplicity both visually and audibly. Firstly, the homes of the protagonists are chaotic, messy places, which are in stark contrast to the officially sanctioned brutalist communist architecture;[28] this is made explicit at the ending of *Dolly*, which abandons Dino and his family in an ambiguous urban space, in between their old neighbourhood (and leaky home) as we witness their move towards the bleak mass of high-rise tower blocks, with the ambiguity of this final move tainted with irony, as Dino's voice-over delivers for one final time, his mantra that in 'every day in every way, I'm getting a little better'. Secondly, the chaos of Kusturica's sets is amplified by the continuous movement of and within the frame, with multiple planes of composition and the inclusion of several narrative actions. The music of the soundtracks similarly function in an equally disorderly manner and they are distinguished by unpredictably shifting semantic possibilities and cultural referents. For example, *When*'s theme, the 'Waves of the Danube' waltz, is used as both diegetic and extra-diegetic music, arranged in a number of different ways, played in slow or fast tempo, in minor and major keys, and provides affective amplification of key moments, such as the orchestration of the weightless looping in the sky of Ankica's glider or, alternatively, as an ironic commentary that provides a contrast between the grandiose and romantic connotations of the waltz and the trashy train toilet where Mesa and Ankica have their brief and 'cheap' sexual encounter.

Kusturica's cinematic style therefore uses chaos and disorder productively, constructing a formal context within which the children of his films not only find a comfortable home in the 'mess' but are pivotal to its creation. It is because of their celebration of messiness that Kusturica's films are often described as 'mad', focusing on far from normal characters, taking place in bizarre settings and situations, involving unreal storylines and supernatural cause–effect relations. Adam Phillips provides some explanation for the productive connection between insanity, artistic creation and childhood in his observance of the following comment by D.W. Winnicott: 'Through artistic expression we can hope to keep in touch with our primitive selves whence the most intense feelings and even fearfully acute sensations derive, and we are poor indeed if we are only sane.'[29]

In their demonstration of the ability of art to connect with intense but suppressed and denied feelings, Kusturica's films enable us to go beyond the officially sanctioned and sanitized versions of history and to delve into the acute sensations of the messy everyday life in pre-1990 Yugoslavia. In that respect, as I have demonstrated, the role of the children in his films is crucial. By articulating the lives of the young protagonists as rooted in the everyday and effecting the messy proliferation of historical detritus, the films capitalize on the affective values invested in the bubbles and the bubbling-up of childhood, which serve to burst simplistic accounts of history that would otherwise negate the complexity of lived experience. The children are not mere symbolic tokens at the hands of a masterful if slightly insane film director. As this chapter has hopefully demonstrated the children are invested with a complex agency that is in itself irreducible to a simple and orderly category.

While the three films are set against a very grim political and historical background, their tone is celebratory. This is not just because the children manage to discover happiness and joy under these conditions but also because the films feel exuberant, full of energy and humour and are extremely pleasurable to watch. Kusturica's films of the 1980s place their affection and establish an alliance with children who summon the resilience needed in order to get on with their lives despite their experience of oppressive, irrational, communist governance. And while more recent Kusturica films have turned up the volume (in the literal and metaphorical sense) in their celebration of everyday chaos, they are nothing but a natural continuation of his early tendency to complicate historical order with the messiness of life. The caustic criticism levelled against *Underground* and subsequent films is discursively akin to the communist desire for order. For many adult critics, Kusturica's films infuriate in their childlike messiness and become anathema to all those who demand tidy versions of 'good versus evil' history, a tidiness that ignores the moral and political complexity and messiness of lived experience and the horrific reality of the Yugoslav wars. As with the obsessive, desperate but beautiful ordering of the world that T.S. Spivet creates, in the chaos, the trauma, the betrayals and the loss that underpin Kusturica's films and Yugoslavian history, an incoherent but wonderful world emerges in the celebration of the disruptive and creative agency of childhood.

Notes

1   'L'imposture Kusturica', *Le Monde*, 2 June 1995; 'La propaganda onirique d'Emir Kusturica', *Liberation*, 30 October 1995.
2   Slavoj Žižek, 'Multiculturalism, or, the cultural logic of multinational capitalism', *New Left Review*, no. 225 (September/October 1997), pp. 28–51, p. 39 (emphasis in original).
3   For a comprehensive survey of the changing international critical attitudes towards Kusturica's films see Goran Gocic, *The Cinema of Emir Kusturica: Notes from the Underground* (London: Wallflower, 2001), esp. pp. 36–46.

4. Dina Iordanova, *Emir Kusturica* (London: BFI, 2002), esp. pp. 1–43.
5. Ibid., p. 38.
6. All sub-headings are quotations from Reif Larsen, *The Selected Works of T. S. Spivet* (London: Harvill Secker, 2009). Page numbers are indicated in parentheses. I was reading the novel at the same time as thinking about this chapter and Spivet's attempts to 'map his world' have very much permeated my reading of Kusturica's films.
7. Defined as anyone under 18 in 'A Summary of the United Nations Convention on the Rights of the Child', *Unicef*, https://www.unicef.org.uk/rights-respecting-schools/wp-content/uploads/sites/4/2017/01/Summary-of-the-UNCRC.pdf (accessed July 2021).
8. See Claudia Castañeda, *Figurations: Child, Bodies, Worlds* (Durham, NC: Duke University Press, 2002).
9. Jacqueline Rose, *The Case of Peter Pan: The Impossibility of Children's Fiction* (Philadelphia, PA: University of Pennsylvania Press, 1993), p. 10.
10. 'Summary of the United Nations Convention on the Rights of the Child'.
11. Michel Foucault, *The History of Sexuality, Volume 1: An Introduction* (New York: Pantheon, 1978), esp. p. 46.
12. See for example Kusturica's interview in the DVD (Artificial Eye) of *Do You Remember Dolly Bell?*
13. The mortally wounded Perhan falls from a bridge into an open wagon of a cargo train, where he dies in a large box. In the scene that follows, he lies dead in his coffin.
14. Paranormal qualities of characters are used more widely and not exclusively in relation to children in later Kusturica films.
15. Adam Phillips, *Going Sane* (London: Penguin, 2006), p. 93.
16. Larsen, *The Selected Works of T. S. Spivet*, p. 91.
17. The ability of Tito to 'glue together' Yugoslavia has 'magical', almost paranormal, undertones, something that Kusturica focuses on, most evidently in *Underground*, where national cohesion is ironically described as Tito's 'secret formula'.
18. See for example an advertisement in *The Sunday Times*, 31 May 1953, which invited visitors to tour 'Jugoslavia' from North to South.
19. Judith Keene, 'The filmmaker as historian, above and below ground: Emir Kusturica and the narratives of Yugoslav history', *Rethinking History*, vol. 5, no. 2 (2001), pp. 233–53, p. 234.
20. Ibid.
21. The case of Hicks is a perfect example of what might constitute cultural messiness; almost completely unknown in Britain he became a major star in Italy largely due to his appearance in the Blasetti film.
22. 'Dolly Bell' is the name that the sex-worker of the film and Dino's romantic interest have adopted.
23. A big hit at the time Celentano competed with the song in the 1962 San Remo festival, an internationally significant annual event televised or broadcast by radio to many European countries in the 1960s.
24. Gocic, *The Cinema of Emir Kusturica*.
25. Often the political hostilities between communist nations were played out in sporting events; notorious in that respect was the Hungary–USSR water polo semi-final ('blood in the water match') of the 1956 Olympic Games.
26. For a more detailed account of Tito's break with Stalin see Keene, 'The filmmaker as historian'.
27. For a discussion of the binary see Chris Jenks, *Childhood* (London: Routledge, 1996), esp. pp. 70–80.

28 For a photographic documentation that celebrates the architectural style in the USSR context, see Frédéric Chaubin, *CCCP: Cosmic Communist Constructions Photographed* (Cologne: Taschen, 2011).
29 Cited in Phillips, *Going Sane*, p. 92; Phillips speculates that the quotation has been relegated to a footnote in Winnicott's 1945 paper on 'Primitive emotional development' because of the implication that 'what adults feel is mad is normal for the child'.

8 THE CHILD IMPRISONED IN HISTORY: CRYSTALLINE COMMUNITY BUILDING IN *O ANO EM QUE MEUS PAIS SAÍRAM DE FÉRIAS* (BRAZIL, 2006)

David Martin-Jones

In the 2000s a transnational trend emerged across several Latin American cinemas towards films exploring national pasts under military rule through a child protagonist. Several such films were set in the 1970s, including five from the Southern Cone: *Kamchatka* (Argentina/Spain/Italy, 2002), *Machuca* (Chile/Spain/UK/France, 2004), *O Ano em Que Meus Pais Saíram de Férias/The Year My Parents Went on Vacation* (Brazil, 2006), *Paisito* (Uruguay/Spain/Argentina, 2008), and *Infancia clandestina/Clandestine Childhood* (Argentina/Spain/Brazil, 2011). This chapter focuses on *O Ano em Que Meus Pais Saíram de Férias*, which situates its child protagonist, Mauro (Michel Joelsas) in a cinematically reconstructed 1970.

O Ano attempts to reclaim the national unity fostered by the 1970 World Cup from its association with the military dictatorship's self-promotion, which used imagery, songs and slogans drawing on the success of the national team. An alternative 'local' view of the past is offered by focusing on the inhabitants of an ethnically diverse neighbourhood of São Paulo, Bom Retiro. This community provides Mauro with a sense of global/local belonging which, whilst clearly identified as 'Brazilian', is posited as coexisting with national celebrations over World Cup victory, as opposed to being entirely defined by them. The film also depicts the military persecution of the population that marked the era, and the neighbourhood's resulting resistance to, or studied ignorance of, the association of the nation's sporting success with its military government.

This is not to say, however, that *O Ano* offers a radical revision of history. Carolina Rocha has argued convincingly that the film illustrates the 'still prevailing discomfort to fully revisit' the period of the national past under dictatorship in Brazil.[1] Rocha sees this in particular in the film's backgrounding of political events[2] and the focus on a child protagonist who has only a partial view of history.[3] I would add to this that in many ways the film's alternative view of the past rests on a cinematic construction of an ethnically diverse community in line with the myth of racial democracy which has structured Brazilian national identity throughout most of the twentieth century. Even so, whilst I would not go so far as to contradict Rocha by suggesting that *O Ano* readdresses the past directly, I argue that it does seek to separate the sense of community and patriotic support for the national team aroused by the World Cup victory from the government's use of the same event for self-promotion as a nationally representative regime. In this way *O Ano* sets out to reclaim the past, in the service of the future, by challenging the way in which the footballing success was co-opted to legitimize the dictatorship. Thus my interpretation falls in line with approaches like that of Laura Podalsky, who sees certain genres of Latin American filmmaking as permitting 'audiences to re-examine past social traumas in ways disallowed by the legalistic discourses surrounding public debates about accountability'.[4] To uncover how this process works in *O Ano*, and indeed the integral role of the child protagonist, I take a theoretical approach, drawing on Gilles Deleuze, to the film's narrative, *mise en scène*, cinematography, montage and characters.

O Ano em Que Meus Pais Saíram de Férias

O Ano begins with a young family in flight from the military state (1964–85). The parents drop off Mauro at his grandfather's flat in Bom Retiro and flee, promising to return in time for the World Cup. However, they leave Mauro without realizing that his grandfather, Mótel (Paulo Autran), has died of a heart attack that morning. Locked out of his grandfather's flat, but with no way of contacting his parents, Mauro is begrudgingly befriended by his grandfather's neighbour, Shlomo (Germano Hauit). Gradually Mauro finds a place within a community of friends in his new neighbourhood, amongst the intermingled Eastern European Jewish, Italian and Greek immigrant populations. When his parents do not initially return as promised, during the World Cup Mauro occupies his grandfather's flat, bonds with local children, especially his neighbour, Hanna (Daniela Piepszyk), local left-wing students and the regulars of a local bar. At the film's conclusion, Brazil's World Cup victory is overshadowed by Mauro's mother's (Simone Spoladore) sudden return. She is in great pain, after capture and torture by the military government. His father will never be seen again. The film closes with Mauro and his mother leaving the country together.

O Ano was made on a budget of US$3.5 million, by Gullane Filmes and co-producers, including Globo Filmes,[5] the cinema arm of the Globo Network.[6] It was released during what Carlos Eduardo Rodrigues, the executive director of Globo Filmes, describes as their second phase of development. This saw a conscious move away from the production of movies associated with television, and the release of several films which performed well internationally, such as *Cidade de Deus/City of God* (2002).[7] As Elaine Guerini notes, the production involvement of Miravista, Disney's Latin American label, with *O Ano* 'automatically guaranteed distribution in Latin America through Buena Vista International'.[8] The film was well received internationally, premiering in competition at Berlin, winning prizes on the festival circuit (in particular in Latin America), placing amidst the final nine films nominated for the Oscar for Best Foreign Language Film, and screening in over twenty countries.[9] Yet, despite its international appeal, the story is deeply rooted in national concerns and clearly engages with Brazil's national history. It does so, specifically, through the figure of the child.

Director Cao Hamburger wanted to revisit his childhood in the film. Although born in 1962 and therefore slightly younger than 12-year-old Mauro during the World Cup, Hamburger's film is autobiographical. His parents, both university lecturers and left-wing militants, went on 'vacation' during his childhood,[10] a memory that arose when he was recalling the 1970 World Cup. This confluence of memories created the inspiration for this, Hamburger's second feature after *Castelo Ra-Tim-Bum, O Filme/Castle Ra-Tim-Bum* (1999), which was based on the children's television series Hamburger created in 1995.[11] Both Hamburger and his co-scriptwriter Claudio Galperin knew, intimately, life in the district of Bom Retiro, traditionally a neighbourhood which attracts newly arrived immigrants,[12] during the 1970s. However, as Bom Retiro has changed – in terms of population density, traffic and a demographic now constituted of Korean and Bolivian diasporas as opposed to the Greek, Italian and East European Jewish communities of the time – they decamped the film's production to Campinas, outside São Paulo. There they were able to reconstruct the period setting in an 'authentic' looking neighbourhood, filming in a deserted apartment block on Rua Luzitana. In this setting, *O Ano* reconsiders history by self-consciously depicting Mauro as a child imprisoned in time.

Imprisoned in a crystalline layer of history

The recent Latin American trend to which *O Ano* belongs evokes the cinematic exploration of traumatic national transformations of the child-focused films of post-war Italian neorealism (e.g. Roberto Rossellini's *Roma, città aperta/Rome, Open City* (1945) and *Germania anno zero/Germany Year Zero* (1948) or Vittoria de Sica's *Ladri di biciclette/Bicycle Thieves* (1948)). Much like the Italian films, in the Latin American films the child is witness to events that they only partially understand but which transform their young lives.

Yet *O Ano*'s rather polished aesthetic treatment of the working-class community of Bom Retiro – akin to its Argentine, Chilean and Uruguayan counterparts in its avoidance of too gritty a social realist or 'documentary' aesthetic – contrasts with other Brazilian films that focus on socially disenfranchised children. Films like *Pixote* (1981) and *Central do Brasil/Central Station* (1998) are arguably closer to Italian predecessors, as Antonio Traverso notes, due to their similarities with the stylistic, thematic and aesthetic concerns of neorealism.[13] For Traverso, these earlier Brazilian films 'focus on the figure of children against the landscape of historical events', representing childhood as 'a state that requires the negotiation of homelessness, violence, sexuality and survival'.[14] *O Ano* positions Mauro somewhat differently. Not only is he granted a home, he also escapes the social and economic privations of his counterparts in the earlier films, although he does lose his father to the military regime. The film also contrasts with the Italian neorealist narratives that are set in the 'present' of post-war Europe, since, like its Latin American counterparts, *O Ano* positions Mauro in history and, in this specific instance, through a process of aesthetic imprisonment that can be uncovered using Deleuze.[15]

In the *Cinema* books, Deleuze draws on Henri Bergson's philosophy to argue that certain films, which he termed 'time-images', allow a glimpse of the virtual whole of time, or duration, as conceived by Bergson.[16] In this model of time the past is shaped like an inverted cone, constructed of myriad, stacked up, virtual layers of time, each layer a different moment in, or memory of, the past. This model was used by Deleuze to explain the 'time travel' of protagonists in films by post-war European directors like Alain Resnais and Federico Fellini, in which protagonists navigate virtually through time, leaping or slipping between virtual layers of the past as they drift between present-day reality and past history, in fantasy, dream and memory.[17] Thus, in the time-image, protagonists might be more accurately described as 'seers', rather than 'doers', whether they are witness to movements of a vast encompassing duration which catches them up within its virtual shifts, or simply mesmerized by the everyday passing of time.[18]

For Deleuze, the child, as seer, has a special role to play in the emergence of the time-image in post-war European cinema. He considered the child's supposed 'motor helplessness' conducive to a greater awareness, a greater capacity for 'seeing and hearing' than adults have.[19] Deleuze argues that, in films like the Rossellini trilogy mentioned above, children are more susceptible to an awareness of the passing of time (what Deleuze terms the 'pure optical situation'[20]), due to their lesser ability (in an adult-oriented world at least) to act in a way that will influence their situation. In short, the child is the ideal 'seer' of the cinema of the time-image.

Such a view is, of course, open to question, and in a previous work I argue that, whilst these post-war European neorealist films might give this impression about the child because they are filmed encountering history in the making (situated in action taking place in the present, or at least, as close to it as one might get with cinema), things are different when the child is reacting to events ('seeing and hearing') in a recreated past. This is the case, I have shown, in the Argentine film *Kamchatka*, for example.[21] There is a distinction to be drawn, then, between the child seer 'situated *in* history, as it happens, or … figured *as* history as it is recreated'.[22] When history is created, with hindsight, the child seer may well function more as a surrogate who offers a conduit into the past for the viewer, and, depending on the timing, perhaps even for a generation who were children at the time in which the film is set. In which case, the child is still valued for their capacity to witness or absorb the situations they encounter. Yet they are just as much of interest (due to the recreated nature of their encounter with situations, their experience of the 'time' they lived through) as portals into the past for a generation seeking a way to inform the present (and future) from this revisiting of their childhoods. Certainly this is the case in the trend of Latin American films identified above, including *O Ano*. Accordingly, the Deleuzian category of the time-image which seems best suited to explaining the function of the child seer in *O Ano* is that of the crystal of time in its seed/environment form.

O Ano reconstructs a version of Bom Retiro in 1970 as though it were a discrete layer of Deleuze's Bergsonian cinematic time. Whilst this is evident in the retro clothing, cars and 1970s decor generally (equally true of most period films), what demonstrates its existence as a time-image is its self-conscious evocation of its virtual existence as a reconstructed layer of time through the use of mirrors and other reflective surfaces. Positioned at the heart of the myriad reflections that characterize the film's layer of time is a Deleuzian 'crystal of time', oscillating around Mauro, which captures, in a single image, the moment in which time splits into an actual present that passes and a virtual past that is preserved.[23] The crystal is thus the moment in which time's virtual layers are formed, and its indiscernible oscillations of momentarily coexisting past and present are the process through which the cone of time is constructed.

For Deleuze, the crystal is evident in various figures, the most 'familiar' being the mirror, which, in its virtual reflection of the actual, demonstrates this process of time's perpetual splitting:

> Oblique mirrors, concave and convex mirrors and Venetian mirrors are inseparable from a circuit … This circuit itself is an exchange: the mirror image is virtual in relation to an actual character that the mirror catches, but it is actual in the mirror which now leaves the character with only a virtuality and pushes him back out-of-field … The actual image and *its* virtual image thus constitute the smallest internal circuit … Distinct, but indiscernible, such are the actual and the virtual which are in continual exchange.[24]

As Ronald Bogue clarifies in *Deleuze on Cinema*, Deleuze is referring to 'a particular vision of the world-as-reflection, as infinite mirrorings … More than a mere theme, the world-as-reflection is a way of seeing and one that issues from a particular conception of time.'[25] The mirror image, then, is an expression of 'the smallest internal circuit' of time, articulating the divisive nature of duration glimpsed in the crystal. *O Ano*'s 'world-as-reflection' – its *mise en scène* populated by mirrors, windows, car ornaments, bumpers and windows, television screens, and even the shiny pendulum of a grandfather clock – provides the broader manifestation of this view of our temporal existence. For this reason we can say that *O Ano* self-consciously constructs one virtual layer of the Brazilian past. The film's creation of a world-as-reflection foregrounds a reimagining of history, the offering of an alternative view on the past, that is occurring on this reconstructed virtual layer of time.

The child's role is integral to this process because this particular crystal of time oscillates around Mauro, a character through whom the disparate demographics of the local community are able to coalesce. Mauro and his milieu form the seed/environment[26] – a coupling that Deleuze considers to be one of the three primary figures in which we discover the crystal of time:

> It is the same circuit, which passes through three figures, the actual and the virtual, the limpid and the opaque, the seed and the environment. In fact, the seed is on the one hand the virtual image which will crystallize an environment which is at present amorphous; but on the other hand the latter must have a structure which is virtually crystallizable, in relation to which the seed now plays the role of the actual image.[27]

The seed is first visible when Mauro arrives in Bom Retiro with his parents. He is depicted inhabiting a seed-crystal at the heart of this virtual environment as he looks out of the rear windows of his parents' Volkswagen Beetle, staring up at the skyscrapers of São Paulo. He is shot from outside the car, the city reflected off the window and paintwork of the car so that his upturned face is overlaid with (reflected) images of the city. Here virtual (reflection, environment) and actual (little boy, seed) are seen to coexist in a mutually informing relationship. Thus, initially the past is seen as a crystal whose reflecting facets imprison Mauro in this layer of time. His confinement is further emphasized when, inhabiting his deceased grandfather's flat, Mauro's every movement is reflected back at him by the *mise en scène*, in mirrors, television screens and windows, as he lives in hope of his parents' return. Moreover, Mauro is repeatedly pictured looking out of the glassed-in balcony of his grandfather's flat, the reflection of the street outside overlaid onto him by the glass, again creating the oscillation between virtual and actual, seed and environment, found in the crystalline internal circuit of time. This figure of the boy behind glass, looking out in hope, overlaid by a reflection of a recreated past, further emphasizes how trapped he is in this layer of time.

In this way, we see Mauro's connection to this environment, the virtual surroundings that he will come to actualize in his role as seed. It becomes evident that Mauro's only escape from the past as prison is through his local community. The neighbourhood's multicultural bonding around the World Cup campaign is posited by the film as a way to recuperate an authentic sense of national pride it engendered, as distinct from the military regime's promotion of itself on the back of the national football team's victory. In this process, Mauro functions as the 'actual-image' that crystallizes the apparently 'amorphous' environment of the community into an overarching 'Brazilian' sense of belonging or identity, since it is his presence and actions which bring together the various immigrant population facets (and in this respect their various histories) in his interactions with his new friends and neighbours.

The child seer in *O Ano*, then, is intended to indicate how, in the present, Mauro's generation might come to look back on their childhood (as though seeing and hearing the past as a 'pure optical situation') so as to consider how best to live in the future. As David Deamer explains with respect to Deleuze's seed/environment relationship, 'the present is a seed, the future a virtual environment in relation to the seed, a virtual succession which subsists and insists within the seed image'.[28] Hence Mauro, in a recreated 1970 present, is the seed which can populate the Bom Retiro environment he encounters, but also a seed able to crystallize the potential for a new Brazilian identity in 2006 ('the future virtual environment') through the encounter between a certain generation of viewer and a proxy seer into their own childhood ('in relation to the seed'). Thus the image of Mauro arriving in the family Beetle, a period indicator if ever there was one, encapsulates his role as seed (as Deamer summarizes, a 'seed image… encompasses the environment as if it were a miniature scene within a sphere of opaque glass. The seed is the seed of an environment; and the environment is the mise-en-scène of the seed'[29]) with respect to what he can offer the national future, from out of the past.

Reimagining nation through local community

Before I explore how this process of crystallization functions aesthetically, it is necessary to fill in a little of the historical background. In a national context where the origins of Brazilian national citizenship have been described by James Holston as 'inclusively inegalitarian',[30] *O Ano* reimagines a diverse but temporarily unified Bom Retiro community which considers itself as Brazilian whilst ignoring or rejecting the trappings of nationalism associated with the dictatorship. As Roberto Schwarz wrote in an essay composed between 1969 and 1970, at that time, the dictatorship did not necessarily attempt to construct an inclusive or authentic sense of national identity with which to mobilize the entire national populace:

> What chance did the government have of forging a real national ideology? If it needs it, it is only because it has to confront subversion. In the previous situation it preferred to do without it, since in essence it is a government associated with imperialism, with demobilisation of the people and with technological solutions, to whom any verifiable ideological commitment will always seem like a limitation.[31]

Accordingly, the regime's focus was on the promotion of a façade of nationhood, using techniques which can be described as 'banal nationalism', following Michael Billig's notion of the 'daily reproduction' of the nation through such mundane signifiers as national flags hung in public places.[32] Yet this 'banal' legitimacy of military rule was used to provide cover for brutal state repression. Schwarz again:

> [A]t the end of 1968… the existence of a state of revolutionary war in Brazil was officially recognised. To stop it spreading to the masses, police repression became really tough, denunciation of acquaintances was encouraged and protected from reprisals, torture took on terrifying proportions, and the press was silenced. As a result, the importance of ideology increased, all of which meant a proliferation of Brazilian flags, of propaganda leaflets, and the setting up of courses in gymnastics and civic values for university students. The phraseology of law-and-order patriotism, suddenly back in favour, could be found everywhere.[33]

In *The Politics of Military Rule in Brazil 1964–1985* (1988), Skidmore concurs, noting that the Médici years 'saw the "national security state" in its purest form'.[34] Whilst successful in economic terms with over 10 per cent economic growth, there was also evidence of growing social inequalities, along with censorship and the brutal repression of the population.[35] This was especially true of the military's 1968–72 anti-guerrilla campaign, which provides the backdrop for the film.[36] Skidmore notes how, under President Emilio Garrastazu Médici (1969–74), the government's public relations machinery used television to promote the military regime's view of 'Brazil's national unity, its new purpose, its disciplined march towards the company of developed nations'.[37] Skidmore observes:

> One of the AERP's [*Assessoria Especial de Relações Públicas*/Special Advisory Staff on Public Relations] most effective techniques in this effort was to link soccer, popular music, President Médici, and Brazilian progress. Médici was good material for such a campaign. He loved playing the father figure, and he was a fanatical soccer fan. AERP exploited both … Médici predicted Brazil would win the cup, and they did … The country got an official holiday to acknowledge the carnival-style celebrations already underway. Médici received the team in the presidential palace, gave each player a tax-free bonus of $18,500, and basked in the endless photos with the players and the huge silver cup … The presidential PR staff lost no time in following up on the World Cup glory. The catchy marching tune, 'Pra Frente Brazil' ('Forward Brazil'), written for the Brazilian team, became the government's theme song and was played at all official events. A multitude of posters appeared showing Pelé leaping aloft after scoring a goal and next to him the government slogan '*ninguém segura mais este país*' ('Nobody can stop this country now.')[38]

This link between football and the imagining of the nation is perhaps no surprise. Football has been at the heart of constructions of Brazilian identity since the 1930s.[39] Yet in *O Ano*, the same imagery used by the dictatorship for self-promotion is reconsidered in relation to a global/local identity. Whilst the film maintains the seemingly racially inclusive image of a national identity underpinned by the myth of racial democracy, the local community offers an alternative view of national belonging to that of the superficial nationalism promoted by the military regime. In *O Ano,* then, a period of great economic prosperity is reimagined as a time when the state actively persecuted the population, and when patriotic sentiments aroused by football victory did not necessarily extend to support for the military regime.

Football

The predominant theme through which the community crystallizes around Mauro, in terms of narrative, montage and cinematography, is football. In contrast to the numerous televised games featuring the Brazilian national team, a neighbourhood grudge match provides an initial community focus to the narrative. This is an occasion for Mauro's voice-over to describe the ethnically diverse constitution of the neighbourhood.

> São Paulo is so big there are people from all over the world supporting every possible team. Shlomo is a Polish Jew. Now he's always talking to Ítalo, who's of Italian descent. Irene's dad's Greek. But her boyfriend… [Black Brazilian Edgar unveils his face and afro hairstyle from under his motorcycle crash helmet]… I think he's the grandson of an African.

In diegetic terms, Mauro's voice-over makes sense of his environment to assist the viewer in recognizing characters. However, his apparent belief that the origins of members of the community will mean that they have divided allegiances in the World Cup is not borne out by events. Although the local football match is constituted of Italian immigrants on one side versus the Jewish diaspora and the Black Brazilian Edgar (Rodrigo dos Santos) on the other, all of the community ultimately support the Brazilian national team. The entire scene – the players on both teams and the local crowd, including Shlomo, Mauro, Irene (Liliana Castro) and their friends and neighbours – constitute a united national community. This is an identity that is Brazilian, but also and at the same time local, and yet ethnically specific due to its global origins.

Hamburger notes his decision to depict the community of Bom Retiro in this way in order to counter preconceptions that international audiences have of Brazil as 'all forests and favelas'. Instead, 'The movie shows a facet that most foreigners don't know; the Brazil of the immigrants and how they are blended together, respecting each other's differences.'[40] Thus *O Ano* offers a different view of Brazil to the *favelas* and violence of films like *Cidade de Deus,* or *Tropa de Elite/Elite Squad* (2007), which are often internationally considered to be representative of Brazilian cinema, or perhaps even Brazilian life. In line with a broader movement that Tatiana Signorelli Heise observes in contemporary Brazilian cinema, for 'reformist' films which focus on the potential for nationally representative cultural practices such as football to unify Brazil in terms of class and race,[41] *O Ano* invites us to consider the community in Bom Retiro as a different vision of how local inhabitants interpreted their sense of belonging to the imagined community of the nation in 1970. For this reason, the film contrasts the national team's endeavours on the global stage with the neighbourhood teams, of varied international origins, interacting at a local level.

The montage and cinematography situate the viewer within this community in order to emphasize that their local support for the national team was tempered by local experiences of state repression. For example, during the only scene in which mounted police and military arrest militant student activists, the editing suggests that the entire community are eye witnesses to the raid. A bewildering montage provides different points of view at street level, including positions from amongst the crowd and within nearby buildings. This manner of filming so as to place the viewer amidst the community recurs on several occasions, not only to integrate the viewer into the community at, as it were, eye level, but also to illustrate the ability of the neighbourhood's population to separate their pride in the national team from the related propaganda of the national government, due to their first-hand knowledge of state repression.

Most effective in making this separation are the montage sequences which accompany the televised games. Initially, Mauro is figured as central to the actualizing community within the diversely populated environment. For example, he is positioned at the centre of a montage which introduces the neighbourhood, when he is depicted in various apartments being hosted for lunch by the building's inhabitants. Then, when the World Cup starts, this montage extends beyond the apartment, as though radiating out from the central position of Mauro whose shouts of 'foul' and 'goal' are echoed by those of the groups enjoying the game elsewhere. These echoes within the environment include not only Mauro's immediate, mostly Jewish neighbours, but also neighbourhood scenes of various ethnic groupings watching the football, such as the nearby left-wing students and the patrons of the Greek bar.

When the players are lined up and the national anthem is playing, it is noticeable how little attention is paid to television screens, as the local denizens engage in conversation. On other occasions Shlomo reads not a national daily newspaper but the *Tribuna Israelita* (a Jewish newspaper) and the left-wing students express - verbally - their solidarity with the Czechoslovakian team due to their shared political beliefs, even if their physical celebrations humorously betray their true support for Brazil. However, despite the local inhabitants' obliviousness to the banal nationalism accompanying the games, whenever Brazil scores a goal the montage unites the different parts of the community in its celebrations, as the ethnic identities around the neighbourhood are brought together by this communal event, our central focus for which is Mauro.

Their shared sense of belonging, whilst clearly located in relation to an imagined Brazilian identity (they are all cheering for the national team) does not necessarily extend to loyalty to the nationalist rituals that accompany the game, such as paying respect to the national anthem. Rather, the Bom Retiro community is shown to identify more with the various local identities of its inhabitants (be they religious, ethnic or political) than with banal signifiers of the nation, such as Brazilian newspapers which might foster a sense of national belonging. Mundane symbols of national belonging are not so much unnoticed amidst daily routines, as they would be, following Billig's rationale, if they were effectively working to construct a shared sense of identity.[42] Rather, they are purposefully ignored by a community that – due to events like the disappearance of Mauro's parents and the arrest of the students – is not blind to the machinations of the military state, or its impact on the lives of Brazilians.

This use of montage has its most pointed effect during the World Cup final, when scenes of the national team celebrating, often appropriated by the dictatorship to promote the military regime, are here deliberately reappropriated by the film to construct its alternative view of collective identity. When Pelé heads Brazil's first goal against Italy, the footage on the small black and white television in Irene's father's bar fills the screen. The edit cuts immediately to Mauro and Hanna in the bar, celebrating together. We cut back to the television, as Pelé leaps into the arms of teammate Jairzinho, exactly the type of image utilized by the dictatorship. We cut back to the bar, where Irene and Edgar sneak a celebratory passionate kiss behind Irene's father's back. The montage returns us to the television coverage, now framed as an image playing on a television set, a new establishing shot from which the action opens out onto the interior of a nearby apartment in which three elderly Jewish men celebrate. Finally we cut back to a shot of everyone celebrating in the crowded bar.

With this montage the film equates the national team with the locally united community of immigrants. Pelé and Jairzinho celebrating together find new, alternative 'mirror' images in the Jewish girl Hanna hugging Mauro (his father Jewish, his mother of Italian descent), the inter-ethnic kiss between Irene and Edgar, and the Jewish and various other European communities (Italian, Greek, etc.) in the apartment block and the bar respectively. By very deliberately replaying the images of victory previously utilized by the dictatorship in its public relations campaigns, in a montage that relinks them to a diverse range of ethnic identities interacting at a local level, the film tries to imagine an alternative history of national belonging.

Absent father/local fathers

The various characters with whom Mauro interacts further this historical reimagining, or crystallizing, of Brazilian community in 1970s Bom Retiro. Mauro, temporarily separated from both parents at the start of the film, and permanently from his grandfather and father by the end, interacts with three surrogate fathers: Shlomo, Edgar and Ítalo. They offer three 'entrances'[43] into the film's reconstructed layer of the past, three facets of the crystalline environment with which Mauro can attempt to oscillate (one might say, thus to germinate), as seed. Ultimately the identity which he embodies, like the diverse community, does not have a singular teleological origin. Each of his virtual fathers, rather, is suggestive of the different histories and identities that intermingle at a local level in Bom Retiro.

Like Mauro's grandfather, Shlomo belongs to the community of Ashkenazi Jews who settled in Brazil, including many arriving during or after the Second World War.[44] Shlomo is initially reticent to help Mauro, especially after he discovers that Mauro is not circumcised and, despite his father bring Jewish, is unaware of Jewish customs. Shlomo is persuaded to help Mauro by the local Rabbi, who compares Mauro to Moishale (Moses) left in the bullrushes in the Old Testament story. Eventually Shlomo begins to look after Mauro, and from Shlomo and other members of the Jewish community Mauro learns the traditions of his Jewish heritage. He also brings the Jewish community into contact with the other neighbourhood populations as Shlomo seeks help in finding Mauro's father from Ítalo.

Mauro appropriates many of the personal effects of his grandfather, trying on his grandfather's hat and using his leather gloves for goalkeeping. Rooting through his drawers, Mauro discovers photographs of men at a harbourside (suggestive of his immigrant heritage) and one of his grandfather and father together, his grandfather in the hat that Mauro now wears. Later Mauro proudly tells Hanna that his grandfather fought against the Nazis in the Second World War. There is thus a clear engagement with both a Jewish identity and an immigrant history in the film, as Mauro 'tries on' a new heritage learned from Shlomo and inherited from his grandfather. This cinematic recognition of the Jewish population of Bom Retiro is telling for the film's reimagining of history. Historically the dominant discourses on Brazilian identity typically excluded Jews from the normative positions of white, European and Christian. As Jeffrey Lesser notes in *Welcoming the Undesirables*, under the myth of racial democracy that has structured discourse surrounding Brazilian identity in the twentieth century, 'Jews were deemed by many politicians and intellectuals as non-white and non-European – a dangerous "other" to whom immigration rights should be denied.'[45] Elsewhere, Lesser observes that there was 'a 20th century history of attacks on Jews, blacks, Japanese and Middle Easterners' in Brazil,[46] and Bom Retiro's Jewish community had previously been portrayed in a very negative light by Brazilian commentators.[47]

Racial democracy, which James Holston positions as a contemporary manifestation of much older Brazilian discourses on citizenship that are 'inclusionist and racist simultaneously',[48] has its origins in the work of Gilberto Freyre in the 1930s, who argued that Brazil was a racially inclusive democracy. Although some scholars have recently attempted to recuperate Freyre's thinking in terms of his views on culture and 'the sharing of values among community members',[49] his influential position has nevertheless been variously critiqued, for instance by Edward E. Telles in *Race in Another America*, for eliding the reality of racial inequality in Brazilian society,[50] and by Amós Nascimento for 'imposing one biological, historical, linguistic, or cultural ideal of 'nation" that remains European and suspends the pluralistic perspectives and claims of different groups and subjects'.[51] Yet whilst *O Ano* offers a somewhat idealized, inclusive image of Brazilian community, very much in line with the conventional myth of racial democracy, it does at least use Mauro, unusually, to foreground the Jewish community's presence and to show the interaction between the Jewish and neighbouring communities in Bom Retiro.

Although *O Ano* can be viewed as part of a further transnational movement in Latin America of films focusing on Jewish families or Jewish communities – e.g. *El abrazo partido/Lost Embrace* (Argentina/France/Italy/Spain, 2004), *Whisky* (Uruguay/Argentina/Germany/Spain, 2004)[52] – by depicting this oft-neglected demographic of Brazilian society the film also recognizes what Nascimento describes as the 'plurality of "Brazils"', and their individual histories, which challenge homogenizing discourses like that of racial democracy.[53] Shlomo's role as first surrogate father to Mauro, then, provides an 'entrance' to the Bom Retiro Jewish community which at least acknowledges its existence as one of many 'Brazils' on this layer of the past.

Mauro's second surrogate father is the Black Brazilian, Edgar. Like Shlomo, Edgar plays his part in the adoption of Mauro by the local community, rescuing him from the crowd and taking him home on his motorcycle when he gets too close to the military crackdown. Mauro begins to idolize Edgar when he makes a vital penalty save whilst playing in goal for the local Jewish team, Mauro's voice-over tells us: 'And suddenly I knew what I wanted to be. I wanted to be black and fly.' We then cut to Mauro's hands in close-up, in the apartment, as he tries on his grandfather's leather gloves and begins to practise goalkeeping saves, leaping around on his grandfather's bed. In this way *O Ano* brings the Jewish community together with the Black Brazilian Other, putting them both, as it were, in the same team. This move acknowledges their respective lack of acceptance historically, even if both were apparently considered to be included in Brazilian society. In doing so, the film further stresses the unacknowledged role played by the Jewish community in the construction of Brazil, and Brazilian identity, by equating them with the role models offered by the national team's black players (including Pelé, Jairzinho, Everaldo et al.). Here, Edgar, as a Black Brazilian goalkeeper, after all, stands in opposition to the military, as he literally saves Mauro from the police and soldiers as though still playing a role for the Jewish community who are sheltering him. The entrance to the community offered by Edgar, then, is one that leads to a replacement of the government's use of images of the national team's Black Brazilian footballers with the local experience of life under dictatorship. Here such nationally representative figures as Pelé are replaced by the local and no less inspirational Edgar, who can foster a global/local identity by protecting and solidifying Mauro's identification with his Jewish immigrant roots.

Finally, Mauro's father's friend, the left-wing student Ítalo, briefly offers Mauro a glimpse of his father's possible return when he spends the night in Mauro's grandfather's apartment whilst on the run. Ítalo represents the young, persecuted generation to which Mauro's parents belong, who are defined by their education and beliefs (in particular, Marxism) as much as their immigrant traditions

(Mauro's father is a non-practising Jew who has married an Italian woman). The two play table football together the following morning. Mauro plays in goal, as he and Ítalo recreate his relationship with his father, with whom Mauro plays table football at the start of the film. As Ítalo lines up his free kick, Mauro asks for news of his parents' whereabouts. The camera remains trained on Mauro as the dialogue proceeds. Rather than provide a conventional reverse shot of Ítalo, focus racks to bring Ítalo's reflection into focus in a mirror to Mauro's right, before racking back to Mauro. As Ítalo explains to Mauro that his parents are on vacation, and that he will soon have to take a vacation, Mauro appears almost to be conversing with a virtual image of his father. The blurry image of Ítalo in the mirror suggests an equation between the two men, whilst also hinting at Mauro's father's likely fate, which is to be murdered by the dictatorship, and left only as a virtual image in the memory of his loved ones. Inevitably, the entrance into the past offered by Ítalo, Mauro's third surrogate father, is also not the ideal solution, as he too is forced to take a 'vacation'. However, through the three possible fathers (Shlomo's Jewish tradition, Edgar the locally inspirational Black Brazilian, the educated and youthful Ítalo), Mauro has experienced a variety of Brazils that contrast with any overarching equation of Brazil with a single figurehead, such as Pelé, or Médici.

The figure of the goalkeeper that Mauro aspires to become is ultimately an amalgam of his father's advice about the difficult job of being a goalkeeper with which the film starts, his grandfather's gloves, Mauro's idolization of the local team's goalkeeper Edgar, and his brief, virtual re-enactment of his relationship with his father with Ítalo. Therefore this is as much a community-influenced goalkeeping position as it is one associated with a perhaps more typical identification between son and father, or national government and populace. The fact that there is no single father figure available to Mauro resonates with ongoing debates that draw links between fathers and nations in films from Latin American countries.[54] In many ways similar to *Central do Brasil*'s alternative vision of the national cultural identity of the state as a fraternal society (in the absence of a responsible patriarchal authority), *O Ano* offers a diverse local community instead of the military regime's propaganda of unity. By becoming-goalkeeper as a response to the collective, Mauro attempts to actualize the 'amorphous' environment of Bom Retiro, momentarily bringing the various denizens into focus through his actions, and thereby intertwining their histories and potentialities. What is most striking about *O Ano*, however, is that ultimately Mauro fails in his attempt, and has to leave.

Backward glance into history

O Ano does not have a happy ending. Mauro as the seed is not able to populate the environment during this cinematic visit to a turbulent layer of Brazil's past. This is perhaps not entirely unexpected for as Deleuze argues, 'certain seeds abort and others are successful'.[55] Prior to the ultimate victory of Brazil in the final, Mauro walks back to the apartment block through the empty streets. The rest of Brazil is watching the game on television. Mauro is depicted as though walking an empty celebratory parade route, hung with bunting and littered with paper, as one might in the aftermath of a triumphant procession. The off-screen noise that accompanies his prolonged, lonely, sad walk, as Mauro realizes that his parents have not returned home, are fireworks that evoke distant gunshots. The past that we access via Mauro in a moment like this seems as though it were a virtual, alternate reality, clearly one at odds with the celebrations which the military regime capitalized upon to promote their legitimacy.

The emptiness of the national football team's victory for the many Brazilians who suffered or disappeared under military rule is further emphasized when Mauro, returning to the apartment disheartened, glumly tells Shlomo that 'Brazil is winning', only to be confronted by the sight of his wounded mother on the bed, and the news that his father will never return. As Mauro is reunited with his mother, the film cuts to footage of the joyous national team, and the people of Brazil celebrating in the street, enforcing the film's alternative view of a national history and victory.

At the very end, Mauro leaves Brazil with his mother. His voice-over states his position as an exile in a manner that describes his individual position, but also that of a generation abandoned or persecuted under military rule:

And that's what 1970 was like. Brazil won the World Cup for the third time, and without thinking about it and not really understanding how, I ended up becoming what is called an exile. I think exile means having a dad who is so amazingly late he ends up never making it home again.

Mauro's history is ultimately that of an immigrant whose heritage passes through Brazil (his grandfather's arrival being due to the disturbances in Europe caused by Nazism and the Second World War) and whose life accordingly moves on again, into exile. His seed does not populate the environment of the 'cracked' crystal,[56] due to the divisive actions of the military state in cracking down on political opposition, which leads to the division of Mauro's family and also makes impossible his role in crystallizing a sustainable community.

However, through its depiction of an ethnically diverse community united in its support of the national team, the film does successfully establish an alternative history of 1970s Brazil. It retains the focus on the amalgamated identities of the immigrants that make up Bom Retiro which we might expect of the myth of racial democracy. Yet, in the sad departure of Mauro, *O Ano* places a different emphasis on the global/local identity of Brazil, a country in which immigrants flow across national borders and where their local existence may or may not allow them to put down roots – always dependent on the political imagining of the nation by the ruling powers at the time. Hence Mauro continues the trajectory of his grandfather, a Polish Jew fleeing the Nazi regime in Europe, taking flight in turn two generations later from the dictatorship in Brazil.

Mauro's backward gaze – from the departing Beetle, as his mother drives him away from Bom Retiro – is a recurring device in world cinemas. Typically it evokes a sense of nostalgic longing for a past that has definitively passed.[57] This gaze into the past is often granted to children, especially in the cycle of Latin American films which includes *O Ano*. The role of the child thus offers a form of engagement with the crystalline facets of this virtual layer of history, through Mauro's interaction with his surrogate fathers, who are in turn representative of the community's diverse histories and identities. However, unlike *Central do Brasil*, in *O Ano* it is not possible to reunite the family in a manner that identifies the family home with the national homeland.[58] Instead, an alternative construction of history is offered and the film marks a distinction between the official national discourse promoted by the government and the ethnically diverse community it purported to represent, whose loyalties were as much local (the neighbourhood of Bom Retiro), and global (the immigrant traditions) as they were national (the football team). What is crucial about the role of the child in *O Ano*, then, is that he is able to offer a way of reimagining the past, so as to offer a different future for the generation he represents. Like Mauro in Bom Retiro, such a future is one around which the whole of Brazil can potentially crystallize anew, as a (national) community.[59]

Notes

1 Carolina Rocha, 'Children's views of state-sponsored violence in Latin America', in Carolina Rocha and Georgia Seminet (eds), *Representing History, Class and Gender in Spain and Latin America: Children and Adolescents in Film* (London: Palgrave Macmillan, 2012), p. 97.
2 Ibid., p. 92.
3 Ibid., pp. 90–1.
4 Laura Podalsky, *The Politics of Affect and Emotion in Contemporary Latin American Cinema* (London: Palgrave Macmillan, 2011), p. 22.
5 Elaine Guerini, 'Brazil', *Screen International*, no. 1585 (2007), p. 13.
6 For an introduction to the Globo Network and Globo Filmes, see Lisa Shaw and Stephanie Dennison, *Brazilian National Cinema* (London: Routledge, 2007), pp. 36–40; Courtney Brannon Donoghue, 'Globo Filmes, Sony and franchise filmmaking', in Cacilda Rêgo and Carolina Rocha (eds), *New Trends in Argentine and Brazilian Cinema* (Bristol: Intellect, 2011), pp. 51–66.
7 Jùlio Carlos Bezerra, 'A decade of work and success', *Revista de Cinema*, vol. 22, no. 3 (2008), p. 22.
8 Guerini, 'Brazil', p. 13.
9 Belisa Figuerio, 'Cinema of Brazil program increases co-production by 200%', *Revista de Cinema*, vol. 22, no. 3 (2008), p. 39. Distribution in the USA was through City Lights Pictures, Elaine Guerini, 'Cao Hamburger', *Screen International*, no. 1619 (2007), p. 12.
10 Guerini, 'Cao Hamburger', p. 12.
11 Guerini, 'Brazil', p. 13.
12 Jeffrey Lesser, *Negotiating National Identity* (Durham, NC: Duke University Press, 1999), p. 1.

13 Antonio Traverso, 'Migrations of cinema: Italian neorealism and Brazilian cinema', in Laura E. Ruberto and Kristi M. Wilson (eds), *Italian Neorealism and Global Cinema* (Detroit, MI: Wayne State University Press, 2007), pp. 165–86.
14 Ibid., p. 178.
15 David Martin-Jones, *Deleuze and World Cinemas* (London: Continuum, 2011), pp. 69–99; David Martin-Jones, 'O "opsigno" de Gilles Deleuze em *Machuca* (2004): cinema e história após a ditadura militar'/'Gilles Deleuze's 'opsign' in *Machuca* (2004): cinema and history after military rule', in Antonio Carlos Amorim, Silvio Gallo and Wenceslao Machado de Oliveira Jr (eds), *Conexões: Deleuze e Imagem e Pensamento e…* (Rio de Janeiro: DP et Alii, 2010), pp. 33–48.
16 Gilles Deleuze, *Cinema 2*, trans. Hugh Tomlinson and Robert Galeta (London: Continuum, [1985] 2005), pp. 1–23.
17 For an introduction to the existing body of work on Deleuze and cinema, see David Martin-Jones and William Brown 'Introduction', in Martin-Jones and Brown (eds), *Deleuze and Film* (Edinburgh: Edinburgh University Press, 2012), pp. 1–17.
18 Deleuze, *Cinema 2*, p. 2.
19 Ibid., p. 3.
20 Ibid., p. 2.
21 Martin-Jones, *Deleuze and World Cinemas*, pp. 69–99.
22 Ibid., p. 76 (emphasis in original).
23 Deleuze, *Cinema 2*, 66–94.
24 Ibid., p. 6.(emphasis in original).
25 Ronald Bogue, *Deleuze on Cinema* (London: Routledge, 2003), pp. 132–3.
26 Deleuze, *Cinema 2*, pp. 67–9.
27 Ibid., p. 72.
28 David Deamer, *Deleuze's Cinema Books* (Edinburgh: Edinburgh University Press, 2016), p. 146.
29 Ibid., p. 149.
30 James Holston, *Insurgent Citizenship* (Princeton, NJ: Princeton University Press, 2008), p. 41.
31 Roberto Schwarz, *Misplaced Ideas* (London: Verso, 1992), pp. 138–9.
32 Michael Billig, *Banal Nationalism* (London: Sage, 1995), p. 6.
33 Schwarz, *Misplaced Ideas*, p. 138.
34 Thomas E. Skidmore, *The Politics of Military Rule in Brazil, 1964–1985* (New York: Oxford University Press, 1988), p. v.
35 Ibid., pp. 106–7, 124.
36 Alfred Stepan, *Rethinking Military Politics* (Princeton, NJ: Princeton University Press, 1988), 33–4; Marcos Napolitano, 'A chronology of Brazilian political history', in Adriano Nervo Codato (ed.), *Political Transition and Democratic Consolidation* (New York: Nova Science Publishers, 2006), pp. 151–64, pp. 154–5.
37 Skidmore, *The Politics of Military Rule in Brazil 1964–1986*, p. 111.
38 Ibid., pp. 111–12.
39 Eduardo P. Archetti, 'The spectacle of identities', in Stephen Hart and Richard Young (eds), *Contemporary Latin American Cultural Studies* (London: Hodder Arnold, 2003), p. 118; Alex Bellos, *Futebol: The Brazilian Way of Life* (London: Bloomsbury, 2002), pp. 36–7.
40 Guerini, 'Cao Hamburger', p. 12.
41 Tatiana Signorelli Heise, *Remaking Brazil: Contested National Identities in Contemporary Brazil* (Cardiff: University of Wales Press, 2012), p. 87.
42 Billig, *Banal Nationalism*, pp. 37–59.
43 Deleuze, *Cinema 2*, p. 86.

44 Karen Backstein, 'The year my parents went on vacation', *Cineaste*, vol. 33, no. 2 (2008), p. 54; Henrique Rattner, 'Economic and social mobility of Jews in Brazil', in Judith Laikin Elkin and Gilbert W. Merkx (eds), *The Jewish Presence in Latin America* (Boston, MA: Allen and Unwin, 1987), p. 189.
45 Jeffrey Lesser, *Welcoming the Undesirables* (Berkeley, CA: University of California Press, 1995), p. 176.
46 Jeffrey Lesser, 'Challenges to Jewish life in Latin America', in William Frankel (ed.), *Survey of Jewish Affairs* (London: Blackwell, 1991), p. 232.
47 Jeffrey Lesser, '"Jews are Turks who sell on credit"', in Ignacio Klich and Jeffrey Lesser (eds), *Arab and Jewish Immigrants in Latin America* (London: Frank Cass, 1998), p. 47.
48 James Holston, *Insurgent Citizenship* (Princeton, NJ: Princeton University Press, 2008), p. 70.
49 José Luiz Passos and Valéria Costa e Silva, 'Freyre's concept of culture in *The Masters and the Slaves*', in Carmen Nava and Ludwig Lauerhas Jr, (eds), *Brazil in the Making: Facets of National Identity* (Oxford: Rowman & Littlefield, 2006), p. 64.
50 Edward E. Telles, *Race in Another America* (Princeton, NJ: Princeton University Press, 2004), pp. 6–10.
51 Amós Nascimento, 'Colonialism, modernism, and postmodernism in Brazil', in Eduardo Mendieta (ed.), *Latin American Philosophy: Currents, Issues, Debates* (Bloomington, IN: Indiana University Press, 2003), p. 133.
52 For a fuller discussion, see Carolina Rocha, 'Jewish cinematic self-representations in contemporary Argentine and Brazilian films', *Journal of Modern Jewish Studies*, vol. 9, no. 1 (2010), pp. 37–48.
53 Nascimento, 'Colonialism, modernism and postmodernism in Brazil', p. 128.
54 Deborah Shaw, 'The figure of the absent father in recent Latin American films', *Studies in Hispanic Cinemas*, vol. 1, no. 2 (2004), p. 85; Lúcia Nagib, *Brazil on Screen* (London: I.B. Tauris, 2007), p. 41; Shaw and Dennison, *Brazilian National Cinema*, p. 110; Stephen M. Hart, *A Companion to Latin American Film* (Woodbridge: Tamesis, 2004), p. 181.
55 Deleuze, *Cinema 2*, p. 87.
56 Ibid., p. 82.
57 John Caughie, 'Representing Scotland', in Eddie Dick (ed.), *From Limelight to Satellite* (London: BFI/SFC, 1990), p. 25.
58 Nagib, *Brazil on Screen*, p. 44.
59 Thanks to Antonio Carlos Amorim, Susana Oliveira Dias and staff and students at the Laboratory for Journalism Studies (especially the Masters in Diverse Sciences and Cultures), at the Faculty of Education, State University of Campinas. Your input was generously given, and extremely influential. Thank you to Mark Harris also, and Soledad Montañez, Stephanie Dennison, Tatiana Signorelli Heise and Carolina Rocha for feedback on initial drafts. Thanks to Tatiana Signorelli Heise for allowing me to read extracts from *Remaking Brazil* (2012), and Carolina Rocha for extracts from *Representing History, Class and Gender in Spain and Latin America* (2012), in both cases prior to publication.

9 BEGINNINGS AND CHILDREN

Lalitha Gopalan

In the denouement of Dadasaheb Phalke's *Kaaliya Mardan* (1919), the film cuts from scenes of Krishna's childhood mischief on land to an underwater playground: through double exposure effects, we watch Krishna dropping himself into the river bed, the domain of the many-hooded snake, Kaaliya, who is feared by the villagers for having poisoned their river. Krishna lands on Kaaliya's fanned hood and coiled body and is soon in the snake's grip. A fight ensues, a battle between god and demon. On screen we see a pile of the coiled serpent's body writhing vigorously while Krishna pulls at its tail, which we know is as an ingenious way to subdue Kaaliya's capacity for strangling. In a series of cutaways we see Krishna's friends bemoaning his premature demise, a conclusion that seems in keeping with Kaaliya's invincibility. When the film returns to the river we see Kaaliya's many-hooded head above water but now firmly under the control of Krishna, who is dancing gleefully whilst straddling the subjugated serpent. Through a set of double exposures we see Kaaliya's wives rising from the waters and beseeching Krishna for mercy. This final section of the silent film is a widely known mythological story of the god Krishna's many antics as a child, a precocious, divine child, that here Phalke brings to life in what scholars have identified as the dominant style in his 'mythological' genre: the tableau presentation of set pieces from popular myths.[1]

The child actor whose adorable frolics are idealized on screen is Phalke's own daughter Mandakini, who has recounted to her father's biographers that she was cast through a series of random incidents in a familial setting: her father's narration of the stories excited her and it was these reactions that Phalke anticipated she would be able to reproduce on screen. Dressed up as the young Krishna with a feathered crown on her head and flute in hand, Mandakini appears to be enjoying herself on a set wrapped by sections of a coiled snake; obviously an outsized prop shaped as a snake is a source of jest rather than fear. To scholars writing on this pioneering figure of cinema in India, Phalke's fascination with the medium's possibilities lay in the direction of movement within the frame, such as the tableau scenario in *Kaaliya Mardan* rendered credible by flailing movements; in other films such as *Krishna Janam*, Ravi Vasudevan has noted the use of dissolves, or more precisely double exposure effects.[2] Considered together these effects were deployed in the mythological genre in a manner that is well suited to such manipulations in the *mise en scène* and in-camera editing. In the infancy of cinema and under colonial conditions, Phalke's experiments have been read variously: his canny use of the mythological genre appears as a subversive attempt to outflank colonial censorship, while at the same time reiterating certain impulses of nationalism undergirded by Hinduism. However, the formal experiments with image composition are less conclusive. Recalling a genealogy that is surely related to Méliès's own fascination with the fantastical possibilities afforded by moving images when in its infancy in France, Phalke's proclivity for choosing set pieces from Hindu myths in the early years of cinema in India appears an innovative way of exploiting the cinematic apparatus's potential for bolstering tricks and sleights of hand, as well as upholding its ability to capture movements through space and eventually become visible through the projection of light. And as Phalke and his heirs gave shape to narrative cinema, the attendant economies of genre and stardom were not far behind; the mythological genre is introduced and his daughter Mandakini emerges as the first child star.

As Phalke's endeavours have been written into the annals of a history of national cinema as the primogenitor of cinema in India, it seems banal yet tempting to call attention to a twinned beginning – the infancy of narrative cinema in India wrapped up in the antics of a child actor turned star – since this origin story has come to dominate the study of cinema in India. For example, Mandakini's debut - as noted in Dilip Ghosh's documentary on child stars in Indian cinema, *Aadhi Haqeqat, Adda Fasana* (1990) – suggests that her appearance as Krishna is the beginning of a long history of Indian cinema's fascination with children on screen.[3]

The double exposure effect in *Kaaliya Mardan* as a hallmark of Phalke's ingenuity has mesmerized filmmakers who have not hesitated to insert and quote the finale to emphasize their own stabs at experimentation. For instance, Reena Mohan's *Kamlabhai* (1992) recounts the rise of the other woman, the other first lady of the Indian screen, from Phalke's stable of actors, but cannot help inserting the double exposure of Mandakini's slow drop towards Kaaliya's supine body. In a series of relays, it is precisely this aquatic scene that is repeated in Ranjan Palit's essay film *In Camera* (2011) – Palit also worked as the cinematographer for Mohan's film. Both citations recognize Phalke's originality whilst carving a place for their own interventions: Mohan's film is a groundbreaking effort to complicate the biopic genre of non-narrative films; Palit's film, similarly, offers a meditative reckoning of a cinematographer's career over twenty-five years. Complicating the citation protocol is Amit Dutta's Student Diploma film, *Ksha Tra Ghya* (2004), which prolongs the connection between child and novelty by inserting the double exposure of Krishna entangled in Kaaliya's folds and subsequently bifurcating the details in his own revision of Phalke. In Dutta's film, with a considerable distance from the original, we see a man picking up a mobile phone that morphs into a snake, an effect achieved through a cut, here an in-camera trick and not a post-production editing rhythm. Dutta finds an equivalence for the child but not immediately, and in fact the doppelganger for Mandakini's Krishna is dispersed across other parts of the film as a rambunctious boy rampaging through the rooms of a home. As we see, Dutta's own critically acclaimed film shuffles images to enhance cinema's relationship to magic tricks that are most potently delivered though the rhythm of cuts, thus contributing to *Ksha Tra Ghya*'s well-deserved reputation as a landmark film in the emerging field of experimental filmmaking in India while deploying a technology from the 1930s – the Mitchell camera.

The decades intervening between Phalke's conscription of Mandakini and Dutta's insertion of a snake as mobile phone, proliferate with signals in the cinemas of India that further emphasize the place of the child in feature films and its indispensability to those cinemas. While children abound in other-language cinemas, it is worth exploring how their arrival on screen in India coincides with shifts in film form and style.

There are many such originary moments in Indian cinema; however, the longue durée after independence throws up a different kind of cinema that is very much at odds with the mythological genre and responds keenly to the postcolonial reality of poverty, development and progress, films that are not far from and are indeed inspired by the preoccupations of Italian neorealism. In this conjuncture, in India, Satyajit Ray's *Pather Panchali* (1955) is the urtext. Ray's film deserves the encomiums that have declared it a canonical text in world cinema; its appearance on various film lists is a facile way to reiterate this point. As the first part of 'the Apu Trilogy', the film borrows the structure of the Bildungsroman by unfolding the protagonist's chronological development from boyhood to manhood. Amongst the many readings of the film there are those that have suggested the direct influence of Jean Renoir's filmmaking of *The River* (1951) in India – perhaps most evident in Ray's choice of outdoor locations. Richard Allen's close reading of the film's form provides us with a consideration of its style with a discriminating reading of the off-screen space, inferred through a rich soundtrack. This companionate reading feeds my own exploration of the relationship between children and scale in *Pather Panchali*: particularly in the composition of images and rhythm of editing.[4]

'The train scene,' as it is known widely, offers the most riveting play of scale. It begins with Apu and his sister Durga wandering away from home and towards the Kaash fields. The camera drops its centre of perspective to show us the children in full shot and at times, in medium close-up, when in repose and conversation; such a drop in the centre of the frame is not unusual in a narrative where the camera accommodates the varying heights of its actors to convey a 'normal' height differentiation between human figures. The Kaash grass, in full bloom, towers over the kids when they rest and effectively camouflages them as they walk desultorily through the fields, mimicking the movement of the feathery stalks. Dwarfing the human figures, the reeds of the grass appear as giant foliage, a trick of scale (*trompe l'oeil*) that is enhanced by the low-angle shots of the camera. As the kids huddle under the blossom, Durga alerts Apu (and by extension the spectator), to a sound off-screen, a train whistle that heralds a rushing train that mobilizes a sudden shift in perspective. There are several shots in this segment but I want to focus on the series of images that follow when the train is captured in long shot, emerging into the frame, right side, with billowing smoke from the far ground, where the film then cuts to a pan. The camera swings shakily right to left to a space into which the train is yet to arrive and cuts to an extreme long shot, revealing Apu's dash towards the tracks; Durga, we note, is no longer in this frame. In a different rhythm, with less unsteadiness, the camera swings left to right from the other side of the tracks to capture Apu running towards the camera. The film cuts and the frame drops below the compartments and is now situated to record the moving wheels of the train, where, through the gaps of the moving wheels we can discern a human figure on the other side of the tracks-Apu. We now see that he is barely as tall as the wheels of the locomotive, diminutive, just as a child is expected to be in Quattrocento perspective. It is this classical arrangement of human figures set against a vanishing point that critics, including Allen, have commented on, implying that the film's preferred plane of action encourages us to accept the film's homage to neorealism. Strictly speaking, according to the conventions of continuity promoted by Hollywood and other cinemas that came under its influence, the camera has actually crossed or disrupted the 180-degree line of action and in effect, corrects our perception of scale. In this elegant flip over the axis of action, the children, more specifically Apu, are corrected to their 'actual' size in relationship to the machine; the earlier impression that encouraged us to imagine either giant children or dwarfed figures running among Kaash grass is retroactively corrected so that we come to understand, with certainty, that the foliage is not oversized flora planted in a fantasy film, but credible vegetation whose length has been heightened by shortening human figures, revealing that children in their natural diminution can participate in tricks of scale in which the world appears differently.[5]

However, shoring up discourses of post-war neorealism forecloses the film's expansive investment in the archive of world cinema. Apu's small figure in relationship to the speeding train also recalls the series of images from the finale of Eisenstein's *Strike* (1925): in this sequence a troop of horses ridden by Kulaks are rearing to attack the strikers. Minutes before the advance, there has been a tense stand-off between the Kulaks and the soldiers as seen by women and children on the edge of the frame. From this group, an infant has wandered into the legs of the horses. The low-angle camera position captures the infant in full shot amongst the columns of legs; a menacing sight that provokes his chaperone to retrieve him, moments before the legs kick off as the Kulaks begin their assault on the workers. Although not a pure metaphor this sequence is freighted with metonymic potential and prefigures the cruelty of the Kulaks; in a later sequence we see them toss babies from high apartment floors. Children and infants are rendered innocent in both *Strike* and *October* (1928), their helplessness metonymically extended to the working class.

Another commensurable comparison worth mentioning in regards to the low-angle position of the camera is from Ozu's famous mode of composition, particularly his 'tatami shots'. However, the dominant reading of Ozu's films favours the adults in the *mise en scène*. In *Tokyo Story* (1953), for instance, scholars have long commented on how the static low-angle shots have us observing adults in conversation in a room with right angle corners and sliding screens. The hallmark of Ozu's style is not to 'break' classical Hollywood style that observes the 180-degree line of action, but instead opts for a 360-degree space of action, thus promoting a different language of continuity. Consider, for instance, a scene in Tokyo in which we find parents and grandparents arranged in a conversation circle. In this rhythm of editing, the camera focuses on adults seated with legs folded on tatami mats, their restrained demeanour contrasts sharply with the tantrums of the young boy, Isamu, who rushes in and out of the frame exhibiting his petulance. We see Isamu and his brother in full shot since the camera is already situated lower to capture the scene amongst the seated adults, a position that accentuates the children's smallness, in contrast to the large adult torsos in plain sight. In an exceptional moment in *Tokyo Story* we see in long shot and in the same frame, the grandmother and Isamu standing together in the garden, so that their differences in height emphasize the generational gap between them.

Ray's singularity has either been framed by scholars as emerging from within Bengali culture, or as an auteur in world cinema, whose style displays a promiscuity of influences akin to a cinephile's archive. A not unreasonable assumption; as one of the founders of the Calcutta Film Society, in 1947, Ray wrote quite passionately about world cinema in essays that were subsequently collected in his *Our Films, Their Films*.[6] What is of interest for me is the place accorded to the film society's activities by Ray in the development of film culture in postcolonial India. Whether Ray influenced the policies of the Ministry of Information and Broadcasting (I&B) is not evident but, in a curious series of coincidences, it is worth observing how in an attempt to foster film culture among children, the Ministry of I&B – with the strong endorsement of India's first prime minister, Jawaharlal Nehru – established the Children's Film Society (CFS) in 1955, the very year *Pather Panchali* was released. The coincidence of interests between India's first prime minister, and a filmmaker in the making, is yet to be written beyond the confines of hagiographies, but what we can hazard is the pervasive influence of the discourse of 'sentimental education' in postcolonial and post-war national cultures in which both figures participated. Ray was not involved directly in CFS activities but his various other films made explicitly for children have been embraced over the years by this institution for purposes of exhibition. A glance at the roster of films produced by CFS confirms Ray's influence on its filmmakers; albeit not the melancholic despair of *Pather Panchali*, but work that is more evident in the light-hearted fantasies and detective stories that he made for children, such as *Parash Pather, Sonar Kela*.[7] A study of these films commissioned by CFS and the structure of subsidies and exhibition conditions deserve a fulsome exploration, but are beyond the confines of the present chapter.

Pather Panchali's influence travels in other directions too, since the impression it made on subsequent generations of filmmakers remains substantial, especially those graduating from the national film school, the Film and Television Institute of India (FTII, established in 1964 by the Ministry of I&B to improve the quality of filmmaking in the nation), which was subsequently realized in the form of various 'New Wave' film movements in regional cinemas. 'New wave' film movements worldwide conjure images of 'Young Turks' breaking free from the dictates of studio and conventional filmmaking, and a supplement makes its way into this pithy sketch in the shape of a film whose protagonist is a child. Truffaut's *400 Blows* (1959) sits beside Godard's youthful *Breathless* (1960) as signposts in the birth of the French New Wave; Hou Hsiao-hsien's *Summer at Grandpa's* (1984) mobilizes Taiwan's New Wave, which subsequently included Edward Yang's children-centred *Yi Yi* (2000). In the 'second' wave of the Taiwanese New Wave, filmmakers acknowledge previous 'new waves': in Tsai's film *What Time is it Over There?* (2001), the protagonist, at various moments, watches Truffaut's *400 Blows* on his television monitor and an ageing Antoine Doinel makes a cameo appearance in the Paris section of the film. And Hou's own second act in Taiwanese New Wave includes a remake of Lamorrise's child-centred film, *The Red Balloon* (1956) as *Flight of the Red Balloon* (2007). Critics have similarly long remarked on the ubiquity of children in the Iranian New Wave of the 1990s, and Majid Majidi's films provide the most obvious examples of privileging children. Simply put, children abound in New Wave films despite – or because of(?) – the impression of youthful rebellion that the concept connotes. So, it follows that the motif of children and trope of childhood should surface in one of the regional new waves in Indian cinema, the 'Kannada New Wave'.

By the time a child-centred film arrives in this short period of astounding films the New Wave is well under way, with works made by writers and theatre aficionados. In this context, a useful framing is afforded by M. Madhava Prasad who cites *Chomana Dudi* (1975) and *Samskara* (1970) as landmark films, based on well-known novels of the modern literary movement in Kannada that shaped New Wave cinema.[8] Into this robust filmmaking scene arrives Girish Kasarvalli – fresh from FTII with his groundbreaking student diploma film, *Avshesh* (circa 1975). Legends circulate that though Kasarvalli never officially graduated from FTII, his diploma film was his passport into professional filmmaking. His first feature film, *Ghatashraddha* (1978), was an extended treatment of his student film and fits quite easily within the dominant social and political preoccupations of the Kannada New Wave cinema; but with a difference – since as Prasad suggests, it is narrated from the point of view of a child, Nani.

Prasad's elegant reading of the film demonstrates how Kasarvalli's figuration of space rearranges the earlier forays of other films in this film movement. The narrative revolves primarily in a Brahmin milieu, with minor but not significant challenges to this hierarchical and highly ritualized ambience in the form of an inter-caste relationship. Nani is sent off by his father to a religious school (Vedic learning) that is located in a village away from his home. The film observes, in detail, the quotidian rituals of upper caste Brahmin life that are akin to other films preceding it but, in this instance, from the young boy's perspective, so that we, as viewers, experience the claustrophobia and patriarchal dimensions of this milieu, most pointedly rendered in Nani's growing friendship with a Brahmin widow, Yamuna. Yamuna's sexual independence disrupts the routine activities of the community that ostracizes her socially – when witnessed from Nani's point of view, we can see the gross injustice meted out to her. The final shot of the film deserves reiteration. The patriarchal dictate of the community performs a ritual ostracization (*Ghatashraddha*) by shaving off Yamuna's hair. In tandem, Nani is escorted out of the village by his father and the scene is set in the outskirts of the village: from Nani's point of view, we see – in long shot – Yamuna, head shaven and grief-stricken, standing under a large Peepal tree that fans out like an umbrella in the distance. Nani's reaction prompts us to find this image shocking. The film closes on this image. Kasarvalli has openly admitted to being influenced by Ray's filmmaking but unlike Apu's awestruck wonder at the moving locomotive that we see in *Pather Panchali*, *Ghatashraddha* accords the assumed innocence of a child's point of view within a carefully established ethics of viewing. The Brahmin habitus is no longer a neutral space in the film but rather a claustrophobic space where change is presented from Nani's perspective.

The Kannada New Wave was short-lived – as Prasad notes – and Kasarvalli has long outlived its scriptures by directing films that have moved him away from the themes besieging both *Avshesh* and *Ghatashraddha*. In an uncanny way, however, critical reception of his films has not completely exhausted the discussion on *Ghatashraddha*'s originality. In the late 1980s soon after the release of *Tabarne Kathe* (1987), Kasarvalli was asked by the editors of *Deep Focus* to respond to his well-known moniker, '*l'enfant terrible* of Kannada New Wave', an outdated (childish) designation that decidedly returns him (and us) to his two primary films as the dominant texts through which we should approach his oeuvre.

As much as new waves and art house films have enlisted children as protagonists to inaugurate a shift in style, both drastic and slight, children similarly crowd popular cinema. Among the different linguistic cinemas of India, Hindi films have nurtured and exploited child stars in family melodramas, socials, and romances: Daisy Rani, Master Alankar, Master Raju, Sachin and Sarika are all popular star monikers. In Tamil cinema, Kamal Hassan's previous history as a child star is considered as a separate phenomenon from his adult success as actor, director and filmmaker. Whilst child stardom deserves exploration as a much-needed corrective to adult dominated star studies, it is worth returning to film itself to note how children revise other crucial mainstays of popular cinema: genre structuring and authorial signature.

Among contemporary narrative filmmakers it is no exaggeration to state that scholarship has identified the feature film director Mani Ratnam as having a distinct signature, legible across both Tamil and Hindi cinemas.[9] That he shifted the course of popular cinema in the 1980s and 1990s in regards to film style is now beyond dispute, notwithstanding the controversial reception of his films.[10] In my own readings of his style I have remarked particularly on his reworking of song and dance sequences through figures of metaphor and metonymy in relationship to narrative continuity. At times, children appear as part of the dancers' entourage or more obviously as part of the unit in family dramas. Reconsidering his films through the lens of childhood, it is remarkable to see the ubiquitous presence of children in his films and how they serve a narratological function and as rhetorical figures. In his two gangster films, *Nayakan* (1987) and *Dalapathi* (1991), children are less widely dispersed throughout the narrative but nonetheless make for an arresting presence in pre-credit sequences. An Oedipal drama besieges the opening sequence in *Nayakan*: a son watches his father, a trade union leader, being shot by the police and subsequently runs away from the southern town of Tuticorin to Bombay. He emerges into adulthood as a gangster who challenges the law and has scant respect for the police. The pre-credit sequence thus offers an explanation for the protagonist's biography in classic Oedipal terms: the son chooses a profession that betrays the father's yet avenges his death. The narrative is suffused throughout with doublings and logics of vengeance in which children reappear before becoming criminal men. Thus in *Nayakan*, the logic of lawless activities hinges on a traumatic childhood of witnessing violence and flight. Released a few years later, *Dalapathi* returns to this logic by updating the epic Mahabharat. The film opens with the birth of a child who is abandoned and placed onto a moving train by a teenage mother and is soon adopted by a childless couple. His subsequent recruitment into a criminal gang pits him against his biological brother; pleas for peace from his ageing birth mother are dismissed as being too late. In different ways therefore, both films open with a damned childhood ignited by abandonment, which provides the narrative drive for their adult gangster heroes.

It is no coincidence that in Ratnam's family dramas children are not solely consigned to film openings, a genre that he substantially revises by reworking the more popular romance genre that conventionally ends with a happy union of a couple. In contrast, his films narrate moments that occur beyond the closures offered by the conventional popular romance, either by propelling the film into a marriage or a family drama. The recursive plotting of family dramas in his films frequently depends upon the children to precipitate narratives that ironically threaten their own ontological status. For example, in *Anjali* (1990) the eponymous, mentally retarded child dies at the end of the film. Through the twists and turns in the narrative, we have learned how a couple and their two young children have struggled with the slow integration of Anjali – the youngest child. Initially presumed dead at childbirth by the family, and by extension the audience, Anjali's birth and apparent death precipitate a crisis in the marriage through a series of misunderstandings: the wife assumes the husband is unfaithful. But as the film unfolds, we, along with the family, discover that while the father is indeed harbouring a secret, it is that he is caring for Anjali. Rather than burden his family with the care of their daughter, he has colluded with a doctor to arrange secretly for her care. Once confronted with the knowledge of their missing sibling and daughter, the family lobbies for Anjali's return to her birth family despite her disabilities. However, the film never completely erases the father's doubts that a normal and healthy family unit can incorporate an ailing child – despite rousing efforts at integration. At the end of the film, Anjali therefore, perhaps conveniently, succumbs to her death. At this point, the soundtrack of the film replays a song from an earlier sequence, which depicted the children in the neighbourhood playing with Anjali. This time, however, the film closes with a shot of the empty wheelbarrow that the kids had previously deployed to wheel Anjali around in the song, establishing a shot whose metaphoric meaning is keenly available through metonymic reminders. Therefore, despite the goodwill apparently expended by the family, the film ultimately confers with the father's initial hesitation regarding the viability of a normal family when caring for a member with a disability.

Although *Anjali* was a box-office success and won national awards for the Best Child Artist, Best Audiography, and Best Regional Film in 1992, it does not blunt the punitive drive of this closing sequence that asserts a normative ideal of the family. Yet the final shot of the wheelbarrow, a metonymic reminder of happier times in the life of family is more ambivalent, though equally decisive on the matter of Anjali's absence. Through this closing sequence, the film posits the child with a learning disability features as 'a structuring absence' of the normal family unit. The death of the child therefore offers no real sense of closure for the viewer, since the empty wheelbarrow prompts us to recall the family's initial intolerance to her additional needs. Ultimately, if the film has apparently been a long lesson in educating the family – and by extension the viewer – on the issue of learning difficulties, by ending the film with the death of the child and thereby restoring 'normalcy' this reflects the family's own inability to cope with such apparent aberrations in the long run.

Another inconclusive ending, even more burdened with double meanings, is literalized in *Bombay* (1995), which provides twin sons for a couple who get married against the religious sentiments of their hidebound parents (he is Hindu and she Muslim).[11] The depiction of a Hindu–Muslim family with twins apparently offers an ideal image of communal harmony, a utopian ideal in a secular national culture. But this ideal is achieved only after being tested by patriarchal rejection at home and through the brutal antagonisms in the city of their choice, Bombay. On the one hand, the twins reverberate this doubling by standing together as figures of unity; on the other hand, they fall apart into polar antagonisms represented by the charred ruins of their shared *mise en scène*. In the final moments of the film – after the male protagonist has quelled the rioters in Bombay – the film ends with images of communal harmony. The family finds itself: first the twins find each other and together they spot their parents. The final shot of the film is a dissolve constituting two images: four members of the family huddled in an embrace that is superimposed on the detritus of the riots in the city streets.[12] It appears at first, therefore, that the family has prevailed despite being thrown asunder by the antagonisms besieging the city and particularly their neighbourhood. However, the dissolve simultaneously evokes another scene, a *mise en scène* of ruin that is the backdrop of this tight embrace. Each image informs the other, producing its own doubling effect. In both *Anjali* and *Bombay*, therefore, children emerge as allegorical figures supplying us with closures that are ambivalent.

In an uncanny relation to these two earlier films, Ratnam's *Kannathil Muthamittal* (2002) grapples with adoption. A couple adopts a third child who has been abandoned by her birth mother at a refugee camp for Sri Lankan Tamils in Tamil Nadu. Long scenes of domesticity display a happy and affectionate family enlivened by the antics of their three children. However, once the adopted daughter learns of her actual birth history, the film steers away from family drama to political theatre in Sri Lanka. The adopted parents accompany their daughter as she searches for her mother in the war-torn regions of Jaffna. In the final sequence of the film, on a rainy day, the birth mother materializes in guerrilla fatigues to meet her daughter and pleads with her to allow her to join her and her adopted parents and return to India. Yet the film eschews this possible ending. Instead, we watch the revolutionary soldier/birth mother retreating into the ruins and gun smoke while the film cuts to a family portrait: father, mother and adopted daughter under an umbrella looking into the distance (although we assume that they are looking at the receding figure of the birth mother). The film's rendition of the family portrait as the preferred final shot interestingly evicts the two birth children who have been left behind in India in favour of the parents embracing their single adopted child. Adoption is therefore signalled as a powerful metaphor for an India-centred solution to the Tamil separatist movement, a quiet acquiescence that disentangles Tamils from their struggle for sovereignty in Sri Lanka. At the same time, the image suggests that the family itself undergoes its own bifurcation, and by evicting the birth children from the final portrait there is a suggestion that presents a possibility of 'two families', a solution that has long been forwarded by the Tamils in Sri Lanka. As is the case with the other two films directed by Ratnam, in the closing moments of *Kannathil Muthamittal* one meaning begets another and each resolution hinges on the figure of the child.

In the last decade, Tamil cinema has undergone a resurgence that I have called, elsewhere, a 'cruel cinema'.[13] These more recent films are vastly different from the urban milieu depicted in Ratnam's films and instead exhibit a familiarity with the working-class neighbourhoods of Madurai, where desultory young men provoke endless fights, all set against a masculine fan culture that is devoted to the film star Rajnikant. Nevertheless, even in these later films, children recur in such a way as to coax us to see them as apposite responses to Ratnam's genteel ambience. In this cycle of films, the escalating violence unleashed by the young men finds an anterior place in a brutal Oedipal struggle against patriarchal forces which implicates fathers, stepmothers and older siblings, resulting once more in causal scenarios linked to childhood that open films such as *Veyyil* (2006) and *Paruthiveeran* (2007) in which the young men play victimized children. In these texts and in other films, children appear in the narrative either as a sideshow or in the *mise en scène* of a family – as is the case in *Pudhupettai* (2006) and *Subramaniapuram* (2008). In fact, many of these films are emphatic about casting children as victims in family and neighbourhood dramas whose resolutions are damned and violent.

Pasanga/Children (2009) is an odd supplement to 'cruel cinema' and casts children as protagonists and adults as the sideshow. Here, children, not young men, hurl epithets at each other and launch into quarrels that do not diminish their violent potential, yet they seem comical; in large part because these sequences are rendered in slow motion. The extended duration of a scuffle in slow motion shots retains a childish bravado but cannot help recalling the attenuated violence of adults seen in the other films in 'cruel cinema'. *Pasanga* therefore disassociates childhood from innocence, and in that rupture provides a moratorium on ideas of a 'sentimental education' long associated with the genre of children's film.

That the image of the child on screen indicates a perceptible shift at every turn in the form and style of narrative in Indian cinemas seems conclusive. That these alterations in style and form extract a price is most evident on a film set, which is where I found myself in July 2012. Kannan's zombie film, *Daayan*, was under production at a defunct engineering factory. The cavernous factory floors had over one hundred zombies with their walking dead white countenance watching a child apparently on the verge of being sacrificed at an altar. This captivating moment was a finale, after a chase through a thicket of overgrown roots and ruins that had been shot earlier in the day. The camera was focused on two adult actors circling around a crying child whose fate was being decided by their different wills. On the other side of the camera, wincing in deep pain was the cinematographer Saurabh Goswami, carrying an Arri Alexa, which weighs about ten pounds with the magazine loaded. Tall, at six feet, Saurabh had spent a number days shooting the child whose short stature demanded that the cameraman shoot him kneeling, a position which when sustained over many days, wreaks havoc on the kneecaps. That the sacrifice was scheduled as the last workday for the child actor was a welcome relief to Goswami's knees that had already surrendered to the gruelling schedule of shooting a child for two months. Labour pains mark all births, scars that may also be borne by the cinematographer's body during the emergence of New Wave cinemas and shifts in style.[14]

Notes

1. The large prop is either a man in a snake suit or a prop moved on a mobile platform being pulled hither and thither by strings.
2. See revised version of earlier essays on Phalke in Ravi Vasudevan, *The Melodramatic Public: Film Form and Spectatorship in Indian Cinema* (New York: Palgrave Macmillan, 2011).
3. Thanks to K.U. Mohanan for recommending this film.
4. Richard Allen, '*Pather Panchali* (1955)', in Lalitha Gopalan (ed.), *Cinema of India* (London: Wallflower Press, 2010).
5. An inverse reading based on *a priori* knowledge of scale regarding machines and flora yields the following for a viewer familiar with machines, the scale of children versus

the running train in classical composition is self-evident; for the viewer familiar with these tall reeds, the tricks of scale promoted by me are irrelevant.
6   Satyajit Ray, *Our Films, Their Films* (Bombay: Orient Longman, 1976).
7   A study of these films commissioned by CFS and the structure of subsidies and exhibition conditions deserve a fulsome exploration, but are beyond the confines of the present essay.
8   M. Madhava Prasad, 'Ghattshradda (1978)', in Gopalan (ed.), *Cinema of India*.
9   See Lalitha Gopalan, 'Nayakan ... ', in *Cinema of Interruptions: Action Genres in Contemporary Indian Cinema* (London: BFI Publishing, 2002). For an extensive reading of Ratnam's style, see Lalitha Gopalan, *Bombay* (London: BFI Publishing, 2005); Swarnvel Easwaran Pillai, 'Iruvar', in Gopalan (ed.), *Cinema of India*.
10 See the critical reception of both *Roja* and *Bombay*.
11 See my detailed reading of the film in Gopalan, *Bombay*.
12 In my interview with Mani Ratnam he asserts that this dissolve was a mistake and that he meant to have a sequence of images: shots of the ruined city followed by the tight shot of the embracing family. That is not how the film arrived to its viewers, so the option of sequential stringing of images remains a hypothetical option.
13 See Lalitha Gopalan, 'Film culture in Chennai', *Film Quarterly*, vol. 62, no. 1 (2008); also the Tamil Film series that I co-programmed with Anuj Vaidya, 'Cruel cinema: Tamil New Wave', 2011, at University of California, Berkeley Art Museum and Pacific Film Archive (BAMPFA), https://bampfa.org/program/cruel-cinema-new-directions-tamil-film%E2%80%82 (accessed July 2021).
14 Thanks to Roberto Tejada for lending his ear on matters both great and small. I dedicate this essay to my parents, for sustenance through a summer of misery.

PART FOUR

BEYOND CINEMA

10 THE CHILD IN SURREALISM: BELLMER, CORNELL, HILLER

David Hopkins

'It is perhaps childhood that comes closest to one's "real life"' wrote André Breton, the surrealist leader, in the First Surrealist Manifesto of 1924.[1] It is now widely understood that, within the surrealist avant-garde, the child was held to be closer to the irrational (via magical thought and fantasies of omnipotence), and to the unconscious, than the adult. This fascination with childhood is routinely mentioned in the literature on surrealism, but rarely isolated for analytic attention. Strangely, our current cultural preoccupation with children's rights, and with children's potential abuse at the hands of adults, has hardly impacted on this field of enquiry, and part of the purpose of this chapter will be to open up some methodological space for a rethinking of the surrealist child. In a sense, the child was everywhere within surrealism, but the adult investments involved in establishing that position of centrality, both among the surrealists themselves and their later historians and commentators, are left unexamined, as if 'childhood' was somehow inviolable or sacrosanct.

It is worth beginning by establishing a few basic principles regarding the surrealist child. One notable example of surrealist child-worship is the notion of the 'femme enfant'. Several photographs exist of members of the surrealist group in 1935 standing respectfully around the 14-year-old child prodigy Gisèle Prassinos as she pours forth the automatic poetry, supposedly issuing directly from unconscious sources and thus uncontaminated by rational control, to which she, as a child, and a girl-child to boot, was thought to be particularly close. Alongside numerous other modernist and avant-garde formations in the early twentieth century, the surrealists aspired in their art and writings to a childlike spontaneity of expression, outside the strictures of formal educational or academic conventions.[2] In broad terms, the surrealist attitude was one that was firmly rooted in Romantic conceptions of childhood, as a state closer to nature and to a form of natural 'innocence', which was itself tinged with Victorian nostalgia.[3] A strong argument for the radical nature of surrealism's position is that it stood in counterpoint to the emphasis on strict parental control and on the unquestioned superiority of adult rational control of the child which was the bedrock, in France in particular, of the paternalistic European cultures of the early twentieth century.[4] A critique of their position would no doubt hinge on their overly romantic idealization of childhood with its kinship to processes of 'othering' that can also be found in the orientalizing and primitivizing currents of Modernism.[5] At the same time, the surrealists were part of the first literary and artistic generation to respond to the tradition of late nineteenth-century psychological thought as it reached its head in the early twentieth century in Freudian psychoanalysis, and therefore had to accommodate the view that children, as well as being conduits for an alternative inspiration and vision, were also actively sexual beings, with complex fantasy lives. This of course was grist to the surrealist mill, insofar as the exploration of sexuality was as central to surrealist concerns as the mining of the unconscious. The two could hardly be separated. Interestingly, though, it is possible to perceive in surrealist art and writing a structural vacillation between conceptions of childhood whereby, on the one hand, the child is seen to represent an opening onto an uncontaminated poetic 'marvellous', whilst, on the other, the child is seen to be unruly and instinctual, disturbingly sexualized.

The dichotomy I am pointing to is rarely cut and dried, and very often surrealist works attest to a confusion or melding of these views of childhood. The proto-surrealist painting by Giorgio De Chirico, 'The Mystery and Melancholy of a Street' (1914), for instance, offers a Victorian-era image of a young girl with a hoop as she walks into a vaguely threatening world in which an animal trailer's door stands ominously open and the massively enlarged shadow of what looks like a male hunter, spear in hand, looms near to that of the child. There is frequently a sense that surrealist artists are thematizing precisely the incursion of sexuality and the irrational into the bourgeois worlds of their turn-of-the-century upbringings. This is surely the case in Max Ernst's collage-novels, especially 'Une Semaine de Bonté' (1934) in which the overstuffed parlours and boudoirs of his childhood become invaded with bird-headed beings. Ernst's 1924 painting 'Two Children are Threatened by a Nightingale' embodies this unease in its very title. But it is also possible to see quite polarized views of childhood in surrealist works, which attest to the root confusion between conceptions of childhood that I have discussed. This can be seen in two relative latecomers to surrealism, Hans Bellmer and Joseph Cornell. In the work of Bellmer, a German artist who entered the surrealist orbit in the mid 1930s, children are often disturbingly violated; in one famous drawing of 1935/6 a child curiously peels up her skin, like a garment, to stare perversely at her own insides; in numerous other images pre-pubescent girls indulge in Sadean fantasies. By contrast, in the work of the American Joseph Cornell, one of the last 'true' surrealists although never, strictly speaking, part of the group, there is, ironically, a reversion to a much more 'romantic' conception of childhood. This is partly an outcome of Cornell's inundation with romantic and symbolist literature (Goethe, Nerval, Poe, etc.) and partly a consequence of his otherworldly personality. Largely confined to the place of his upbringing for his entire adult life, looking after a demanding mother and a crippled brother, Cornell spent hours wandering through the bric-a-brac and curio shops of mid-town Manhattan, searching for the fragmentary objects which he would assemble in an associative matrix in the 'boxes' he produced from the mid 1930s onwards.

What I want to do in this essay is to track the very different conceptions of childhood represented by these artists, and see how they operate, as structural underpinnings, in the work of a contemporary artist who is one of the clearest inheritors of the surrealist tradition, the American-born artist Susan Hiller. In so doing, it may be possible to see how sharply the cultural configuration of childhood has shifted in the eighty or so years since surrealism was at its height and offer some perspective on surrealist child-worship in the process. Film and video works will be privileged in the latter part of this discussion. Film was a central medium within the surrealist avant-garde (in the experimental Dalí/Buñuel collaborations and the work of Germaine Dulac to mention the most obvious examples) but my reason for privileging film is also partly methodological; it has the advantage, over the static mediums of painting, sculpture, assemblage and collage that dominate accounts of surrealism and post-surrealist production, of containing the residues of narrative impulses that help explicate psychological and social attitudes, whereas static objects may more immediately lure us into abstract considerations of aesthetics, iconography, style and so on. At the same time, it seems important here to emphasize that this discussion aims to focus on adult conceptions of childhood and not childhood itself. The question might therefore be: what forms of adult identification with children, and attendant forms of nostalgia and/or regression, are at play in these works? And what might we learn from this, not so much about the fantasies that adults impute to children and their imaginations, but the fantasies and anxieties that adults impose upon childhood?

In 1931, Bellmer's mother, in the process of moving house in the wake of her husband's cerebral haemorrhage, came across a box of Bellmer's childhood toys, which she subsequently sent to him. The collection included broken dolls, linocut magazines, glass marbles, Red Indian disguises, conjuring tricks, penknives, spinning tops, and pink sugar pigeons, and, when Bellmer came to arrange the objects in a shadow box which he called his 'Personal Museum', it further incorporated objects such as a metal Puss in Boots, a gyroscope, toy trains and playing cards.[6] It seems that the arrival of the box of toys acted as a catalyst in Bellmer's artistic development. Along with other highly charged personal events of the period, notably Bellmer's obsession with his adolescent cousin, Ursula, who became his neighbour in Berlin, it directly informed the construction of 'The Doll', the mannequin made up of multiple, interchangeable parts that the artist was to fabricate between 1934 and 1936. This in turn was reproduced photographically in the book 'Die Puppe' (1934) in which Bellmer's text 'Memories of the Doll Theme' serves to underline the self-willed regression that had followed the artists' revelatory re-acquaintance with his childhood playthings, and the way this reconnection was bound up with a recollection of early sexual fantasies. Talking of the association he had made in childhood between confectionery or objects associated with play and thoughts of young girls, he wrote:

> In fact certain objects from their world were always coveted for they were often as fragile as those black Easter eggs with their doves and pink sugary curlicues – so tempting, but thankfully having nothing more to offer… Yet, apart from such baroque confections, a single coloured glass marble was sufficient to extend the bounds of my imagination in disconcerting directions. The marble was less confiding, despite offering a view of its interior in which one could behold the frozen ecstasy of its spirals. It was enthralling. Lured by this miracle, pleated lace flounces nestled around the marble's curves, the lost leg of a little doll curved over it, the lid of a cigar-box inclined to form a threatening perpendicular and the inscription on its surface disappeared up above, beneath the celluloid ball and the corkscrew curls that played about it.[7]

What is noteworthy here is the way that Bellmer combines a remarkable ability to empathize with the proto-fetishistic viewpoint of a child gazing at and through a marble with the emergence of a proto-paedophilic fantasy which he later developed, not only in the construction of 'The Doll' but also in certain drawings of the mid 1930s in which allusions to the decorative adornments of confectionery or clothing and to childish toys such as marbles figure prominently.[8]

Joseph Cornell would himself revert to a box format – not directly related to the 'Personal Museum' of Bellmer, but having interesting thematic connections to it – from about 1936 onwards. For Cornell, the box – small and glass-fronted, and usually either presented in the form of a poetic tableau, or compartmentalized internally to form a kind of jewel casket or reliquary – became his central means of expression. Particularly exquisite examples are the so-called 'Medici' boxes, dating from 1942 to the mid 1950s, in which reproductions of Renaissance portraits by Sofinisba Anguissola, Bronzino and Pintoricchio, pasted to the back of the boxes, are surrounded by compartments containing toy blocks or small balls, producing the overall effect of a penny arcade slot machine. The so-called 'Untitled' (Medici Princess) box of 1948 is especially interesting in terms of the relation to Bellmer for its utilization of the combination of the image of the beautiful young girl and the allusions to childhood games. As Diane Waldman points out, the claustrophobic homage to the unattainable princess could well be understood as an outcome of Cornell's yearning for a female companion/lover. The work dates from a period when Cornell briefly held a factory job, a temporary respite from his normal confinement at home in Queens, New York, looking after his mother and brother. It appears that Cornell met a young woman in the factory at this time, but as his diary reveals, felt unable to consummate the relationship. Diane Waldman notes that the girl in the Medici Princess Box is the ideal of youth and innocence, but as royalty she is unattainable. Cornell, recognizing the futility of his longings, situates her behind glass, making her even more detached in time and place.[9]

There is, then, a deeply melancholic, nostalgic cast to Cornell's evocation of childhood, but it is arguable whether he enters into the self-willed regression of Bellmer. Whatever affinities might be observed between Bellmer and Cornell – and they certainly represent perfect examples of the idealized and sexualized polarities of surrealist attitudes to childhood – they were radically different artists, who have rarely been brought into proximity. Bellmer was self-consciously psychoanalytic in approach. Cornell, however, asserted on one occasion: 'do not share the subconscious and dream theories of the surrealists. While fervently admiring much of their work I have never been an official surrealist, and I believe that surrealism has healthier possibilities than have been developed.'[10] This talk of 'healthier possibilities' may suggest a certain anxiety on Cornell's part regarding the 'darker' aspects of surrealism and it is not surprising to discover that Cornell was a lifelong follower of Christian Science, the religious movement set up in America by Mary Baker Eddy.[11] Whereas Bellmer knowingly nurtured his paedophilic fantasies, Cornell's work, and his personal diaries, often speak of a level of repression that he was surprisingly unreflective about. Yet there is plenty of biographical detail to suggest that Cornell had deeply peculiar relations to young children and women. Mary Ann Caws notes that in his diaries there were voluminous notes about the girls he watched from afar, who were discussed in the pages of his journal in terms of an obsessive childlike personal mythology:

'Tina' (a 'be-bopper' he says) entered into the general domain of his 'fairies' or 'fées' – whom he named according to their clothing or associations. The 'apricot angel' wears orange; the 'fée aux lapins' or bunny fairy is a counter girl who sells toy bunny rabbits.[12]

Cornell even went as far as to arrange tea parties solely for children, and to invite them as privileged guests to his exhibitions.

Given such information, scholars tend to agree that sexual repression was a powerful motor behind Cornell's work: Lindsay Blair notes of certain of Cornell's boxes, that it is 'impossible, for all their emphasis on the innocence of childhood, to ignore the lingering presence of the strong desire that originally caused the boxes to be made'.[13] There has, however, been surprisingly little in-depth psychoanalytic investigation of the work. An exception to this occurs in one of the few detailed analyses of Cornell's work as a filmmaker by Marjorie Keller.[14]

Attending to the theme of childhood in Cornell's work, Keller argues that the construction of the child-figure in much of Cornell's output approximates closely to certain typologies in the writings of Nerval, Lewis Carroll and Goethe, all of whose writings Cornell greatly admired. Keller pays particular attention to Cornell's interest in the figure of Mignon from Goethe's important 'Wilhelm Meister's Apprenticeship' cycle (1795–96) which was extremely well known in Europe in the nineteenth century, partly via Thomas Carlyle's translation into English (1824). A brief summary of Mignon's role in Goethe's epic tale will be helpful here. Having initially become entranced with the child when he glimpses an attractive creature at an inn and is unable to 'declare it a boy or a girl', the book's central character, Wilhelm Meister, subsequently watches Mignon perform her strangely dislocated acrobatic act with a troupe of Italian rope-dancers.[15] After she has been mercilessly beaten by the leader of the company for refusing to perform her 'egg dance', Wilhelm pays for the child to be released from the troupe and takes her as his own servant. Mignon continues to adopt a male identity ('I am a boy, I don't want to be a girl'),[16] looking upon Wilhelm as her father, and only adopts women's clothes after she has witnessed a sexual encounter between Wilhelm and an actress, which is a prelude to her tragic death, brought on by uncontrollable sexual jealousy. Throughout their relationship, Wilhelm is continually moved to pity by the child, sensing that there is something mysteriously injured or lacking about her: 'He longed to take this forlorn being to his heart in place of a child, to feel her in his arms and with a father's love to arouse in her an enjoyment of life.'[17] In his own copy of Goethe's novel, Cornell apparently underlined a passage in which Goethe described a meeting with a painter who produced scenes depicting Mignon's life: 'And thus you might see the Boy-girl, set forth in various attitudes and manifold expression.'[18] Keller argues that it is the gender confusion thrown up by Mignon that Cornell was especially drawn to. Hence, according to Keller, in a late collage by Cornell of 1960, which is actually titled 'Mignon', 'her childhood is combined with an urchinlike appearance. She is very much a boy-girl.'[19] The boyish girl can further be shown to be a recurring motif in many other works by Cornell: just one example is the text-piece produced by Cornell for the American journal *View* as a homage to one of the many Hollywood actresses he idolized, Hedy Lamarr, titled 'Enchanted Wanderer: Excerpt from a Journey Album for Hedy Lamarr', which incorporated a collage of the ethereal-looking actress transformed into a Renaissance boy. Keller goes on to suggest that the psychoanalytic logic of all this might accord with the conclusions reached by Otto Fenichel, one of Freud's followers, who also made explicit use of the Mignon story, alongside other motifs in fairy tales, to develop the idea that the female child, in certain kinds of transgender male fantasy, is unconsciously equated with the penis (the 'little one', as in the name Mignon):

> In feminine men who during childhood or puberty liked to fantasise themselves as girls, the same mechanism is present as in heterosexuals. They fell in love with little girls in whom they see themselves embodied, and to whom they give what their mothers denied them. Very probably this mechanism is also the decisive one in pedophilia. Always such fantasies are combined with the idea of mutual protection: the little woman is rescued by the great man, in actuality, the latter by the former in magical fashion. These women represent not only the man himself who loves them but, in particular, his penis. In the way in which the charm of such figures is generally described one invariably finds a suggestion of their phallic natures. They are *phallus girls*.[20]

Whatever one may feel about the accuracy of Keller's analysis in relation to the specific details of Cornell's work, it is fascinating that, in one of the richest recent cultural analyses of representations of childhood in the nineteenth century in which the child is shown to embody the very notion of 'interiority' for the modern age – Carolyn Steedman's *Strange Dislocations* of 1994 – the figure of Mignon is once again identified as an archetypal embodiment of adult fantasies about children. Having painstakingly examined the development of the nineteenth-century obsession with Mignon as it was carried over into the attitudes of audiences to various performing children – mainly child-acrobats, child-actors and children in melodrama – Steedman concludes that audiences in the nineteenth century identified with the pitiful figure of Mignon since the child represented 'an aspect of the self, and all that the self had experienced and endured. Among all the other things members of that audience wanted, looking at the child, was their self.'[21] Significantly, she too chooses to enlist the help of Otto Fenichel and his psychoanalytic reading of Mignon and Mignon-figures to further elucidate the narcissistic identifications of (male) audiences with the child performers they gloated over,

> Otto Fenichel concluded that the desire of adult men was precisely this desire, for they saw themselves embodied in the child. They sought to rescue, save, *have* that child, he thought, so they might give to her 'what their mothers had denied them', specifically a baby, in more general terms what they had lost, what all of us have lost, which is the baby or child one formerly was.[22]

Whether one chooses to pinpoint the paedophilic valence of this analysis (deriving as it does from Fenichel) or chooses to simply underline the narcissistic process by which the attention to the image of the child answers to an internal sense of loss (which might loosely be allied with the notion of *nostalgia*),[23] the advantage of using the Mignon trope is that it provides an analytic tool for understanding surrealist representations of children which moves us beyond the polarized categories of idealized/sexualized child, as discussed earlier. This tool seems especially helpful in the case of Cornell, where the degree of repressed sexuality positively begs for some mode of elucidation. It makes sense here, however, to return briefly to Bellmer. Images in which the bodies of young girls double as phalluses often crop up in his work, especially in certain late 'Untitled (Phallus Girl)' drawings of the 1960s in which the young women are transformed into vaginas being penetrated by enormous penises.[24] Similarly in certain photographs of his 'Doll' assemblages of 1932–34 and 1935 the articulated parts of the mannequin are swivelled round to suggest the transformation of the entire body into a phallic formation. The paedophilic associations of the latter images are underlined by the succinct explanatory text supplied by the surrealists when certain of these images were reproduced in their magazine, *Minotaure*, in 1934: 'Doll. Hans Bellmer, variations on the assembling of an articulated female minor.'[25] In the past, commentators on

Bellmer have scoured Freud and been quick to talk of the notion of the 'phallic mother' in relation to this kind of imagery. It might have made more sense to look to Fenichel and to the pathetic, dislocated-looking body of Mignon.

It is the work of Cornell, with its poignant overlaying of a celebration of childhood 'innocence' and an attitude of adult 'longing' towards the childish state, that I wish to concentrate on closely, and I want now to focus attention on a small group of films that deal precisely with the conjunction of childhood, acrobatics and entertainment, that figured so prominently in the Mignon story. Marjorie Keller has herself noted the direct parallels with Mignon in the trilogy of so-called 'Collage films', dealing with children which Cornell produced, in collaboration with the filmmaker Larry Jordan, at some point between the 1940s and 1960s: *The Children's Party*, *The Midnight Party* and *Cotillion*.[26] These include fairly obvious motifs such as the girl-boy and the child-acrobat. My purpose, therefore, will not be to simply look for allusions (whether direct or unconscious) to Goethe, but to consider more broadly how we should assess the balance between a celebration of the iconography of childhood and an incipient sexualization of the child in these films, in the broader context of an assessment of the surrealist child.

Cornell's small group of experimental films, in which he spliced together examples from the hoard of old movies and motion-picture stills that he picked up on his curio-hunting trips to Manhattan from Queens, have for a long time been seen as important in terms of 'avant-garde' film history, not least because they were massively influential for a subsequent generation of American experimental filmmakers, such as Bruce Conner, Ken Jacobs, Jack Smith and Stan Brakhage. The most celebrated example is *Rose Hobart* (c.1936), which is largely a re-edited version of a Universal Pictures movie from 1931 *East of Borneo*, but the trilogy of collage films dealing with childhood is especially rich in technical experimentation, with the principles of collage and montage being explored particularly inventively.[27] Interestingly, the three films in question, *The Children's Party*, *Cotillion* and *The Midnight Party* share a great deal of the same found footage, with Cornell combining the images differently, and adjusting the speed of the film and style of editing, as well as introducing new imagery, to produce different emphases. In *The Children's Party* Cornell confronts the viewer with a series of what look like sections of amateur film recording entertainment or vaudeville acts (circus acrobats, trapeze artists, high-wire act, Indian knife-thrower and a performing seal). This is intercut with sections of home-movie material showing children at a party, grouped around a table, apple-dunking (suggesting a Halloween party) or, in the case of a number of shots of very young children, simply staring into the camera and nodding off to sleep. There is also a third category of material in the film that seems to derive from educational films and scientific documentaries: for instance, a didactic section on astrological formations and a haunting fragment from a microscopic film of an amoeba.

The effect of all this is disorientating on first viewing, with the juxtapositions of differing grades and conditions of film and types of imagery appearing quite random, but repeated viewings make it possible to discern a carefully orchestrated narrative logic by which the film falls into two main areas: the 'world' of the children and the 'world' of the entertainers. The entertainer's world, although ostensibly created for the benefit of the children, is presented quite independently, as though containing its own logic. The children become witnesses to this inscrutable, seemingly autonomous, other world, but they never interact with it. They are often presented frontally in 'freeze-frame' images. Sometimes we are presented with the footage from an action sequence of a circus or vaudeville performance followed by a stop-frame image of a child, smiling or grimacing, as though registering the effect of what he or she has 'seen'. (There is an interesting parallel here with a later short film by the Latvian/Israeli filmmaker Herz Franz, *Ten Minutes Older* of 1978, in which the film concentrates solely on the faces of children as they react to a theatrical performance, although the faces of Franz's subjects are mobile whilst Cornell's are poignantly frozen). The film constantly switches between the voyeuristic viewpoint of the camera entering into the sphere of the child/children and the sphere that they are supposedly observing. The latter is not necessarily comforting; there is a sequence in which a 'Red Indian' hurls a set of knives at a wrapped-up woman, skilfully outlining her body with the constellation formed by his daggers, before she emerges, grinning, from her wrappings. The image is made particularly uncanny by the film's absence of sound; there is no reassuring response from the audience to provide us with a cue on how to respond (none of Cornell's collage films has a soundtrack). Frequently, the images of adult performers have a sexual edge. The film is unified, at an almost subliminal level, by a series of sequences which deal with a voyeuristic exploration of the female. In the first of these a woman is seated on a chair held high by a strongman in his mouth. He is forced, in effect, to look up the woman's skirts to do this. A little further on, there is a fragment of film in which a female tightrope walker in a white tutu springs up and down on her rope: the film slows down, and, in close-up, her skirt flies up, revealing her pants. In another sequence, a female trapeze artist in a circus, viewed from below, swings dramatically towards us, displaying her legs. Further on, we see a Busby Berkeley-style line of dancers, kicking their bare legs up in the air.

It might be inferred from this that, although *The Children's Party* apparently deals with images redolent of 'childish innocence' (parties and circuses), it in fact deals, at a deeper structural level, with the theme of children in thrall to the behaviour of adults and, more particularly, to the spectre of sexuality. This is underlined at the end of the film. The penultimate sequence is a lengthy one in which two young girls, dressed as ballerinas, kick up their legs in unison, as though mimicking the earlier sequence of high-kicking adult dancers. There is little doubt that sexuality is creeping up on them, and that they now have become the 'performers'. The final sequence seems to confirm this: in a setting worthy of Méliès, against a 'fairy-tale' backdrop, a naked girl of around ten or eleven years of age, with long flowing hair, poses coyly on horseback. Sitney has discerned a complex allusion to Lady

Godiva here, but it is hard to overlook the uncomfortable, vaguely paedophilic associations of the image.[28] Jody Hauptman, for instance, notes that:

> Echoing the original Lady Godiva, the child has hair so long it covers her naked body... This tiny girl, like the Alice in Lewis Carroll's photographs, has not reached sexual maturity, yet she displays a marked degree of sexuality... Exacerbating the viewer's discomfort is the child's acknowledgement of her own eroticism; looking coyly at us, *she collaborates in the spectacularization of her youthful sexuality.*[29]

In conclusion, it might well be argued that Cornell himself identifies with the children presented in *The Children's Party* and relives, to some degree, his own bafflement in the face of the sexual (a bafflement he seems not to have surmounted as an adult, given his confined lifestyle). The film might thus be seen as a covert exploration of his own sexuality, but the extent to which this becomes inter-fused with his young subjects is distinctly discomforting.

If we now turn to *Cotillion* and look at the way similar technical juxtapositions of freeze-frame and 'action' sequences, along with a sizeable proportion of the same filmic material, are handled, it is noticeable that the effect is more assertively 'abstract' and less concerned with narrative. Here the stop-frame images of the children last for longer and seem to embalm or memorialize the children, suggesting the nature of (still) photography as 'that which has been'.[30] This deathly connotation is especially marked in a sequence where the camera is trained on the face of a sneezing baby. Suddenly the sneezing fit is halted in a freeze-frame image as if the baby's breath has itself been halted. It becomes evident, then, that *Cotillion* is more concerned with mortality, and with reflecting nostalgically on the nature of the fragments of old film that it assembles, than *The Children's Party*. Reworking the same material, Cornell actively de-emphasizes the sexual in favour of the nostalgic.

This, of course, chimes in with much that has been said so far about Cornell's repression of his own sexuality and about a historical moment, in which pre- and post-Freudian views of childhood are simultaneously in play, that helps situate surrealist attitudes to childhood. Arguably, Cornell's collage films of the 1940s sit more directly in a surrealist lineage than his better-known boxes. In the case of the film from the trilogy I have left out of this analysis, *The Midnight Party*, there is a distinctly dreamlike, or nightmarish, quality to it, suggesting that Cornell was dealing more straightforwardly here with the surrealist obsession with the oneiric. But in the case of *The Children's Party* the surrealist inflection arises from the film's 'anthropological' recording of the vagaries of popular culture (more specifically the iconography of children's play and entertainment), an attitude that was directly at the centre of surrealist concerns in the 1930s.

A key strategy of both the 'official' surrealist journal *Minotaure* (1933–39) and the organ of the 'dissident surrealists' headed by Georges Bataille, *Documents*

(1929–30) had been to view the products of Western popular culture (mass entertainment imagery, magazines, advertising, postcards, children's toys and games) as if viewing 'tribal' or 'primitive' artefacts and to thereby reveal the fetishistic and 'magical' latencies underpinning the spell they exerted.[31] In the trilogy of 'collage films' by Cornell there is one oft-repeated frame which seems to emblematize an analogous concern. Emphasized as a freeze-frame, but also run as part of an action sequence, it is the close-up image of a boy with a peculiar-looking party hat, who, after the 'apple-dunking' ceremony indulged in by the children, lifts his face up to the spectator, with his mouth abnormally stretched to accommodate an enormous apple.

This might well be an allusion (whether conscious or unconscious) to the images of tribespeople with masks and facial adornments from the pages of either *Documents* or *Minotaure*, both of which Cornell would have been familiar with.[32] In his first surrealist film *Rose Hobart* (1936), Cornell had already flirted with 'primitivist' imagery, juxtaposing re-edited shots of the star of *East of Borneo* with ones of the natives and landscape of the Indonesian principality of Maradu, the fictional setting for the film. It is interesting to note that, at that time, Cornell's taste for the 'exotic' could arguably be seen as out of kilter with the mood of surrealism, in its official Parisian form. After their principled opposition to the Colonial Exposition in Paris in 1931, which featured their involvement in an anti-colonial exhibition, 'The Truth about the Colonies', the Paris surrealists had become increasingly wary of appearing to uphold colonialist stereotypes.[33] But the allusions to anthropological imagery in *The Children's Party* in fact suggest that, by the 1940s, Cornell had himself become more self-conscious in deploying such conventions. It seems that part of the purpose of these films was to present a kind of quasi-scientific cultural anthropology of childhood, with phenomena such as performing seals or apple-dunking soberly documented as examples of Western ritual behaviour. In this sense, of course, the child is implicitly positioned as 'other', on a par with the 'primitive', but this move is not made without a degree of irony. What makes Cornell's practice especially poignant, however, is the personal investment, akin to mourning, involved in this act of documentation. In a letter written, but not sent, to one of the many female stars Cornell admired from afar, Eva Marie Saint, Cornell wrote 'I am particularly prone to Christmas, from childhood, in the context of New York, snow, magical store windows, (Christmas) Eve, etc, no matter how thin the personal mystique gets hammered out by the world condition.'[34] Cornell's attempt at memorializing this fast-disappearing world is similar to the impulse shown by Bellmer in creating his 'Personal Museum' (box of childhood toys), discussed earlier as a precursor to Cornell's boxes. What the anthropological/nostalgic ambience of Cornell's collage films serves to occlude, however, is the atmosphere of sexuality, verging on the paedophilic, which was present at a submerged level in works such as *The Children's Party*. Cornell's identification with his child subjects, delighted and appalled as they are by the allure of their entertainers, is arguably just as 'unhealthy' as he deemed surrealism to be.

In 1990 the artist Susan Hiller presented an installation in London titled 'An Entertainment', making use of four synchronized video programmes consisting of edited footage of 'Punch and Judy' shows filmed by her at various seaside locations throughout Britain during the 1980s. The critic Guy Brett evoked the effect on spectators of the piece as entering a large darkened space, where they were bombarded with fragments of images, flashed onto the walls, of Punch beating his child, along with imagery such as skeletons, the hanging of Mr Punch, and so on: 'A flash of red clothing, a noose jerked awkwardly up the wall. A pale flat skull, the relentless violence of the beatings which become almost like an abstraction of pain: all these images enter the bright arena and disappear into the darkness again.'[35]

Hiller's work provides a very apt coda to this essay's discussion of the surrealist attitude to the child. The artist is frequently characterized as part of the surrealist lineage, and she herself has made no bones about her debt to the movement, although she has also, understandably, emphasized her distance, as a contemporary artist, from it.[36] It is clear that 'An Entertainment' has certain very clear affinities with Cornell in the way he has been discussed here: it is a 'collage' of kinds; there is a very pronounced anthropological aura to it; it deals with the theme of children's entertainment put on by adults; it reveals the same fondness for the iconography of childish toys and rituals. Whether or not Hiller has seen Cornell's trilogy of 'collage-films' about childhood seems unimportant: her work undoubtedly speaks from within the same cultural idiom.

There are, however, numerous crucial differences. Apart from massive technical and aesthetic divergences (the shift that is effected between film and video being fundamental) the most obvious difference concerns the sheer level of disturbance and violence in Hiller's work, compared with the 'lightness' of Cornell's. As I have argued elsewhere, the spectator of 'An Entertainment' is not merely shown images of Punch and Judy, but is effectively placed, via the staging of the installation, in the position of a child who has to make sense of these ritualistic, hallucinatory images as they flash before his or her consciousness. It as though Hiller has compelled us to adopt the point of view of the children in Cornell's films as they take in acts of knife throwing, sexual provocation and so on, and ratcheted up the effects another 50 or so per cent.

I have argued elsewhere that one of the best ways of contextualizing 'An Entertainment' is in terms of the near-hysteria surrounding the issue of child abuse that was at its height in Britain at the time it was made. (The allegations of Satanic ritual abuse in the Orkney Islands in the late 1980s are one of several examples.[37]) Hiller herself has certainly hinted that abuse, although not necessarily sexual abuse, was one of her concerns. She has said: 'The baby-battering, wife-beating, homicidal violence of the central character too reflects the actual conditions of patriarchy'[38] and, on another occasion: 'I was subjecting myself to what I saw children being subjected to in every Punch and Judy show... the child is being taught something through the terror of ritual.'[39] In British society at large child abuse was, of course, something of a 'discovery' of this period. Carolyn Steedman notes that, writing in 1992, in a review of a classic work by Otto Rank on incest, the journalist Liam Hudson pointed out that it was 'scarcely five years since incest erupted in our midst as a vehicle for journalists in search of copy, and for all those paediatricians, psychologists and social workers who know in their bones that parents do their children irreparable harm'.[40] It is tempting, then, looking back on the surrealist view of the child via the lens of Hiller's recent work, to see her as de-sublimating what had been at issue, deep beneath the surface, in the relatively gentle, poeticized universe of Cornell.

The surrealists of the classic epoch, who had claimed the 'rights' to the imaginative and visionary splendours of childhood long before children had any 'rights' of their own (they have, of course, increasingly been in possession of legal rights since the 1970s)[41] would no doubt have been appalled at the moral censoriousness implicit in Hiller's position. But the surrealist valorization of childhood, which had to reconcile the dawning of a Freudian understanding of sexuality with a conviction of the omnipotence of the child's imagination and desires, could hardly outlive its own paradoxes. One of the central themes of Cornell's 'collage films' was the way that supposedly 'innocent' children (polymorphously sexual as they would be in Freudian terms) mimic and perform more adult versions of sexuality. After all, fantasies, sexual or otherwise, are not just things children possess; they are also things which are thrust upon them, both literally and metaphorically, from an adult world.[42]

Notes

1 André Breton, 'Manifesto of surrealism', in *Breton: Manifestoes of Surrealism*, trans. Richard Seaver and Helen R. Lane (Ann Arbor, MI: University of Michigan Press, 1972), p. 40.
2 For the modernist cult of 'child art', see Jonathan Fineberg, *Discovering Child Art: Essays on Childhood, Primitivism and Modernism*, rev. edn (Princeton, NJ: Princeton University Press, 2001).
3 For a discussion of the child in Romantic literature, see M.H. Abrams, *Natural Supernaturalism: Tradition and Revolution in Romantic Literature* (New York: Norton, 1973), pp. 379–83. See also George Boas, *The Cult of Childhood* (Dallas, TX: Spring Publications, 1990) (originally published by The Warburg Institute, London, 1966).
4 For a discussion of French attitudes to children in the early twentieth century, see Theodore Zeldin, *A History of French Passions. Vol I: Ambition, Love and Politics* (Oxford: Clarendon Press, 1993) (first published 1973), ch. 12, pp. 315–42.
5 For a recent definition of these processes, see Michael Richardson, *Otherness in Hollywood Cinema* (New York: Continuum, 2010), pp. 12–15.
6 Peter Webb and Robert Short, *Hans Bellmer* (New York: Quartet, 1985), p. 26. For a good reproduction of the 'Personal Museum', see also Therese Lichtenstein, *Behind Closed Doors: The Art of Hans Bellmer* (Berkeley, CA: University of California Press, 2001), p. 20.
7 Hans Bellmer, 'Memories of the doll theme', trans. Malcolm Green, in Bellmer, *The Doll* (London: Atlas Press, 2005), p. 37.
8 For examples of these drawings, see Webb and Short, *Hans Bellmer*, pp. 61–4.

9   Diane Waldman, *Joseph Cornell: Master of Dreams* (New York: Abrams, 2002), p. 74.
10 Joseph Cornell, letter dated 13 November 1936, Archives of the Museum of Modern Art, New York; as cited in Dawn Ades, 'The transcendental surrealism of Joseph Cornell', in Kynaston McShine (ed.), *Joseph Cornell* (New York: Museum of Modern Art, 1980), p. 19.
11 For Cornell's devotion to Christian Science, see Lindsay Blair, *Joseph Cornell's Vision of Spiritual Order* (London: Reaktion Books, 1998), pp. 75–7.
12 Mary Ann Caws: *Joseph Cornell's Theater of the Mind: Selected Diaries, Letters and Files* (New York: Thames & Hudson, 1993), p. 33.
13 Blair, *Joseph Cornell's Vision of Spiritual Order*, p. 126.
14 Marjorie Keller, 'Joseph Cornell: the symbolic equation', in *The Untutored Eye: Childhood in the Films of Cocteau, Cornell and Brakhage* (London and Toronto: Associated University Presses, 1986), pp. 98–178.
15 Johann Wolfgang von Goethe, *Wilhelm Meister*, Vol. I, trans. H.M. Waidson (London: Calder, 1977), pp. 83–93.
16 Ibid., Vol. II, p. 10.
17 Ibid., Vol. I, pp. 102–3.
18 Goethe, *Wilhelm Meister's Apprenticeship and Travels*, trans. Thomas Carlyle (London: Chapman and Hall, 1824); quoted in Keller, 'Joseph Cornell: the symbolic equation', p. 103.
19 Keller, 'Joseph Cornell: the symbolic equation'; Cornell's 'Mignon' collage is also reproduced in ibid., p. 102.
20 Otto Fenichel, 'The symbolic equation: girl=phallus', in *Collected Essays*, Vol. II (New York: Norton, 1954), pp. 10–11.
21 Carolyn Steedman, *Strange Dislocations: Childhood and the Idea of Human Interiority 1780–1930* (Cambridge, MA: Harvard University Press, 1994), p. 169.
22 Ibid. Steedman also cites Fenichel in footnote 23, p. 221.
23 Nostalgia is often viewed pejoratively as a fundamentally unproductive, self-indulgent state of mind. However, in surrealist studies it demands greater theoretical attention. Walter Benjamin asserted the importance of the 'outmoded' in surrealism in his seminal essay, 'Surrealism: the last snapshot of the European intelligentsia' (1929), in Peter Demetz (ed.), *Walter Benjamin: Reflections: Essays: Aphorisms: Autobiographical Writings* (New York: Harcourt, 1978), and there are overlaps between a valorization of the 'outmoded' and an attitude of nostalgia within surrealism which await proper elucidation. For recent attention to the notion of nostalgia, see Svetlama Boym, *The Future of Nostalgia* (New York: Basic Books, 2001).
24 See, for example, catalogue nos 212 and 213 in Michael Semff and Anthony Spira (eds), *Hans Bellmer* (Munich and London: Hatje Cantz, 2006), p. 216.
25 *Minotaure (Paris)*, no. 6 (1935), pp. 30–1.
26 For Keller's full analysis see 'Joseph Cornell: the symbolic equation', pp. 139–78. For an account of the making of the films, and Jordan's role in the process, see P. Adams Sitney, 'The cinematic gaze of Joseph Cornell', in McShine (ed.), *Joseph Cornell*, pp. 77–8.
27 For Cornell's position in relation to 'avant-garde' traditions, see P. Adams Sitney, *Visionary Film: The American Avant-Garde 1943–2000*, 3rd edn (Oxford: Oxford University Press, 2002), 315–45. For an overview of Cornell's own production, see ibid., pp. 69–89.
28 See ibid., 81. Unfortunately Adams Sitney's account of the 'collage film' trilogy is seriously confused by the fact that he appears to be referring to *The Children's Party* when discussing *The Midnight Party* and vice versa.

29 Jodi Hauptman, *Joseph Cornell: Stargazing in the Cinema* (New Haven, CT: Yale University Press, 1999), pp. 192–3 (emphasis added).
30 Jodi Hauptman also adopts this kind of Barthesian position on *Cotillion* in ibid., pp. 127–9.
31 For introductory essays on *Minotaure* and *Documents*, see Dawn Ades, *Dada and Surrealism Reviewed* (London: Hayward Gallery/Arts Council of Britain, 1978), pp. 278–39, 228–49. See also Musée d'Art et d'Histoire, Geneva, *Focus on 'Minotaure': The Animal-Headed Review* (Geneva: Skira, 1988), and Dawn Ades and Simon Baker (eds), *Undercover Surrealism: Georges Bataille and 'Documents'* (London and Cambridge, MA: Hayward Gallery Publishing and MIT Press, 2006).
32 Cornell might, for instance, have seen the photographs of tribal head adornments and masks in Dr Ralph von Koenigswald's 'Têtes et Crânes', *Documents*, no. 6 (1930), pp. 353–8. He would also have been aware of *Minotaure*, no. 2 (1933), an issue devoted to the 'Mission Dakar-Djibouti 1931–1933'.
33 For a detailed discussion of the 'Truth About the Colonies' exhibition and subsequent shifts in surrealist aesthetics see Adam Jolles, *The Curatorial Avant-Garde: Surrealism and Exhibition Practice in France, 1925–1941* (University Park, PA: Pennsylvania State University Press, 2013), pp. 93–173.
34 Cornell Papers, Archives of American Art, 1055: 126, undated letter draft to Eva Marie Saint, *c*.1960, cited in McShine (ed.), *Joseph Cornell*, p. 93.
35 Guy Brett, 'Susan Hiller's Shadowland', *Art in America*, April 1991, p. 142.
36 For Hiller on surrealism, see Alexandra Kokoli (ed.), *Susan Hiller: The Provisional Texture of Reality. Selected Talks and Texts, 1977–2007*, pp. 213–30.
37 See David Hopkins, *Childish Things* (Edinburgh: Fruitmarket Gallery, 2010), pp. 69–76.
38 Susan Hiller, as cited in Brett, 'Susan Hiller's Shadowland', p. 143.
39 Susan Hiller, interview with Stuart Morgan, in *Susan Hiller* (London: Tate Publishing, 1996), p. 44.
40 Liam Hudson, *The Times Literary Supplement*, 24 July 1992, pp. 7–8; cited in Steedman, *Strange Dislocations*, p. 165
41 The publication of the 'Convention on the Rights of the Child' by the United Nations in 1989 was indicative of an increased sense of the importance of children's rights in the late twentieth century. (Formal declarations of children's rights had been made, however, in 1924 by the League of Nations and in 1959 by the United Nations General Assembly.)
42 My thanks to Karen Lury for her helpful comments on this essay. Slightly modified sections of it (dealing with Cornell/Mignon and Bellmer/toys) also appear in my essay 'Re-enchantment: surrealist discourses of childhood, hermeticism and the outmoded', in David Hopkins (ed.), *A Companion to Dada and Surrealism* (Chichester: Wiley-Blackwell, 2016). The argument of this current essay is, however, substantially different.

11 MIND HOW YOU GO: CHILDREN AND THE PUBLIC INFORMATION FILM

Andrew Burke

Looking back, the 1970s now seem like a golden age for the public information film in the UK, particularly for those aimed at children. The structuring irony of many of the most memorable public information films from this era intended for young viewers is that, in order to promote safety, they chose to depict peril. These public information films *target* children, not simply in the sense that it is a genre aimed at a young audience, but that they *take aim* at the very children they represent on screen. To be young in a public information film from the 1970s is to be put at risk, even sacrificed, for the greater good. From the dangers of crossing the road to the risks of shallow water to the hazards of the farmyard, public information films from this era see peril everywhere and depict a world that tests and targets the children they represent, often sacrificing them cinematically to promote public safety. The injunction to *Mind How You Go* (1973), to take the title of one of the most iconic public information films, is a simple instruction to its young viewers to take care crossing busy roads, but it also serves more generally as the key to understanding the genre itself. In the safety-related public information film, the world is a dangerous place, one filled with innumerable threats and hazards that attract the youthful, naive and unguarded. In cataloguing the sheer range of possible accidents and tragedies that might occur in the most ordinary of circumstances, public information films aimed at young viewers create a world in which children face injury or death at every turn. Within the space of these films, 'mind how you go' is as much a terrifying threat as it is a cautionary instruction or gentle warning.

In what follows I will to look at a number of public information films from the 1970s that transform the world of the child into a space of temptation and terror. My argument is that these films draw on the generic conventions of suspense and horror to do their work. This accounts not merely for the grisly images of maimed accident victims that are the stock-in-trade of public information films from this era, but more importantly for the ambient sense of menace and doom that characterizes them. Ultimately, I think that these films are more interesting for their tone than for their content. However shocking the images of blood and violence might have been, the atmosphere of these films is somehow even more disturbing and distressing and sticks more resiliently in the memory. I will return at the end of my analysis to the idea that it is precisely this sense of unease that makes these films subject to nostalgic remembrance, but for now I want to turn to a film that exemplifies the way in which the public information film sacrifices lives on screen in the hope of saving them in reality.

Tone and atmosphere generate a kind of eerie surplus to the basic lessons of farm safety that John Mackenzie's *Apaches* (1977) was ostensibly produced to convey. Commissioned by the Health and Safety Executive and made under the auspices of the Central Office of Information (COI), Mackenzie's short film presents a complete catalogue of child fatalities, as a group of kids succumb each in turn to farm-specific forms of grisly death. The conceit of the film is there in its title. The kids in Mackenzie's film play cowboys and Indians.[1] They are imagined as, and imagine themselves to be, the eponymous Apaches, a brave tribe of fierce warriors whose native terrain is the countryside around the farming village in which they live. Their identification as Apaches, however, assumes a more profound significance in light of the way in which death diminishes their ranks. The film imagines the children as a tribe not made for the modern world and doomed to extinction when faced with the danger presented by the technologies of modernity.

The film begins with the kids playing in the hills above the village, costumed as Apaches and planning their attack on the town below. The title and credits appear in a typeface that immediately identifies the film as drawing on the history of the western. It is projected against a shot of a big sky with drums echoing softly on the soundtrack, and the children are silhouetted as they run along the crest of the hill. The film is narrated by one of the children, Danny, who is the chief of this adolescent tribe. He introduces his fellow warriors in voice-over and explains that they are at war because they are 'tired of the broken promises of the great white father'. Two things are interesting about this scene. First, it establishes the force of the children's imagination. They imagine the damp green of the English countryside to be the desert landscapes of Arizona or New Mexico, the traditional terrain of the classic western. This act of adolescent imagination proves fatal as their fantasies will prevent them from perceiving the clear dangers of the farm. Nevertheless, much of the power of *Apaches* comes in the way that it represents a child-centred rural geography. The spaces of the countryside are transformed through the imaginative play of its young characters and part of what makes the film feel so uncanny for adult viewers is the simultaneous familiarity with and inaccessibility of this experience of landscape. As Owain Jones argues, there is an otherness to childhood and the child-specific experience of space that renders it uncanny:

> Yet children are always, in some respects, on their own, in other places, and *need* other places and other spaces (as in other spaces of solitude, solo play,

dens and such like (Ward 1990). Riddell (2006, p. 31) talks of 'the tribal cruelty, companionship, and wonderment that makes children's lives as *separate and as magical* as they have always been' (my emphasis). In other words, distances and intimacies are simultaneously present within child–adult relations. It is the affective geographies of their distant, other world which I feel are vital to what children's lives are. They are thus vital to children's geographies yet also very difficult to address.[2]

In drawing on the conventions of the western, *Apaches* finds generic form for the affective geography of these rural children, who are represented as being embedded in a world that is open to play but filled with hazard. Moreover, the western's conventional sense of melancholic loss about the disappearance of the tribe connects, for adult viewers at least, with the impossibility of fully experiencing again the child's imaginative engagement with landscape. I will return to this idea in my conclusion, but for now I want to establish that *Apaches* is about loss: not simply the accidental deaths of the children, but also the melancholic attachment we retain to the childhood experience of place once we become adults. Second, the scene suggests that the children have been betrayed by a society that has colonized the landscape of their childhood play. There is some suggestion of negligence, with the parents failing to protect the innocents from the dangers of the adult world, the hazards of the farm as a modern, industrialized space. To draw on Jones once more, the film, in order to represent the hazards of the modern countryside, retains an idea of the rural idyll.[3] The sense that these accidental deaths are deeply tragic rests upon the idea that the countryside is the natural home of childhood and with the industrialization of agriculture also comes the loss of innocence of rural childhoods. Children in this romanticized, elegiac scenario become the doomed Apaches of the western as they succumb to the dangers of this transformed space.

There are, of course, profound ideological consequences to the way in which the film grafts the preventability of accidental adolescent death onto the ideological morass of the western. The film combines the elegiac and the fatalistic in the figure of the child pretending to be an 'Indian'. The children are doomed from the start as they assume the role of a tribe under siege, their accidental deaths rehearsing the final historical stages of the genocide of westward expansion in America. As such, the film inherits the conventional ideological problems of the traditional liberal western in its representation of the children as the innocent, yet inevitable, victims of progress and industrial expansion.[4] The children are represented as noble savages who must be protected from their own naivety and ignorance about the modern world and its dangers. Just as the conventional western demands the death, assimilation, and/or subordination of the Native Americans that appear on screen as the opponent of the white protagonists, so too does this particular subgenre of the public information film demand either the death of its young characters or their submission and subordination to a paranoid, if grown-up and mature, logic that sees danger everywhere and in everything.

While the generic coordinates of the western provide *Apaches* with its basic allegorical frame, its tone derives from the way in which it combines elegy and anxiety. As soon as it establishes the identity of the kids as Indians, as a doomed tribe, the film becomes an exercise in finding increasingly inventive ways to dispense of its young cast. In so doing, it brings together the realistic and the horrific. The set-up of each death involves both explaining the game the children are playing and showing the hazards of the farm as a space of work. The first child dies whilst the children are engaged in a game of wagon train. The warriors ambush a farm tractor that stands in imaginatively for the vehicle of colonial expansion. When Kim, the younger of the two girls who are part of the group, manages to jump on the trailer being pulled by the tractor, she shoots the young man driving with her toy gun. He playfully shoots back, thumb cocked with his index finger as the trigger, but when the tractor hits a rut in the muddy farmyard it throws the young girl forward and beneath the wheels of the moving vehicle. The film cuts to an image of blood splattered on the toy gun which, cracked and broken by the weight of the trailer and its load of hay, stands in for the crushed body of the child itself. The soundtrack goes eerily silent as the kids look on at the corpse that remains unseen by the viewers. Then, to underscore the gravity of the consequences of this dangerous play, the scene shifts in time and space to the children's school and we see the headmaster remove the nametag from Kim's hanger outside her homeroom. Even though the child's death is telegraphed and anticipated by a whole set of generic markers and clues that commonly structure safety films, the sequence is shocking not least because of the speed with which the fatal accident occurs and its consequences are registered.

The other children each die in turn, their deaths linked to a game gone awry. Some of these games extend the imaginative world of the western, but these are complemented by other forms of play, either drawn from the classical repertoire of childhood games or from popular culture. Tom falls into a slurry pit and drowns trying to escape capture during a game of kick-the-can; Sharon suffers immensely after inadvertently drinking some poison in a mock ceremony to the gods after a game of ambush the fort; Robert dies when a gate falls on him while playing *Starsky and Hutch*.[5] In each instance, the film toys with expectation, setting up potential accidents only for the child to step out of the way or avoid the danger in the very last second. Nevertheless, and rather perversely, the film demands each child's death and ruthlessly exploits the sense of dread as close scrapes give way to fatal incidents. As such, *Apaches* at times feels something like a slasher film in the brutality of its inexorable, deadly logic. Carol J. Clover provides a definition of the slasher film that resonates strongly with the narrative arc of *Apaches*: 'At the bottom of the horror heap lies the slasher (or splatter or shocker or stalker) film: the immensely generative story of a psychokiller who slashes to death a string of mostly female victims, one by one, until he is subdued or killed, usually by the one girl who has survived.'[6] The children in *Apaches* are targeted by circumstance rather than by a psychokiller, yet the film reproduces the basic narrative form of the slasher film, not least in how its children are picked off one by one until the last has learned the lesson of safe play.[7] The key here is the way that *Apaches* appeals to other generic and narrative forms in order to represent its young characters as victims. In this process of victimization, the film both indigenizes and feminizes the children. They become the doomed Apaches in a genre, the western, structured around their extermination and they become the feminized victims of an unseen and terrifying homicidal force akin to the psychokiller of the slasher film. As resolutely as the western or slasher film demands that its aboriginal or female characters must die, so too does the shock-based safety film require that its young cast be exterminated or eliminated.

In *Apaches*, the element of horror is also amplified by the look of the children. Almost uniformly blond, blue-eyed and androgynous, they are not unlike the flaxen-haired, glassy-eyed children in the *Village of the Damned* (1960). Even though they do not share the malevolent coldness of the children in the earlier film, they nevertheless retain some small portion of their weirdness, not least because once they start dying in sequence both nature and civilization seem against them. The relative absence of adults enhances this sense that the children are a force unto themselves, embroiled in a losing battle with a hostile universe that is eliminating them one by one. There is a basic instability here: on the one hand, the children in *Apaches* are innocents, sacrificially killed in order to help save their peers in the audience; but on the other hand, the fact that the children are so ruthlessly targeted combines with their slightly creepy homogeneity to make them seem like a malevolent force that must be eliminated. They are somehow innocent and sinister simultaneously and this, I would argue, is a result of the frantic generic mixing that both structures and defines Mackenzie's film. *Apaches* draws primarily on the western and the splatter film for its structure and narrative shape, but the look of its country children also connect it to forms of rural horror and to tales of the supernatural and the uncanny, which in England at least have long been associated with the isolated countryside and those ways of life disappearing in the face of modernization.[8]

With only two of its original six children remaining, the film adopts an even more sombre tone near its end as rain descends on the village and it is enveloped by an atmospheric gloom. The game that Danny and Michael play is strikingly morbid. In voice-over Danny explains, 'the Apaches have fought well against great odds. Our braves are few and the white man is many. We have no food. Winter is coming. Our people will starve. We have been robbed of our homeland, but we shall return. We shall survive. I, Geronimo, must gather together our scattered people and we shall survive.' Having commanded Michael to remain in the hills 'to protect the lodge of our fathers', Danny goes alone to the village below. There is a conspicuous contrast here with the opening sequence. The sun is setting, the wind gusts audibly on the soundtrack, and Danny is isolated in a bleak and unforgiving landscape. The tone is autumnal and there is an air of complete desperation. Danny, as Geronimo, announces that he is going to make peace with the 'white eyes' and to learn from them the art of survival in the modern world. In terms of the film's structuring conceit, this capitulation could be read as Danny's realization that he must adhere to the rules of safety, yet the film has him helped onto a tractor parked on a muddy hill by an adult who merely tells him to 'be careful'. When he inadvertently releases the brake, the tractor rolls down the hill, picking up speed until finally veering off the road, tumbling down a steep incline and killing Danny upon impact with the ground below. There is an inescapable perversity to Danny's death, since by this time he embodies all the melancholy of tribal surrender. Danny, as the chief, must die to satisfy multiple generic demands, both in terms of the film's allegorical allegiance to the western, its stylistic and tonal connection to the horror film, and its identity as a public information film for children that emphasizes safety through shock. At the film's end, only Michael survives. We see him at the graveside during Danny's funeral. He has lost his tribe, all his friends are dead, but he has also been, to extend the allegorical logic of the film itself, assimilated, uncomfortably dressed in a suit and tie at the Christian funeral of his tribal chief. The film does not linger on him, nor does it give him some kind of trite speech that would show that he has learned the lessons of safety as a result of this series of fatal accidents. The image of Michael is one of profound melancholy, of the last of the Mohicans, robbed of his land, his culture and his pride, but also of a child who has lost all his friends.

Throughout the film the accident scenes have been punctuated by short sequences that show a family preparing for a wake. It is only after the tractor accident and funeral that the film reveals that the wake is for Danny himself. He narrates the film from beyond the grave. This spectral narration adds yet another uncanny dimension to the film, but it is also weirdly flat in terms of emotion. The film as a whole is oddly affectless. Not only do the children not react when they see their friends die, they seem largely unaffected by these deaths generally. They continue to play and bear none of the psychological scars that should rightly come with the serial fatality of their closest friends. This criticism surely misses the point of the film and demands a level of psychological realism from a genre, the safety film, for which it is not the highest priority. Nevertheless, this lack of affect connects *Apaches* ever more strongly to the horror film, which likewise demands a kind of emotional and cognitive discontinuity on the part of its characters who in sequence must, against all logic, go back into the house or into the woods for the sake of the plot. The film might strive for a kind of quiet intensity in order to dramatize the seriousness of the accidental deaths, but the eerie silence only manages to lend the children an air of resigned fatalism and to assign the parents a deeply unsettling sense of indifference.

Apaches is perhaps in a class of its own with its distressing hybridization of the western and horror cinema, yet there are other safety films that approach it in terms of fatality and bloodiness. *The Finishing Line* (1977) and *Building Sites Bite* (1978) likewise rely on shock to convey their messages of safe play. There are also a number of driving safety public information films which rely on accident scenes for their impact, most notably *20 Times More Likely* (1979). But from here I want to turn to films that are less bloody but no less psychologically disturbing in the way that they mobilize fear and anxiety to promote safety and security. There is an enduring creepiness to *Lonely Water* (1973), a 90-second public information film primarily designed to air during breaks between children's television programming. Commissioned by the Royal Society for the Prevention of Accidents, the spot aimed to reduce drowning accidents that occurred as a result of play near rivers and ponds, or around water on construction sites or waste ground. The film is narrated in voice-over by 'The Spirit of the Dark and Lonely Water', a hooded figure of death who watches over, perhaps even compels, children to engage in the kind of reckless and heedless behaviour that results in drowning. Given voice by Donald Pleasance, the Spirit is not merely a malevolent figure, but a perverse one, taking pleasure in the deaths he both witnesses and also seemingly orchestrates.

As with *Apaches*, the creepiness here resides in the film's construction of a universe that targets children, that lures them to their deaths through the temptations the world offers. The film opens with a low-level tracking shot over a murky swamp, eventually settling on the hooded figure of the Spirit shrouded in mist. As the Spirit tells us, this kind of Hammer horror landscape may seem the ideal site for terror and death, but it is not actually where he is at his most potent. The scene shifts to a building site where four kids try to retrieve a football from a rain-filled hole. Cheered on by the other children, the brashest of the bunch inches his way down the muddy slope reaching for the football with a stick. It is no surprise when he slides down into the murky water and cannot escape. The chillingly eerie element here is the way in which the film switches to the drowning child's point-of-view and shows us the Spirit silently approaching in the background, unnoticed by the other children who simply do not know what to do to save their friend. A second child drowns when the branch he is hanging on to breaks as he reaches with his net to catch fish from a pond. The lesson here is that the greatest danger is not in the conventional landscapes of the horror film, but in the most banal of sites and spaces. The Spirit specifically targets three types of children, 'the unwary, the show-off, the fool', all of whom fail to recognize the hazards of the everyday. But the terror of the film derives from how it gives this childhood inattention and negligence spiritual form and constructs a world view in which children do not simply make errors of judgement or fail to prevent the preventable, but are tracked and targeted by a malevolent force that lays in wait for such moments. When the film settles on a 'No Swimming' sign alongside a river near an illegal tipping site, there is a kind of gleefulness in Pleasance's voice as he explains, 'Only a fool would ignore this, but there's one born every minute.' The targeted victim in this final scenario, however, is saved by 'sensible children' playing nearby, whose attentiveness to safety neutralizes the Spirit's power. Nevertheless, the Spirit is confident enough to announce, 'I'll be back', as his cape sinks into the murky water. The artificial echo of the Spirit's voice signifies his defeat but also, in a trope drawn from the horror film, heralds his eventual return.

Even more than recklessness, it is inattentiveness that is the primary cause of death in both *Apaches* and *Lonely Water*. The equation of safety and mindfulness is a common one in public information films of all sorts, but it takes on a certain urgency in those targeted at children. *Mind How You Go* is largely free from the blood and shock that characterize many of the safety films for children made in the 1970s, yet, despite its relative gentleness, there is still something revealing in the way it constructs the world as a place that preys on childhood inattentiveness and distraction. The film, commissioned by the Department of Education, begins on a suburban high street with Valerie Singleton, the host of the renowned BBC children's magazine programme *Blue Peter*, demonstrating the safe way to cross a busy road. She draws her lesson from the then recently published *Green Cross Code* (1970), which sought to simplify the basic procedures of pedestrian safety so that they could be remembered by even the youngest of children.

After this opening didactic sequence, which mimics the conventions and format of an on-location magazine-style report, the film shifts to the fictional story of a young boy, Graham, who must safely navigate his way to and from school. Graham's problem is that, as his father puts it, he is prone to 'mooning about'. His tale is, as the credits have it, 'told by' Singleton, the storybook phrasing suggesting that this public information film is geared towards a very young audience who might learn best from a simple story rather than a more complex or startling cautionary tale. Graham nearly steps out into traffic on his way to school, but escapes with only a warning from a lorry driver who has to slam on his brakes. Graham is admonished by the driver, who asks him, 'Why don't you look where you're going? They don't teach you nothing at school?' This is an oddly self-reflexive moment for a public information film in that it raises the very question of who is responsible for conveying this basic safety information to children, of versing them in the safety protocols of modern urban life, for which crossing the road stands metonymically.

As Michael Brooke explains, *Mind How You Go* was distributed free of charge 'to encourage schools, local education authorities and road safety officers' to show the film.[9] Combined with possible television broadcast on both public and private networks and screenings in cinemas before commercial films, there is a diffuse set of bodies, sites and contexts in and through which public information films target their young audience. Their reach and impact seems best explained in terms of governmentality, a concept Michel Foucault developed in part to explain the process by which individuals are subject to, and internalize, all kinds of rules and routines that regulate the self and enable productive self-governance.[10] Even though learning how not to be run over by a car is surely one of the less pernicious aspects of this process of social integration and compliance, it does illuminate the odd dynamic that generates the uncanny atmosphere of many of these films. One of the consequences of the state assuming this task of edification and protection is the projection of a world that is both dangerous and sinister.[11] This process is clear enough in *Apaches* and *Lonely Water*, where fate seems to take gleeful aim at vulnerable children, but even in the seemingly innocuous *Mind How You Go* Graham is subject to a world that requires his absolute vigilance.

Mind How You Go is not subtle in driving home the necessity of absolute alertness. Following Graham through his school day, the film show numerous times when he lets his attention lapse. Helpful and caring teachers gently admonish Graham but also repeatedly drive home the message that you must always look for both danger and opportunity. During a field trip to the zoo, one teacher tells Graham to look carefully at how a bird of prey is 'looking and listening all the time in case of danger. Because when he's not living in his cage, he's a wild animal and there is danger all around him.' Later, having given up the ball a little too easily during a football match, Graham is told by his Physical Education teacher, 'you must remember to look around you before you move'. The effect of these clearly telegraphed lessons is faintly comic in the way they foreshadow Graham's eventual revelation that they apply to everyday life as much as to the natural world or football pitch. Despite the comedic effect, which even the youngest of viewers might find somewhat corny and patronizing, there is a specific world being constructed here, one that is defined by the omnipresence of danger and the necessity of vigilance.

The film drives this point home even more strongly when it has Graham pass by the scene of an accident on his walk home. A young girl has been struck dead trying to cross the road and a tracking shot from Graham's point of view shows the ambulance attendants covering the body, although his perspective is partially blocked by the legs of those gathered around the scene. No blood is shown, yet it is all the more disturbing for the way in which Graham seems the intended recipient of the message. In a perverse way, this young girl died to save Graham, to drive home for him the lessons of the day. Sure enough, when later tempted to cross the road at a busy junction, Graham is overwhelmed and initially cannot bring himself to do it. The film presents a terrifying montage of cars and lorries streaming by, their force and immensity emphasized by the angled shots that replicate the perspective of a child. A few tilt shots also suggest a level of psychological disorientation and anxiety. Graham is frightened and presumably the children watching the film are meant to be as well. He retreats to the window ledge of a corner shop to calm himself and to think things through. It is at this point that the various lessons of the day return to him, indexed precisely to the tenets of the *Green Cross Code*. Spectral images of his teachers, his schoolmates and the birds of prey appear above his head and the accompanying aphorisms about being visible, looking and listening, and seeing the way is clear before you move resound in his head. The echo effect is somewhat reminiscent of *Lonely Water*, but more importantly it establishes that the rules that should govern his behaviour have been wholly internalized. In a rather benign way, it signals that lessons have been learned, but there is a slightly more sinister aspect to the echo since it suggests that this learning ideally becomes a voice inside our heads, guiding us from within rather than from without. The electronic processing of these voices, the special effect that partially dehumanizes them and amplifies their insistence and force, ensures its overlap with those kinds of sci-fi horror that address autonomy and fears of being controlled. The film itself has a happy ending as Graham successfully makes his way home and Valerie Singleton returns to stress the importance of the *Green Cross Code*. Nevertheless, there are several moments in the film that are more complex and distressing than they may initially seem.

While *Mind How You Go* focuses on the process by which a child internalizes the necessity for vigilance, the last two films I want to examine target adults. *Absent Parents* (1982) is a 40-second public information film about the dangers of leaving very young children unaccompanied around water. It begins with a group of children playing indoors on a climbing structure, but juxtaposes this with shots of a child outdoors walking along the very edge of a wooden bridge that crosses a shallow creek. In a clever bit of cross-cutting, the image of a girl falling off the play structure alternates with that of the girl falling into the creek. The message is clear: what might be a harmless fall inside might be deadly outside if it occurs near water. As Tony Dykes observes, this scenario is 'every parent's nightmare', and the short is reminiscent of the opening scene of *Don't Look Now* (Nicolas Roeg, 1973), in which an unsupervised young girl playing outside drowns whilst her parents are busy bickering inside.[12] The look of the film, with its crisp cinematography and bold colour palette, also invokes Roeg's film. The girl is not wearing a red rain jacket or boots, yet red is the dominant colour and the film exploits the almost spectral pastiness of the children in a manner that emphasizes their fragility but also visually links them to the kids in *Apaches*. The ghostliness of the children invokes their death despite its prevention and points to the way in which their parents would be punished and haunted by any lapse in attention, no matter how brief. The message of the film is about the need for constant surveillance, and this point is driven home by the weird over-enunciation that distinguishes the voice-over: 'Never let small children out of your sight if you know they can get anywhere near water, however shallow. Children love water, but water can kill.' Once again, the natural world is transformed into a malevolent force or entity that attracts and targets children, luring them to a death that seems calculated rather than accidental.

Sewing Machine (1973) preys on parental guilt as ruthlessly as *Absent Parents*. Directed by John Krish, whose post-war documentaries have recently been re-evaluated and rediscovered, this minute-long filler film is specifically about temporality.[13] An on-screen countdown timer begins at one minute and works its inexorable way to zero. The voice-over announces, 'this minute, the one you see being eaten up, is the last one of this little girl's life'. With the spectre of death hanging over the remainder of the film, Krish follows the child as she ignores her mother's command to stay on the pavement and away from traffic. The mother is just inside, at her sewing machine, but the child runs free. The problem, as the narrator explains, is that children are too easily distracted and this makes them supremely vulnerable: 'When this child crosses the road because she sees her best friend, what she will not see or hear is the car that will knock her down. The sudden excitement blots out everything else. All she can hear and see is inside her own head. It is that simple. It is that deadly.' The timer reaches zero as the impact occurs. This is heard but not seen. The film focuses instead on the mother's stunned reaction as she comes to realize that the crash she has heard involves her child. The film's force resides in the ruthless brutality of the clock. It is neither nature nor the machine that demands this child's death, but simply time itself, which has been determined in advance and reaches zero with a mechanical coldness.[14] Unlike in the later *Absent Parents*, where the mother is offered a reprieve by saving her daughter from the shallow creek and hugs her closely out of the fear of having nearly lost her, *Sewing Machine* lingers on the horrified and anguished face of the mother for several seconds after the counter reaches zero. These seconds are excruciating as they invite the viewer to identify not simply with the abjection of tragic loss but with the guilt that is its inevitable companion. But what binds *Sewing Machine* to the other public information films discussed here is its transformation of the ordinary into a space of peril for unwitting and inattentive children. The young girl in *Sewing Machine* seems especially joyous and carefree, which is what, quite cruelly and sadistically, makes her the ideal child protagonist for a safety-oriented public information film.

Although the production of public information films continued into the 1980s and 1990s and even continues into the present day, the 1970s seem a high-water mark for the genre. This assessment is probably influenced by the temporality of nostalgia itself: those targeted by these films are now in a position to write about them, buy compilation DVD packages, obsessively assemble YouTube playlists of obscure examples, or even make films that draw on the language and vocabulary and replicate the tone and feeling of films half-remembered from childhood viewing. As much as DVD technology has played a part in the compilation and redistribution of public information films, the internet, with its tendency to accumulation and aggregation fuelled by its ever-expanding bandwidth, seems central to the rediscovery of these films in recent years.[15] But this technological explanation is surely only part of the equation. The contemporary fascination with these films has something to do with feeling as well, not simply the affective force of hazy childhood memories but the sense of loss that these ageing films embody and trigger. Memory here is as likely to be prosthetic as actual, in that the sense of loss does not accrue only to those who lived during that time or experienced these films as contemporary warnings rather than historical artefacts.[16]

The broader power of public information films from the 1970s, I would argue, derives from their status as a remnant from a world that to a large degree has disappeared. This world was defined by a kind of 'technocratic utopianism' that understood state intervention into everyday life as both necessary and desirable,[17] an understanding which has steadily been eroded since the election of Margaret

Thatcher's Conservatives in 1979 and the rise of neoliberalism as a state ideology in the UK and elsewhere over the past thirty years. Writing about a cohort of musicians (The Focus Group, The Advisory Circle, Belbury Poly) who take the atmosphere of public information films from the 1960s and 70s as inspiration for their sample-based evocations of the recent past, Simon Reynolds argues that a shift has taken place, among some at least, in the way this period is remembered and represented:

> This lost era of planning and edification represented a paternalism (or perhaps maternalism, given its association with free milk for schoolkids or BBC children's fare like *Watch with Mother*) that rock'n'roll in some sense rebelled against by celebrating desire, pleasure, disruptive energy, individualism. But by the early 2000s, these bygone ideals of progress started to acquire the romance, pathos and honour of a lost future. The idea of a 'nanny state' didn't seem so suffocating and oppressively intrusive any more.[18]

Nevertheless, the work of these artists retains a sense of the weirdness and creepiness of many of the public information films upon which they draw. Indeed, the bureaucratic, even slightly robotized female voice that introduces The Advisory Circle's *Mind How You Go* EP aims to soothe but sounds eerily sinister when she delivers the mandate of this fictional governmental body: 'The Advisory Circle. Helping you make the right decisions.' This clarifies the way in which the original films resonate in the present. I would argue that they are not simply the trigger for a nostalgia that misses the safety and security of an innocent past but rather are compelling precisely because of the way in which they blend fear and forward-thinking, paranoia and a sense of progress. These films persist in memory, they haunt the present, not because they represent an idealized safe world, but because they imagine a world in which adventure, imagination and possibility go hand in hand with risk, danger and uncertainty. Given this understanding, it is scarcely surprising that many of the most affecting public information films are the ones that feature children. In them the sense of loss is doubled. Not only do they evoke the imperfect, lost era of welfare state interventionism, but also a kind of childhood, free-ranging and in need of instruction of how to play safely, that has largely disappeared in a contemporary world where restraints and restrictions on children's play have increased dramatically. As such, I would argue, to contemporary viewers of *Apaches*, the film presents not simply the lost world of the 1970s with all its technocratic ambitions and collective aspirations fully in view, but also a lost world of childhood in which play still trumped prevention. The sinister tone and sheer excess of *Apaches* as well as other public information films about safety that targeted children might have been the stuff of nightmares in its day, but oddly enough, in retrospect, anxiety becomes allure and nightmare turns nostalgic.

Notes

1. For more on the long history of 'playing Indian' and the political significance of such appropriations and identifications, see Rayna Green, 'The tribe called Wannabee: playing Indian in America and Europe', *Folklore*, vol. 99, no. 1 (1988), pp. 30–55; Philip J. Deloria, *Playing Indian* (New Haven, CT: Yale University Press, 1998).
2. Owain Jones, '"True geography [] quickly forgotten, giving away to an adult-imagined universe". Approaching the otherness of childhood', *Children's Geographies*, vol. 6, no. 2 (2008), pp. 200–1.
3. Owain Jones, 'Idylls and othernesses: childhood and rurality in film', in Robert Fish (ed.), *Cinematic Countrysides* (Manchester: Manchester University Press, 2008), pp. 189–90.
4. As Edward Buscombe explains, the idea of the 'Vanishing American' can be traced back as far as the eighteenth century, but perhaps finds its most powerful expression in the 'melancholic nostalgia' that characterizes Edward S. Curtis's photographs of Native Americans taken in the first decade of the twentieth century. Edward Buscombe, *'Injuns!' Native Americans in the Movies* (London: Reaktion, 2006), p. 70. The cinema draws on Curtis's sentimental fatalism in the development of the western and oscillates between assimilation and attrition in its representation of the fate of Native Americans on screen. Buscombe argues, 'the cinema offered two main routes towards extinction. In the one the Indian gracefully acknowledges that his time has come and consents to fade from the scene, agreeing to become progressively assimilated into white culture until the last traces of Indian identity have been effaced. In the other, the Indian, almost invariably a mounted warrior of the plains, defiantly fights against the white advance but is inevitably defeated' (ibid., pp. 80–1).
5. *Starsky and Hutch* (ABC, 1975–79) was a hugely popular American TV police series broadcast in the UK by the BBC from 1976.
6. Carol J. Clover, *Men, Women and Chainsaws: Gender in the Modern Horror Film* (Princeton, NJ: Princeton University Press, 1992), p. 21.
7. Clover tracks the emergence and development of the slasher film in the 1970s, paying special attention to the way in which the genre provides 'a clearer picture of current sexual attitudes' than more mainstream fare from the era 'not despite but exactly because of its crudity and compulsive repetitiveness' (ibid., p. 22). The production date of *Apaches* in 1977 places it in the midst of the first cycle of 70s slasher pictures, the most famous of which is *The Texas Chainsaw Massacre* (1974). Interestingly, Donald Pleasance appears in another key and later film from this era, *Halloween* (John Carpenter, 1978.)
8. Although he focuses primarily on American examples, David Bell usefully sketches out the basic generic variations of the subgenre, including its connection to the slasher film, in 'Anti-idyll: rural horror', in Paul Cloke and Jo Little (eds), *Contested Countryside Cultures: Otherness, Marginalisation and Rurality* (London: Routledge, 1997), pp. 94–108. But *Apaches* also fits with a strain of 1970s British cinema and television that sees the countryside as a haunted, dangerous and creepy place, including *The Owl Service* (ITV, 1969–70), *The Wicker Man* (Robin Hardy, 1973), *Penda's Fen* (BBC1, 1974) and *Children of the Stones* (ITV, 1977). Children frequently play a key role in these works, either as the adventurers who can see the continuing presence of the past or as representatives of that still living past who seem somewhat out of place in a modernized present. For more on children, the weird countryside

and its connections to horror, see Rob Young, 'The pattern under the plough', *Sight and Sound*, vol. 20, no. 8 (2010), pp. 16–22.
9   See Michael Brooke, 'Mind How You Go', *BFI Screen Online*, http://www.screenonline.org.uk/film/id/1402597/index.html (accessed 14 July 2021).
10 Foucault develops the concept of governmentality in a lecture delivered at the Collège de France in 1978, drawing primarily on examples from the sixteenth to eighteenth centuries. Governmentality, he argues, includes not simply questions of statecraft, but extends to questions of self-governance and, crucially, the 'government of children and the great problematic of pedagogy'. Michel Foucault, 'Governmentality', trans. Pasquale Pasquino, in Graham Burchell, Colin Gordon and Peter Miller (eds), *The Foucault Effect: Studies in Governmentality* (Chicago, IL: University of Chicago Press, 1991), p. 87.
11 For a study that draws on Foucault's concept of governmentality in order to analyse state-subsidized documentary filmmaking, see Zoë Druick, *Projecting Canada: Government Policy and Documentary Film at the National Film Board* (Montréal and Kingston: McGill-Queen's University Press, 2007). Druick develops the category of 'government realism' to describe films produced by the National Film Board of Canada in the period after the Second World War (ibid., p. 23). Even though the films I analyse here depart from orthodox realism, they nevertheless continue the process in which state-subsidized films communicate and transmit ideas about self-governance and safe conduct. Indeed, there is a way in which the subcategory of UK public information films from the 1970s I am analysing here constitutes a kind of 'government horror' in the way they mix safety and shock.
12 See comments from Tony Dykes in his essay in the accompanying booklet for the BFI DVD release of *The Best of COI: Five Decades of Public Information Films* (the most recent version, including Dykes original essay, is April 2020).
13 In an interview with Kier-La Janisse, John Krish speaks at length about his work on public information films for British Transport and, while he does not mention *Sewing Machine*, he does recount the hostility he faced from concerned parents about his rail safety film *The Finishing Line* (1977). For more, see Kier-La Janisse, 'School of shock: Q+A: John Krish on railway scare film "The Finishing Line"', *Fangoria*, 23 June 2013, http://www.fangotv.com/school-of-shock-qa-john-krish-on-railway-scare-film-the-finishing-line/ (accessed 7 April 2017).
14 The countdown timer links *Sewing Machine* to contemporary fears of imminent nuclear attack and to the *Protect and Survive* (1975) series of animated public information films. This series of twenty films detailed the steps to take in the event of a nuclear strike and is renowned for its chillingly detached and pragmatic approach to surviving thermonuclear war. Produced by Richard Taylor Cartoons, the same company responsible for the animated *Charley Says* safety films featuring the eponymous and much-loved accident-prone orange tabby, the *Protect and Survive* series disturbs because it normalizes and naturalises nuclear war, making it seem imminent rather than merely possible. These films connect with fictional representations of life after nuclear war such as *The War Game* (BBC, 1965) and *Threads* (BBC2, 1984) in the way they combine the pragmatic and the catastrophic, but they share their sense of anxiety-driven preparation with public information films that deal with more everyday tragedies.
15 For more on the connection between expanded bandwidth and the production and circulation of cultural knowledge, see Will Straw, 'Embedded memories', in Charles Acland (ed.), *Residual Media* (Minneapolis, MN: University of Minnesota Press, 2007), pp. 3–15.

16 Alison Landsberg developed the concept of prosthetic memory to name those memories that 'originate outside a person's lived experience and yet are taken on and worn by that person through mass cultural technologies of memory'. Alison Landsberg, *Prosthetic Memory: The Transformation of American Remembrance in the Age of Mass Culture* (New York: Columbia University Press, 2004), p. 19.
17 Simon Reynolds, *Retromania: Pop Culture's Addiction to Its Own Past* (London: Faber & Faber, 2011), p. 339.
18 Ibid., p. 338.

12 'WE KNOW WHAT IT'S ACTUALLY LIKE': VOICE, DIALECT AND SELF-EFFICACY IN SCOTLAND'S *UNDERSTANDING CINEMA* PROJECT

Jamie Chambers

Discussing representations of children in Scotland's 2014 *Understanding Cinema* project, Luke Davies, the 11-year-old director of *L<3B*, remarked to me that 'adults tell [children] what they think it's like to be a child, what they think it's actually like. But we know what it's *actually* like.'

In the cinematic arena, children are perennially spoken for, spoken about and spoken 'towards', with rarely an opportunity to speak *for themselves*. Children's perspectives and subjectivities are referred to in cinema to the point of fetishization, their perspectives constructed by adults, frequently underscored with a sense of nostalgia about the untainted innocence of child perspectives. The *Understanding Cinema* project, modelled upon *Le Cinéma, cent ans de jeunesse* (*CCADJ*) programme from Cinémathèque Française, creates opportunities for Scottish children to make films of their own. One of *Understanding Cinema*'s defining characteristics as a school-based programme of film education is the manner in which it encourages participants to make films about their own lives, and thus voice a sense of their own particular 'dialect': an articulation of 'film language' mediated by children's own sense of location and identity and thus a sense of their own, located filmic 'voices'. Alongside this prioritization of 'dialect', *Understanding Cinema* simultaneously pursues an inextricable sense of *self-efficacy*; through a contention that, in learning to voice located aspects of the self through cinema, children might also develop a greater sense of self-confidence and social agency. Whilst these objectives may well seem utopian when contextualized within the discourses of critical pedagogy, my experience working as a practitioner on *Understanding Cinema* between 2013 and 2014 (the experience upon which this essay is drawn) has provided the opportunity for in-depth, qualitative exploration of the project's approaches to dialect and self-efficacy, and has found *Understanding Cinema* to achieve considerable yet contingent success in both.

In broader terms, this chapter explores a strange sense of circularity about the place of children in neorealist cinema, and the place of neorealist technique in children's film education in programmes. Children are frequently the subject of neorealist cinema, from Giuseppe and Pasquale in *Shoeshine* (Vittorio de Sica, 1946), Bruno in *Bicycle Thieves* (de Sica, 1948), Maria in *Bellissima* (Luchino Visconti, 1951) and Pasquale in the second episode of *Paisan* (Roberto Rossellini, 1946), to (if we employ Robert Sklar and Saverio Gioachinni's notion of a refracted 'global neorealism'),[1] Apu in Satyajit Ray's trilogy (1955–59) and Ahmed and Mohamed in Abbas Kiarostami's *Where is The Friend's Home?* (1987). Christopher Wagstaff has speculated as to why neorealist filmmakers continually returned to children's perspectives:

> [C]hildren are, in social terms, ideal embodiments of *sermo humilis* (lowered voices) … De Sica has returned repeatedly to their rhetorical use in his elecutio. He uses them thematically, it is true; but stylistically they fit very well Auerbach's definition of sermo humilis: the 'sublime' (being human) expressed through a 'lowly' style, embodying a voice too low to make itself heard in the adult world.[2]

Given their deep roots in cinematic neorealism, *CCADJ* and *Understanding Cinema* can fittingly be seen to engage a disparate 'community' who have long lacked representation in cinema's 'politics of recognition'. Children themselves can perhaps be seen as something of an 'othered'/'undered'[3] or 'subaltern' group.[4] To echo Edward Said's loaded quotation of Marx, the pervading paternalist logic upon children's place in cinema seems to be that 'they cannot represent themselves, therefore they must be represented'.[5] *Understanding Cinema*'s employment of neorealism is thus intriguing; for whilst the project aims to engage cinematically with the 'lowered voices' of children, the expectation is that children do so largely *themselves*, rather than via neorealism's somewhat paternalistic claim to articulate the 'lowered voices' of marginalized communities from outside. The question *Understanding Cinema* thus presents its practitioners is how then to assist children in articulating their own neorealist 'dialect' without that assistance becoming an epistemic imposition in itself. Media scholars such as David Buckingham and Michelle Orner[6] have expressed considerable scepticism regarding the affordances school-based creative projects create for children to express their own 'authentic voices'; 'authors have challenged the emphasis on "student voice" in so-called critical pedagogy: the notion that students can be "given" a voice by the teacher and that they will then use this to speak some kind of subjective truth is, they argue, an illusion'.[7] Can a neorealist-inspired programme of learning then hope to afford children any degree of self-expression that is not merely interpellated by adult notions of what a child's 'authentic voice' should be?

It would seem important at the outset, however, to relativize such notions of 'epistemic imposition' as being located, contingent phenomena, rather than essentialized and overreaching catch-all allegory. Whilst all teaching arguably is a form of epistemic imposition, different programmes of learning should be seen to create simultaneous impositions and affordances for their learners. It would therefore seem important for critical theories of pedagogy to move beyond simplistic and determinist conceptions in which authoritative voices inevitably interpellate and eclipse children's own potential for self-representation, towards a perspective taking into account the unruly, contingent and over-determined experience of practice 'on the ground'. To what extent does *Understanding Cinema* afford opportunities to voice aspects of the 'dialect' of the located self, amidst an adult-driven programme of learning? To what extent did the children's representations of their own lives articulate their own experience, and to what extent where they mediated and shaped by myself as the children's teacher/practitioner?

This essay will focus in particular upon the delivery of the *Understanding Cinema* project and the teaching of what might be considered neorealist filmmaking technique in two Scottish primary schools in East Lothian: P5 (where the children are aged 9 to 10) in Law Primary School (North Berwick) and P7 (where the children are aged 11 to 12) in St Gabriel's Primary School (Prestonpans). The discussion will focus upon issues I encountered as an *Understanding Cinema* tutor working with these two different groups of students, and will look at both the process and outcomes of the programme's seven-month syllabus, alongside semi-structured interviews I conducted with participants and their teachers once the programme had concluded. I will consider case studies of particular students and their films within a broader discussion of the possible benefits such an approach might engender. Whilst the discursive approaches I have adopted belong largely to film studies, I have also attempted to take note of the problematizing positions of media education scholars such as David Buckingham. All the *Understanding Cinema* films discussed below are available to watch online via the links given at the end of the chapter.

Neorealism and Bruno's tears: performances of 'the real'

Understanding Cinema's annual topic is taken from *CCADJ*'s own annually revolving curriculum, arising from the work of French film theorist and filmmaker Alain Bergala. Now an international programme with participants in Brazil, Cuba, Portugal, Spain, Italy, Germany, Austria, Belgium and the UK, *CCADJ* builds upon France's strong precedent of cine-pedagogy, addressing cine-literacy and opening up access to filmmaking in schools and community groups across the world.

Perhaps the core characteristics of *CCADJ*'s (and consequently *Understanding Cinema*'s) approach are the focus on aesthetics and insistence upon a sense of 'dirigisme' or 'direction', interpreted by the Mark Reid of the British Film Institute (BFI) as a series of 'constraints and parameters'. Amanda-Jane Thomson, class teacher of the P5 class I worked with at Law Primary School, described how the project's approach allowed

> [T]he children ... a lot of time to experiment with [different types of shots] and to see how they could use that effectively to create specific meanings throughout their film. Which really is quite different compared to how I would have previously approached filming in the primary school. You know, you would have given them the camera, the camera would have been static, wide angle. We would have shot what happened in front of the camera and there would have been no understanding of what we could do with that camera to create meaning.

Each year participants explore a highly specific aspect of film aesthetics and 'grammar'. *CCADI*'s and *Understanding Cinema*'s topic in 2014 was 'le plan sequence' or 'the long take', a cinematic trope with its own ties to neorealism through the work of the French film critic André Bazin. As postulated by Bazin, the 'long take' is a form of cinema with closer proximity to 'real life', and thus a form of cinema aspiring to greater epistemological 'authenticity' or verisimilitude. Describing filmmaking approaches that prioritized 'long takes' over montage, Bazin described 'the regeneration of realism in storytelling' and how film, through the 'long take', was 'thus ... becoming capable once more of bringing together real time, in which things exist, along with the duration of the action, for which classical editing has insidiously substituted mental and abstract time'.[8]

Bazinian notions that some traditions of representation are inherently more 'authentic' or 'real' than others are deeply problematic. It would therefore seem sensible to frame neorealism at the outset as a genre of cinema that frequently stages compelling performances of 'authentic reality', but does not necessarily possess any privileged relationship with 'the real'. In these terms, 'the real' or 'the authentic' could be seen as akin to an aesthetic, articulating itself through performance. Discussing neorealism's performance of the 'authentic real', Christopher Wagstaff quotes Michaelangelo Antonioni's maxim that 'reality is like an onion: peel off one layer and you reveal another beneath it'. Focusing upon the famous scene in *Bicycle Thieves* where Bruno (Enzo Staiola) cries at his father's actions, Wagstaff contrasts the myth of how the scene was created with a much less idealized account from the director's daughter:

> [De Sica] needed the boy to cry, and was having trouble getting this out of the sunny Staiola. Prompted by the production secretary De Sica surreptitiously put some cigarette butts into Staiola's jacket pocket, and then proceeded to 'discover' them, and scold Staiola for hoarding butts to smoke in secrecy, whereupon the little boy burst into tears ... [But] If you peel off the edifying

anecdote I have just recounted, you uncover another layer where De Sica got Staiola to cry by shouting at him and smacking him.[9]

Aesthetically, Bruno's tears achieve a compelling textual performance of the 'real', the 'authentic', of childhood. As fictional drama, one is intuitively aware, however, that such performances of 'authenticity' are achieved through degrees of artifice, contrivance and pragmatic contingency that may not concord directly with the aesthetic performance of 'realism' achieved textually by the film. Unsurprisingly, the myth surrounding how Bruno's tears were achieved *does*, however, concord with the humanist sympathies pursued aesthetically by the film. The anecdote of the false accusation emphasizes Staiola's innate nobility, integrity and authenticity; his tears arose from the accusation he was ungenerous; that he could have shared something and didn't. Wagstaff's account 'unveils' the means by which this performance may actually have been achieved, through a cruelty highly discordant with the scene's performance of the 'authentic real'; a concealed image of opportunist cruelty standing in stark contrast with the broader humanist claim of neorealism. Bruno's tears thus illustrate the inventive properties of neorealism and the at-times discordant means through which performances of realism may be achieved.

Looking beyond critical unease with notions of 'the real', neorealism has been adopted by a diverse array of global filmmaking projects, as aptly illustrated by Giovacchini and Sklar's discussion of 'global neorealism'.[10] Considering the adoption of neorealist technique by filmmakers as diverse as Satyajit Ray, Ousmane Sembene, Ken Loach and the Amber Collective, one of neorealism's affordances seems to be its engagement with materialist, historical and shared/social lived experience in a manner that would seem dialectical, productive and *useful* for dialect-driven identity projects. As this essay will go on to explore, neorealism might also be seen to serve a particular pragmatic purpose in helping children articulate certain experiences; to perform and represent experiences in a particular way. Whilst the insistence on a particular 'way of speaking' inherent in *CCADJ* is an epistemic imposition, it is an imposition that generates certain affordances. If *CCADJ*'s overriding sense of dirigisme (of 'constraints and parameters') imposes and restricts, *Understanding Cinema* participants are asked to mobilize a particular form of speaking that would seem to allow considerable possibility for the contingent 'voicing', or social performance of the located self.

The *Understanding Cinema* project: parameters and constraints

As an *Understanding Cinema* practitioner coming to the project equipped with the *CCADJ*'s Bazinian philosophy of 'realist authenticity', I was interested by how deeply saturated children's imaginations seemed to be with the tropes of Hollywood. When I first asked students to come up with their own film ideas, the results constituted a literal *kitsch*: zombies, vampires, 'slasher'-killers, evil masterminds and 'smart-ass' one-liners; what seemed to me the refracted cultural detritus of commercial cinema as filtered through the imagination of Scottish schoolchildren. I was not alone in this experience; Mark Reid describes how 'too often young people, given cameras for the first time, imagine they can create mini Jason Bourne-like escapades, set in their school playground'.[11] Big-budget Hollywood associations seemed to underscore many of the children's knee-jerk cinematic impulses on a linguistic level too. 'Tell me abaad it…', 'Tohhhhtally…'; when the cameras started rolling, children would frequently abandon their own native Scottish/English accents to assume an adopted register of glitzy, fetishized 'otherness' gleaned from American entertainment. It was a rhetoric they seemed to have learned through cultural osmosis, and one that felt to me, in representations of their own stories and lives, deeply incongruous and 'inauthentic'. One can identify here a potential clash between my own (perhaps paternalist) sense of what was an 'authentic representation' of the children, and what the children felt was an 'authentic representation' of themselves. My notion of 'authentic representation' involved the children using their 'everyday' voices, wearing their 'everyday' clothes and behaving as I myself saw them behave day to day. Perhaps the children's own notion of an 'authentic representation' of themselves was drawn from more private or personal experiences than what I was able to see, or perhaps it was – at least initially – partially rehearsed in the same terms in which 'authenticity' is represented in children's Hollywood cinema.

This might be seen to reflect what David Buckingham has described as the 'social worlds of production', whereby children's creativity in school-based exercises is frequently a 'negotiation between the interests of the peer group (which are frequently drawn from popular culture) and the criteria of what counts as legitimate "school writing"';[12] in other words, a discordance between the children's own frame of cinematic reference and the references I was pointing them towards. Buckingham's suggestion that media work should be grounded amongst the ready references of children's previous media experience highlights another area of tension with *Understanding Cinema* and *CCADJ*, which both insist upon primary reference to an expansive canon of international art cinema that may well be alien to the majority of participants. Whilst it is easy to frame art cinema as an elitist and 'closed access' form of media literacy, one could equally postulate (recalling the broad, serious frame of Raymond Williams) a curriculum of art cinema uniquely concerned with localized working-class or 'popular' experience.[13] 'Art cinema' (itself an unstable notion) would thus seem to denote merely a *way of speaking*, rather than a specification as to what is said. The diversity of British cinema engaging with working-class experience illustrates the expansive vocabulary and expressivity of art cinema that is, theoretically at least, open to anyone, to say whatever they want to say. Neorealist-inspired programmes like *Understanding Cinema* might thus be seen to broaden that access, creating opportunities to speak in art cinema's supposedly exclusive register.

Whilst not intended to be a Leavis-ite polemic against 'popular' cinema (such a hyper-localist argument taken to its extreme would also preclude children from engaging with the European and global cinema that comprises most of *CCADJ*'s canon), nor to preclude children from expressing imagination, playfulness and a sense of the fantastical in their storytelling, the problem of the hegemonic pervasiveness of Hollywood archetypes would seem to me to be its implicit devaluing or 'othering' of the located self. So all-pervasive was Hollywood amongst the children's cinematic references, and so absent any visible indigenous alternative, that the language and systems of signification of popular cinema were adopted by my *Understanding Cinema* participants as if they were 'universal', the language of the self. When asked to come up with film ideas, my students wanted to write about characters who did not seem to *be* them, and places they had not been to, thus mirroring the sense of 'exteriority' and 'dispossession' their relationships with commercial cinema seemed to engender. One of my students initially wanted to set his film *in* America, somewhere he had never been, but told me he felt was just somehow 'better' and 'less boring' than Scotland. There seemed an implicit sense that children felt their own identities and concerns had no value within a cinematic arena. To be yourself was to be 'boring', 'mundane' and 'commonplace', whereas American accents, 'sassy' talk and superheroes/aliens/zombies were 'cool' and 'exciting'.

Whilst my *Understanding Cinema* participants' aping of Hollywood fantasy could be said to articulate a sense of 'self' through pursuit of 'wish-fulfilment' and a desire for escapism, such as the thematized treatments of escapism in *Billy Liar* (John Schlesinger, 1963), *The Spirit of the Beehive* (Victor Erice, 1973) and *Pan's Labyrinth* (Guillermo del Toro, 2006), or indeed through a sense of both individual and social *play* (which should be seen to be part of the daily 'reality' of children's experience), what seemed particularly problematic to me in the children's early work was the manner in which a borrowed American 'dialect' (whether on a literal level of speech or the more analogous level of content and style) referenced an *exteriorized* and ultimately unachievable, unliveable experience, fetishized by the children as a desirable but unreachable sense of 'otherness'. Ultimately the children's adoption of modalities from popular cinema seemed to me to articulate a sense of alienation. Here Raymond Williams's notion of the 'unlearning of the inherent dominative mode' takes on a very literal significance. In addressing the hegemonic presence of Hollywood the *Understanding Cinema* project, with its leaning towards neorealist filmmaking techniques, focusing on 'dialect' and cultural locality, could thus be seen to provide a potential counter to this sense of alienated, unreachable otherness, and thus a means by which to begin reinvigorating and rearticulating social performances of the located self.

Here one returns to the dilemma of how to assist children in articulating their own 'dialect' without that assistance becoming an epistemic imposition. One of the key problems I encountered was that, inevitably, trying to help children to find their own 'dialect' meant facilitating an 'unlearning' of assumptions about cinema, and thus a certain degree of short-circuiting of their initial instincts. In contrast to the fantastical pleasures of popular cinema a neorealist programme can risk seeming ascetic and, at worst, repressive. As such my concern was to attempt to foster a delicate dual programme of learning and unlearning: to help the children find a sense of their own 'dialect' without me necessarily telling them exactly what that dialect should be, and to encourage them to think more of *themselves* (rather than of far-off glitzy others) without that epistemological shift feeling like a compulsory imposition. Interestingly, as will be discussed below, that 'dialect' took different forms and modalities for different students within the filmmaking process; in places it was articulated through performance and script, and in others through camera placement and direction.

David Buckingham has claimed that 'teacherly attempts at imposing cultural, moral or political authority children experience in their daily lives are very unlikely to be taken seriously. If, as in many cases, they are based on a paternalistic contempt for children's tastes and pleasures, they certainly deserve to be rejected.'[14] My own highly localized experience as a practitioner on the *Understanding Cinema* project does not seem to support these statements. As a figure of authority attempting to steer children away from non-reflexive emulations of popular cinema, my role was certainly paternalistic. My experience, however, was that many children took the project very seriously indeed and produced work within *Understanding Cinema*'s 'parameters and constraints' that ultimately both they and myself considered to be of a high aesthetic standard and commitment.

The *Understanding Cinema* project in practice: Lumière Minutes

The first exercise of three for 2014 *Understanding Cinema* participants was the filming of 'Lumière Minutes'; one-minute documentaries shot from a static perspective, after the fashion of the Lumière brothers. For *Understanding Cinema* participants, the Lumière Minute exercise was simultaneously a first experience of using a camera, framing a shot and cinematic 'observation', whilst providing a decisive first step towards engaging with a greater sense of autochthonous identity. Here the neorealist concern with dialect and 'lowered voices' manifested itself in a commitment to finding interest in the 'mundane' and 'commonplace': to borrow a phrase from Terence Davies, the challenge of the Lumière Minutes exercise was to find 'the poetry of the ordinary'.

As part of Exercise 1, *Understanding Cinema* participants were encouraged to find moments in their day-to-day life which expressed their own 'dialect': a moment that somehow reflected the locality and specificity of their own day-to-day experiences, and thus enacted a certain sense of 'storytelling', and the establishing of perspective. Among my classes there was at first a proliferation of domestic spectacle and exhibitionism – of children looking directly at the camera, of cats in hoodies and dogs performing tricks, of 'over-the-shoulder' shots of children playing video games or outside playing football – much of which seemed to lack the more detached sense of observation and aesthetic diegesis commonly associated with cinematic rhetoric. Unsurprisingly, such footage seemed to draw upon the semi-participatory 'home mode' of domestic video footage, as identified by Richard Chalfen and subsequently explored by Buckingham et al.[15] Maria Pini has characterized the home mode as material created 'if not necessary within the home, then dealing primarily with the "the home", the domestic and the familial. Such material tends to be thought of as private, and as such, its significance closely resembles that of the traditional family photo album.'[16] Contemporary discussion of the home mode has been updated to include camera-phone footage, which Rebecca Willett describes as extending the home mode's possibilities to include both a broader spectrum of locations and acquaintances, addressing either a wider audience online of family, friends and peers, or indeed a narrowing to more private, personal reference.[17]

As *Understanding Cinema* participants were able to watch their Lumière Minutes with the class and get a sense of audience responses (thus learning what might interest those outside their lives and what might not), their work seemed to become more considered, perhaps reflecting a move away from the home mode's semi-private address to family and friends, towards a more reflexive, aesthetic diegesis reaching beyond the home mode to address both their class and me – a demanding, 'artsy', outside tutor. It is interesting to consider the manner in which the communicative act of filmmaking in this sense became increasingly less 'monological' (less undilutedly personal and individual) and came to take into account a growing aspiration and expectation of shared significance with a widening audience. Hanging over *Understanding Cinema* activities was the expectation of a larger audience of strangers, through the possibility of the children's work ultimately being screened on the project's website and at the 2014 Edinburgh International Film Festival. 'Speaking' with a camera thus became an increasingly *social* act for the children, their films increasingly taking on the properties of 'speech acts' that voiced aspects of self, whilst simultaneously being couched in a semi-adopted rhetoric affording the possibility of speaking 'socially'.

The prioritization of the 'aesthetic' moment embodied in group viewings of material (often shot a mere hour previously) reflects a key concern of the *Understanding Cinema* project: the moment at the end of each session when children watched back and discussed their work, and were thus able to evaluate their own decisions (as directors, actors and camera operators) with the rest of the class *as an audience*. Amanda-Jane Thomson identified this moment of evaluation and discussion as being one of the most fundamental aspects of the programme:

> At the end of the session, it came back to discussion, and reflection on what had happened, and evaluating how it had worked… We would put the films on the board and we would have a discussion… about what had worked, why had it worked well, what wasn't so good, how could we make things better.

Here the children seemed to grasp something of the tangle of epistemology and ontology inherent in the notion of cinema fostered by *Understanding Cinema*. Whilst the film was made *from inside* by them, the filmmakers, meaning and aesthetic success came to be defined as much *from outside* by audiences who might well know nothing about them, their lives and their priorities. As such the films deemed successful by the group usually expressed a complex dialectic, a complex 'speech act' performed between these two perspectives.[18]

Watching the responses of their class, children went back and shot more Lumière Minutes which seemed increasingly to become more localized and specific, whilst simultaneously aspiring to a diegesis addressing audiences beyond the extended 'home mode' of camera-phone footage. We saw a community group sanding a boat; a grandparent who owned a hotel setting out cutlery before guests arrived for breakfast; one mother teaching her daughter to read the Koran, and another washing her 2-year-old daughter in the bath. Children seemed to actively enjoy this sense of 'show and tell' and for some participants the exercise began to serve something akin to a complex diary function, shooting upwards of 50 Lumière Minutes in a single evening. The viewpoints started to gain a greater sense of 'transportive' viewing, and thus a sense of basic storytelling. Rather than watching a child staging a to-camera performance, we were starting to be actively *shown* aspects of children's lives through their eyes, in a manner that made a more self-conscious address to a wider audience.

As we moved onto the second exercise (which involved filming a staged dramatic scene as a long take from both static and moving perspectives), I found elements of Hollywood-ized rhetoric starting to creep back into the children's work as we progressed from the documentary approach of the Lumière Minutes to rudimentary staged dramas. The more we moved towards 'drama', the more fantastical the children's stories became, as if the opportunity to be more imaginative was somehow synonymous with 'make-believe', escapism and mythic role-play. (It is important here to note that such a sense of play would seem itself to be part of children's everyday lives, albeit articulated in a different modality to the perhaps more materialist arena of neorealism.) The reintroduction of 'drama' and 'artifice' seemed to draw us back towards the magnetizing influences of mainstream cinema that the Lumière Minutes had helped us begin to unpick and 'unlearn'. Once again I encountered the sense that the children felt their own lives and concerns were not worthy of dramatization, something I resolved to tackle head-on.

Each week, I would draw up a cumulative list of elements that were not allowed in the children's films. Aware that this 'unlearning' necessitated a certain degree of imposition in itself, I attempted (perhaps unsuccessfully!) to make this playful rather than draconian, framing the 'rules' as being like the rules of a game, once again reflecting *CCADJ*'s sense of *dirigisme* or creative restraint. In one instance, I introduced a weekly 'close-up competition', to see who could get the camera closest to its subject, in order to encourage the children to explore camera perspectives beyond the wide shot. I increasingly specified that everyone had to use their own voices, and play characters who were believable analogues for themselves. We talked about how it was important for 'believability' and the transportive claim of a film that events feel as 'real' as possible, aspiring to an aesthetic of verisimilitude. Thus real school bells were more 'believable' for audiences than children making trilling noises off-camera, and real teachers more believable for wider audiences than children playing teachers. One consequence of this process was that, eventually, in each of the children's final films (at both Law and St Gabriel's), there is not one child who isn't either playing themselves or a version of themselves. Each child chose to use their own name in their films, and in particular cases, the film's storylines were based on real-life happenings from the children's lives. Michael Egan, class teacher of the P7 class I worked with at St Gabriel's Primary School, identified the moment where we began to prioritize 'realism' as the moment when the children truly started to 'take possession' and feel a sense of ownership of their work, thus moving from the jokey pastiches of earlier exercises to a greater sense of application. As Egan described:

> I think it was because the kids were tasked to make it as realistic as possible, and when we spoke about that as a group, we kind of said 'you need to use what you've got'. So immediately, it was going to be characters their own age, they were going to use pre-existing settings, the likes of [Prestonpans] tower, the likes of the school building, going down the street, someone's house: this was all available to them and it's immediately authentic. And I think they then just naturally began to use their own names… I think like Luke's film [L<3B], like them all, I think that they've just taken it all very personal and it comes over in the film that its personal issues and that its realistic. I think by saying to them that the films had to be realistic, that was a breakthrough moment. At that point, they started to really take it seriously, and it has shone through.

Similarly noting how the neorealist imperative placed upon an aesthetic of verisimilitude assisted students in finding greater depth of significance in their films, Amanda-Jane Thomson remarked upon the differences between the school-based drama conventions in Scottish schools and this new style of naturalistic, 'neorealist' acting:

> In terms of drama it's been really interesting, because usually you would go to drama and you would kind of go all into these roles which actually children don't have a lot of experience of, but actually if we bring it right back to them, that's where they can play an effective character, if it's something that they've experienced.

As we moved towards Exercise 3, where the children were tasked with making a final 10-minute film utilizing everything they had learnt about the long take, I tried to encourage each of my classes to make sure each film engaged in some way with the children's own concerns, their own personalities and the realities of the situations they were trying to depict. Once again this involved a degree of gentle steering, away from knee-jerk Hollywood homage towards story ideas that demonstrated a greater localized significance to the lives of the children themselves (once again, a moment of tension between imposition and creativity). I encouraged students to investigate the real-life processes they were exploring. At Law, Max's *First Day* explored what would happen if a new student came to school. Max's classmate Elizabeth, playing the new student, was so cast (without intervention from me) by the group because she was the newest to the school and thus the member of the group who most distinctly remembered the emotions associated with arriving at a new school. I encouraged the group to research what *exactly* happened to new students who arrived at Law for their first day in the middle of a term: which member of staff would greet them at the front door and how they would be introduced to the school and their new class. The research was then worked up by the group into the opening sequence of their film with notable maturity.

Elsewhere at Law, Jack's *Blocked* mixed aspects of popular genre (thriller, police procedural, comedy and even a hint of horror) with neorealist 'authentication' and verisimilitude. The film chronicles a mysterious blocking of the school toilets and allows 'behind the scenes' glimpses of the many different layers of Law's institutional structure as they struggle to deal with the problem. Playing themselves, we witness the school janitor bemoaning this new spate of 'blockings', the senior management team debating the best approach to the problem, the Deputy Headmistress making an announcement about the problem at a real school assembly, and finally a pupil council meeting where the terrible truth of the matter is revealed. Interestingly, the senior management team's scene was reshot (without my intervention) by Jack and his group after they watched it back with the class and, having scripted it themselves, deemed the script and performances 'inauthentic' and unconvincing. Having decided that the initial scene – which featured professional women in their forties and fifties reading dialogue written by 9-year-old boys – did not meet the film's overriding tone of 'authenticity', Jack's team subsequently refilmed the scene, encouraging the senior management team to improvise dialogue as they would have done 'in real life'. This resulted in a rendering of a senior management team meeting that the filmmakers and their class felt was more believable for audiences, as can be seen in the final film.

Towards 'embedded' dramatic narratives with *Blue Raspberry* and *Me and Mum*

In my efforts to help *Understanding Cinema* participants find a sense of their own 'dialect' in their films I still found overall that, when called upon to act, participants at Law Primary School in particular frequently returned to more playful, exaggerated and theatrical modes of performance that did not always achieve an aesthetic of verisimilitude. I therefore devised a homework exercise for a smaller group of the children who had responded well to Exercise 1, whereby each participant was tasked with filming a modest, naturalistic storyline to interweave with a selection of 'documentary' moments from their Lumière Minutes. I hoped this might serve to draw their performances into a more 'naturalistic' register whilst creating a film that had a greater performative sense of each child's own voice and 'dialect'.

Bridget Harley, director of *Blue Raspberry*, one of the films produced by this homework task, is a shy girl to whom the imposing 'adult' rhetoric of an interview does not do justice. However, her 'voice' seems highly articulate in *Blue Raspberry*, which 'gives voice' to the lived experience of a trio of young sisters through a grounded childhood perspective rarely seen in cinema. The film revolves around a central conflict between Bridget and her parents, where, against the wishes of her mother and father, Bridget spends her pocket money on 'blue raspberry' sweets, and then eats them secretly, only to be caught, blue-tongued, by her mother. She is scolded, and the film finishes ambiguously, without a definitive sense that any lesson has been learned. The film's linear narrative is interspersed with documentary footage of Bridget's life with her family and sisters, playing on the beach, sledging down the stairs at home, and playing atonal improvisations on the piano. The sea and the girls' relationship to natural landscapes plays a central role of the film, which achieves a striking overall sense of lyricism through elided framings, naturalistic performances and its depiction of the girls' play. There is something striking about the picture of childhood Bridget is able to capture seemingly unawares, and the relative sense in the film of an insider's ontology of childhood. Put differently, *Blue Raspberry* achieves a convincing and compelling performance of 'authenticity'. Bridget has unparalleled access to the relatively unmediated home life of her sisters and her family. She is a trusted family member, and her filming apparatus (a FlipVid camera the size of a mobile phone) is small enough to be fairly unobtrusive. She is therefore a director whose observational presence, whilst not without influence, is perhaps the closest cinema gets to invisibility.

Colin McArthur has discussed cinema's potential to either sentimentalize or demonize the Platonic ideal of childhood, discussing how

> [W]ith regard to the dominant narrative of childhood, the gaping trap that awaits any filmmaker is sentimentality ... Just as there are dominant narratives about Scotland, so too is there a dominant narrative of childhood within which the child is seen as innately innocent, placid, asexual and 'nice'. There is of course, an equally reductive counter-narrative of the innately evil child ... However, certain filmmakers – for example Vincente Minnelli with Margaret O'Brien in *Meet Me in St Louis*, or Victor Erice with the child actors in *The Spirit of the Beehive* – have managed to construct a more complex view of childhood.[19]

What is significant about *Blue Raspberry* is the sense of childhood representing *itself* in a manner that does not engage the sedimented tropes and assumptions of popular cinema. Indeed *Blue Raspberry*'s portrayal of childhood is strangely evocative of *The Spirit of the Beehive* (albeit without the earlier film's politicized subtext), in expressing the sheer wildness of childhood and the looming shadows of the adult world.

For Bridget, the film is about an 'everyday' conflict which finds consonance with the vignettes of daily life captured in her documentary, 'diary'-like Lumière Minutes. Through a complex entangling of interior ontology (the director's perspective on her own life) and exterior epistemology (the prospective adult audience in relation to Bridget's rushes, as mediated through myself, as Bridget's *Understanding Cinema* tutor and editor), the film also speaks to a wider audience, about childhood in the shadow of adulthood. Notably, the experience of expressing herself through cinema (both as an actor and director) seems to have had a positive effect on Bridget's sense of self-efficacy, meaning she was able to make a presentation in front of an audience of 200 people at the Edinburgh International Film Festival, something Amanda-Jane Thomson tells me she would not have been able to do at the start of P5. Here, it would seem, the semi-neorealist imperative to *speak socially* – to voice 'dialect', or aspects of the self through the adoption of ways of speaking that conversely construct significance for a broader audience – seemed of considerable benefit to Bridget's confidence and sense of self-efficacy.

Part of the same exercise, Jamie Thomson's *Me and Mum* (2014) constructs a celebrative, inflected portrait of his hard-working mother, Jo. Like *Blue Raspberry*, the film centres around a modest domestic conflict in which Jo becomes frustrated with her son for his lack of responsibility. Throughout the film Jo is seen working, putting the needs of her family above her own. When Jamie forgets his water bottle on the way to rugby, Jo's frustration provokes a rude response and the two fall out. After reflection, Jamie apologizes to his mother and the two bond whilst giving Jamie's baby sister a bath. The film is built around a complex sense of perspective: of Jamie looking at his mum, and his mum looking at Jamie. Set amongst the daily rhythms of life at home, *Me and Mum* once again has a strong feeling of localized, rooted perspective, and in its specific rendition of a universal story of maternal frustration recalls Shane Meadows's notion that 'to make a universal film ... you need a very particular focus'.[20] Jamie seems aware of both the film's specificity and universality, and how the two are interlinked:

> The bits which felt most real were the bits, the 'Lumière Minutes', the pizza at the start ... It gave you a sense of our life as well. Because you normally see my brothers getting angry at my mum because my mum's forgotten what they've said or something like that. And it shows you what someone's normal life is like. Because there will be mums all over the world – my mum is definitely like that ... they'll think, I hope we're not the only family which does this and that, and what I'd say is 'you're not'. There are loads of people who do the same things as you.

It is interesting to consider how both *Me and Mum* and *Blue Raspberry* employ aspects of the home mode in their intimate recordings of family life, whilst simultaneously repurposing it to address an audience outside an enclosed group of friends and family. Whilst being constituted largely of the normative locations, characters, scenes and events of the home mode, both films take reflexive, aesthetically aware perspectives upon family life in a manner that presupposes a wider audience of strangers outside the family's community of significance.

For an expressive and confident student like Jamie, *Me and Mum* also helped find a register of acting that was more naturalistic than some of his more bombastic performances in class. Indeed, speaking to teachers and participants across the project, there was an interesting consensus that acting for film differed to the theatrical drama classes that are a staple of the Scottish school week. Amanda-Jane Thomson described to me how

> I have some children in my class that in drama, before we started the project, would have been very unwilling to go in and take a role on, sort of realistically. There was a lot of kind of – some that just didn't want to do it, others that would just play up as a result, because it was just too embarrassing to take a role, and to watch some of those children now in front of the camera is just amazing, the confidence in them in front of the camera.

There was a sense throughout the project that film, affording a quieter, more subtle, arguably 'naturalistic' register of performance than theatre, could potentially foster greater confidence of self-expression, and thus act as a gateway to subsequent participation in the more 'exhibitionist' arena of school drama productions. Sabilla, one of the project participants at St Gabriel's, told me how acting in films had given her a new confidence, and in particular the confidence to play the role of 'the parrot' in the school play: 'first of all I didn't want to be the parrot, but now I actually wanted to be the parrot, because then I'm doing more filming, being more confident, 'cos a parrots got lines I can remember. So yeah, I liked filming and it helped me.' Sabilla told me that when she acted in her group's film *L<3B* it was easier to act because she just played a version of herself; 'I was trying to be myself, because I don't want to be anybody else. Because, whenever I be somebody else I feel a bit shy. So I like being myself.' Sabilla tells me that the whole process has given her more confidence and that 'now I can go anywhere, and I don't need to feel shy, and make Sumaiya [Sabilla's twin sister] say it, so I can … say more stuff and say it confident'.

Self-efficacy via narrative analogy: *L<3 B* at St Gabriel's

One of the most remarkable films produced by my *Understanding Cinema* students in 2014 was Luke Davies' *L <3 B* (2014) from St Gabriel's Primary School, Prestonpans; a film with a marked sense of 'dialect' and aesthetic achievement.

L <3 B begins with Luke being rejected when he 'asks out' his classmate Bailey in the playground. He then suffers further indignities at the hands of his mother, his teacher and several of his friends, before earning the affections of Charley, Bailey's best friend. The film was birthed by Luke in response to a discussion I had with the class about the importance of using the camera to convey emotion. Under Luke's direction, a group of students produced a short one-minute, one-shot film where Luke waits uneasily in the foreground, left of frame, whilst Bailey and Charley approach background to foreground on the right. Luke hesitantly asks Bailey if she will go out with him, only to be callously rejected (the sequence which now opens the finished film). What initially struck me about the short was the bravery involved on Luke's part in conceiving a story that placed him in a position of such vulnerability. When I first encountered him, Luke was a shy student, frequently hesitant to express himself in front of the rest of the class. In *L<3B*, however, Luke conceived of a film where, playing himself, he suffers a considerable degree of humiliation from both adults and fellow students. As Luke's teacher, Michael Egan, describes it:

> The big concern when he made [*L<3B*] in his group was how much Luke had put himself out there for public ridicule, bearing in mind that Luke's quite a quiet withdrawn boy in class. Socially I wouldn't say that he struggles, but he's got a very small group of friends who are all of the same gender […] So yeah, I was really surprised when he came up with that film, and I think he almost played himself. I thought there was a lot of Luke in that.

Luke's bravery in 'putting himself out there' in the film did not go unnoticed by his classmates. His co-star Bailey remarked to me that 'Luke was so confident to do all the stuff we had to do, because a lot of people wouldn't have been able to do that. And he made the film the best, I think'.

L<3B's production was underscored by a very complex interplay between the narrative of the film and Luke's own, personal (and much more complex) narrative whilst negotiating P7. There is a sense in Luke's own words that the film gave him a sense of licence and freedom to express himself in ways he couldn't in real life: 'you could just do what you want, say what you want, act whatever you wanted to act'. *L<3B* thus seemed to create a 'safer' forum in which Luke was able to negotiate and explore certain conflicts through a particular performance of self. By 'affording' himself greater social agency in the film, Luke was then, through a complex analogical process where his efforts were validated both personally by himself and socially by his peers, seemingly afforded a greater degree of social agency in 'real life'.

There is a strong sense of 'emotional literacy' in *L<3B*, of exploring issues that are deeply personal to many of Luke's peers and yet difficult to talk about. Another film from St Gabriel's, *Copycat* (based on a real-life falling out between its two lead actors) explores competition, feuds and racism from a 12-year-old's perspective with similar maturity and attention to dialect and verisimilitude. Both films would seem to provide strong vindications of the benefits of helping children find ways to express and explore their own concerns and priorities. Michael Egan described to me how a visiting Quality Improvement Officer remarked upon how the class's film work enabled them to explore complex emotional ramifications of situations affecting children their age. Worries about rejection and peer esteem are an issue for more than just Luke, and when I asked Bailey if *L<3B* 'rang true' in terms of P7 at St Gabriel's, she told me with a pained smile and an awkward cough that 'a lot of people get rejected.' *L<3B* seemed to provide Luke with a vehicle to explore, in a safer arena, emotions and worries which were very real and personal to both him and the class, in a manner seemingly both cathartic and constructive. Michael Egan describes *L<3B* as helping Luke 'really explore his own emotions at a good time in his life', and crucially the project falls just at the end of P7, just as the St Gabriel's P7s are about to make the transition to senior school. Luke himself admitted that the freedom he felt acting in the film 'actually made me feel a bit better. Because I know people would say, "that's a really good film" and stuff like that'. The last time I saw Luke he was, like Bridget, presenting his film before a packed cinema of 200+ Scottish schoolchildren at the Edinburgh International Film Festival, standing under the spotlight with a microphone and laughing happily with his audience about the 'kissy scene' in the film. Compared to the quiet student I had first met six months before, the contrast was remarkable. Egan described to me how the new sense of confidence and self-efficacy Luke seemed to find through *L<3B* has had a knock-on effect in his school experience as a whole:

> His spelling age has gone up from 9 to 13, his reading has improved, I can see a huge difference socially. His pupil comment on his report card is that he felt more confident, and for me, that's all hung off the film topic. I think its the first time he's put himself out there, he's realized that he maybe had a bit more to offer than he thought, and the other kids are viewing slightly differently ... I've watched Luke grow – its transformed Luke's Primary 7 experience. If we hadn't done this, Luke would have had a very different Primary 7. I think academically its just given him enough of a boost. It's almost like by putting himself out there in the film, he's put himself out there in other ways.

Conclusion

The manner in which *L<3B* assisted its participants' personal development would be remarkable in its own right, if the film didn't also achieve such a pronounced aesthetic success. Luke's own cathartic personal trajectory overlaps with the film's bruising emotional diegesis, particularly in the scenes in which Luke is exposed to humiliation at the hands of the girl he 'fancies', his mother, his friends and his schoolteacher, played by Michael Egan himself. Here we could recall neorealism's aspired proximity between history and text, and its emphasis upon couching narratives in relatively materialist, social terms. In drawing tentative conclusions, it is important to underline how the parallel aesthetic and social-developmental success of *L<3B* both seem to arise from the very specific, neorealist-inspired model of the *Understanding Cinema* project. On a script level Luke conceives of a story taken from his own life, from his concerns and his worries, exploring a powerful set of emotions that are very real to P7s at St Gabriel's. Luke keeps his own name in the film, and thus plays an analogue of himself (as do his co-stars), and the performances in the film are largely improvised. It is this neorealist approach that creates the film's robust and aesthetically successful sense of projected 'ontology', of self-sanctioned representation, and thus its bruising emotional power and highly successful performance of 'authenticity'. In parallel with these aesthetic dimensions, the *Understanding Cinema* project's insistence on 'dialect', and articulation of self, means Luke creates a forum in which he is able to explore difficult, *real* issues and concerns via a vicarious sense of self, and thus enact a complex sense of emotional literacy which is beneficial both for him and his classmates who share the same worries. The project's insistence that Luke invests or performs a direct sense of self, as manifested aesthetically through neorealist technique (a 'realness' of the script, improvisatory techniques, long takes) all conspire to create a sense of the self both at work and at play, negotiating the worries Luke and his classmates have 'in the real world', in the safer arena of a film. Therefore, in the case of *L<3B* at least, there seems to be a correlation between a process that attempts to help children realize aspects of their own 'dialect' (in exploring their own issues and concerns through cinema) and a greater sense of self-efficacy.

Luke's story is only one of many, but it is reflective of children's testimonies about the *Understanding Cinema* project as a whole. In spoken and written evaluations conducted across Scotland a considerable number of children commented that the project had made them 'feel more confident'. On a preliminary basis at least, then, there would seem to be significant value in granting children access to filmmaking opportunities, encouraging them to find something resembling their 'own voice' amidst a cacophony of inherited preconceptions from commercial cinema, and in creating a means through which they can 'safely' explore their own emotions, concerns and priorities: in other words, a means of expressing their own 'dialect'.

It is worth acknowledging once again, however, the media studies discourses that would seem to problematize these conclusions. The notion that school-based film projects such as *Understanding Cinema* provide children with the affordance to express 'authentic selves' is an argument that has provoked considerable scepticism from scholars such as Buckingham and Orner. Considering some of the problems underlying the conclusions of this chapter, one must return to the sense of performance inherent in articulations of self in the *Understanding Cinema* project. This essay has largely taken the view that *Understanding Cinema*'s neorealist-inspired insistence on 'dialect' and 'locality' leads to a creative expression of children's voices that could be considered more 'authentic' or 'in tune' with their own day-to-day lives, if not their taste in films: the neorealist 'documentary' claim of proximity between the filmic and the extra-filmic. Despite these more 'localized' narrative frameworks some students eventually adopted at my insistence, there remains, in many of the films, a sense of identity performance, of students donning both a figurative and literal costume that recalls Buckingham's discussion of the 'social worlds of production'. Despite my best attempts, elements of the heightened 'sassy' talk that seemed so alien to my experience of the children's day-to-day speech crept back into some of the films. Jack Hamilton's *Blocked* stages a successful, anti-purist mix of neorealist 'verisimilitude' and popular genre, with its fusion of police procedural and school documentary. Some of the films' narratives implicitly enact a sense of fantasy, wish-fulfilment and myth. Luke gets the girl in *L<3B*, and the film simultaneously affords Sabilla a sense of authority and wisdom when the boys ask her for her advice. (Similarly, Luke's co-star Aidan told me he was playing 'the cool one' in the film). It would seem that no matter what the aspired proximity between film and extra-filmic historical experience, a sense of and a desire for myth-making remains.

Perhaps it is a mistake to see this as a problem, however. Interestingly, *Copycat*'s writers and crew insisted upon weaving opportunities for each of its actors to speak into the narrative, even if this undermined its teleology. There was a sense amongst the group that each child had to have their moment in the spotlight, their chance to be 'heard'. This was an interesting incidence in which I was proved wrong by my students, who politely refused to follow my McKee-ist script logic (that they should cut the 'flashforward' scenes of Sumaiya talking to Stephanie because they were narratively redundant), because they wanted to cleave out space in the film for Stephanie to be seen and heard. Ultimately I believe the film proves me wrong, as the 'flashforward' scenes contribute eloquently to the film's choral aesthetic of generosity and plurality. In this instance, the presence of voice is literal – the film creates the affordance for each one of its characters to literally speak and be heard.

This essay has attempted, pragmatically, to mobilize an unfashionable discourse – the notion of the children's 'authentic voice' and how that might be articulated by creative work in educational contexts – that has been rendered as problematic by various critics in media and education studies. Throughout, I have attempted to locate the discussion somewhere between parallel experiences as a theorist and practitioner, from a perspective that attempts to juggle an awareness of theory with the contingent, unruly and worldlier experience of classroom teaching. Ultimately, it would seem one of the fundamental questions underlying this discussion is perhaps less whether a convincing case can be rehearsed for projects like *Understanding Cinema* allowing children to articulate their 'authentic voices', but rather, what affordances are opened up for children when an idea of 'authentic voice' is pursued pragmatically? As an unworldly ideal, the notion of 'authentic voice' would seem ultimately unachievable. Yet what happens if that impossibility is both accepted and ignored, and a child's 'authentic voice' is viewed as a sort of unreachable destination – a goal that can be strived towards, if not arrived at? Where do we find ourselves if we embark towards such utopian coordinates? The sort of pessimism surrounding 'voice' postulated by Buckingham and Orner would seem to risk a serious degree of determinism; of precluding certain experiences and practices because they risk incurring intellectual dissonance or discomfort when rehearsed in the less-worldly arenas of academic discourse. Whilst it would be disingenuous to claim that the *Understanding Cinema* project allows children unmediated opportunities to articulate a 'pure', 'authentic' sense of their own voices free from any sense of epistemic imposition, it would seem equally disingenuous and deeply determinist to claim that, considering the diverse vocalities present in any given film production, the voices of children filmmakers are not present – strongly present even – in *Blue Raspberry, Me and Mum, New School, Blocked, Copycat* and *L <3 B*.

Understanding Cinema *films*

Copycat (Megan Thomson, Wiktoria Karbowniczek and Sumaiya Alim, Scotland, 2014) http://vimeo.com/groups/257525/videos/100746759

L <3 B (Luke Davies, Scotland, 2014) http://vimeo.com/groups/257525/videos/100150740

The Den (Eve Duncan, Zoe Gormley, Sophie Hetherington, Alex Kane and Reon McSherry, Scotland, 2014) http://vimeo.com/100796087

Blocked (Jack Hamilton, Scotland, 2014) http://vimeo.com/groups/257525/videos/103998120

Blue Raspberry (Bridget Harley, Scotland, 2014) http://vimeo.com/groups/257525/videos/100150741

First Day (Max Mayer, Scotland, 2014) http://vimeo.com/groups/257525/videos/103998121

Me and Mum (Jamie Thomson, Scotland, 2014) http://vimeo.com/groups/257525/videos/103997956

Wednesday (Connal Tolmie, Scotland, 2014) http://vimeo.com/groups/257525/videos/10079

Notes

1   Saverio Giovacchini and Robert Sklar, *Global Neorealism* (Jackson, MI: University Press of Mississippi, 2011).
2   Christopher Wagstaff, *Italian Neorealist Cinema: An Aesthetic Approach* (Toronto: University of Toronto Press, 2007), p. 90.
3   Michael Denning, *Culture in the Age of Three Worlds* (London: Verso, 2004).
4   Gayatri Spivak, 'Can the subaltern speak?', in Cary Nelson and Lawrence Grossberg (eds), *Marxism and the Interpretation of Culture* (Urbana, IL: University of Illinois Press, 1987), pp. 271– 313.
5   Edward Said, *Orientalism* (London: Penguin, 2003), p. xxvi.
6   David Buckingham, *Media Education: Literacy, Learning and Contemporary Culture* (Cambridge, MA: Polity Press, 2003); Michelle Orner, 'Interrupting the calls for

student voice in liberatory education: a feminist poststructuralist perspective', in Carmen Luke and Jennifer Gore (eds), *Feminisms and Critical Pedagogy* (New York: Routledge, 1992).
7 Buckingham, *Media Education*, p. 129.
8 André Bazin, 'The evolution of the language of cinema', in *What is Cinema: Volume I*, ed. Hugh Gray (Berkeley, CA: University of California Press, 1967), p. 39.
9 Christopher Wagstaff, *Italian Neorealist Cinema*, p. 33.
10 Giovacchini and Sklar, *Global Neorealism*.
11 Mark Reid, '*Cinema Cent Ans de Jeunesse*: an integrated film education programme', *AMES* (2014).
12 Buckingham, *Media Education*, p. 128.
13 Considering British cinema alone, the films of the British New Wave, of Ken Loach, the Amber Collective, Bill Douglas, Terence Davies, Shane Meadows, Andrea Arnold and Clio Barnard all explore British working-class and subaltern experience in a manner utilizing the full, aesthetic palette of 'art cinema'. Such a canon would thus seem to challenge the perhaps patronizing presumption that 'art cinema' is completely out-of-step with and out-of-reach of working-class or 'popular' experience.
14 Buckingham, *Media Education*, p. 33.
15 Richard Chalfen, 'Home movies as cultural documents', in Sari Thomson (ed.), *Film/Culture: Exploration of Cinema in its Social Context* (Metuchen, NJ: Scarecrow Press, 1982), pp. 126–37; subsequently explored in David Buckingham and Rebekah Willett (eds), *Video Cultures: Media Technology and Everyday Creativity* (London: Palgrave Macmillan, 2009).
16 Maria Pini, 'Inside the home mode', in Buckingham and Willett (eds), *Video Cultures*, pp. 71–92.
17 Rebekah Willett, 'Always on: camera phones, video production and identity', in Buckingham and Willett (eds), *Video Cultures*, pp. 210–29.
18 One can perhaps identify this as one of the moments of liminality between criticism and creativity that media scholars such as David Buckingham believe foundational to the construction of media literacy: 'for literacy clearly involves both reading *and* writing; and so media literacy must necessarily entail both the interpretation and production of media'. Buckingham, *Media Education*, p. 49. He continues: '[t]here has to be a kind of *translation* from the "passive" knowledge that is derived from viewing or reading – or indeed from analysis – to the "active" knowledge that is required for production or viewing' (p. 132). Indeed it would seem to be one of the key strengths of the *Understanding Cinema* project that textual criticism ('reading') and film production ('writing'/'speaking') are inextricable, with students emulating in practical work the techniques they have just analysed in canonic examples, before once more returning to their seats in the audience to consider the aesthetic achievements of their own work.
19 Colin McArthur, *Whisky Galore! and The Maggie* (London: I.B. Tauris, 1982).
20 Jason Scott, 'From local roots to global screens: Shane Meadows's positioning in the ecology of contemporary British film', *Journal of British Cinema and Television*, vol. 10, no. 4 (2013), pp. 829–45.

INDEX

7 Up!/Seven Up! (1964–) 3, 10, 16, 101–112, 115
10 Minutes Older (1978) 96, 179
20 Times More Likely (1979) 193
400 Blows (1959) 3, 107, 162

Aadhi Haqueqat, Adda Fasana (1990) 158
Absent Parents (1982) 196, 197
'Act Naturally' (1963) 111, 113
A.I.: Artificial Intelligence (2001) 94
Alexander, Katherine 74, 75–77
Ali, Mahershala 86, 87
Alice (through the looking glass) 4, 16
Aligrudic, Slobadan 124, 128
Allen, Richard 159, 167 n. 4
Almond, Paul 101, 105
An Entertainment (1990) 13, 182
Anjali (1990) 164, 165, 166
Apaches (1977) 13, 188–94, 196, 198–99
Aveshesh (c.1975) 162, 163

Bachelard, Gaston 8, 17, 22, 33 n.3, 34n.14
Badlands (1973) 8, 22–25, 34
Banks, Russell 28, 33 n.1
Baron, Cynthia 9, 72, 82, 98 n.3
Barthes, Roland 95, 100 n.25
Bazin, Andre 14, 206, 223 n.8
Beasts of the Southern Wild (2012) 44
Bellissima (1951) 203
Bellmer, Hans 12, 13, 172–75, 177–78, 181, 183
Bennett, Jane 6, 16 n.13
Bergala, Alain 14, 17, 205
Bicycle Thieves (1948) 141, 204, 206
Billig, Michael 145, 149, 155 n.32
Billy Liar (1963) 209
Black Cat, White Cat (1998) 128
Blair, Lindsay 175, 184 n.13

Blue Peter (1958–) 194
Bogle, Donald 85, 98 n.1
Bogue, Ronald 143, 155 n.25
Bombay (1995) 165, 166
Boyhood (2014) 8, 16, 35, 40, 42, 43
Breathless (1960) 162
Breton, Andre 171, 183 n.1
Brett, Guy 182, 185 n.35
Brickman, Barbara Jane 24, 34 n.9
Brooke, Michael 194, 200 n.9
Brooks, Xan 112, 117 n.22
Bruzzi, Stella 10, 101, 116–17
Buckingham, David 204–5, 208, 210–11, 220–23 n.6, 7, 14, 18
Building Sites Bite (1978) 192
Burke, Andrew 12, 13, 187
Butler, Judith 103–4, 109, 114, 116 n.7, 117 n.17, 34

Calcutta Film Society 12, 161
Caouette, Jonathan 10, 101, 113–15, 116 n.7, 117 n.17
Capturing the Friedmans (2003) 10, 101, 105, 111–13, 115
Carnicke, Sharon 9, 72, 82, 98 n.3
Carroll, Lewis 4, 16 n.7, 175, 180
Castle Ra-Tim-Bum (1999) 141
Central Station (1998) 141, 152, 154
Chalfen, Richard 211, 223 n.15
Chambers, Jamie 12, 14, 203
Charley Says (c.1960–1970) 200
Chase, Ilka 72, 73
child
  agency 90, 124
  'becoming' 3, 40
  'bubble' 11, 121, 123, 124, 126, 127, 129
  in/as history 142, 154
  othered/otherness 39, 204

point of view 2, 3, 142
   'seed/environment' 11, 144, 145, 150
   voice 14, 204, 211, 214, 216, 220, 221
Children's Film Society (CFS) 161, 168
Child's Play (1984–1988) 101, 103, 108, 110
Children of the Stones (1977) 199
The Children's Party (1940–1960) 13, 178–81
Chomana Dudi (1975) 162
Le Cinema Cent Ans De Jeunesse (CCADJ) 14, 203–9, 212
City of God (2002) 141, 147
Clandestine Childhood (2011) 139
Cloke, Paul 38, 46 n.12, 47 n.24, 199 n.8
Close Encounters of the Third Kind (1977) 94
Clover, Carol J. 190, 199 n.6
Cooper, Gladys 72, 73
Cornell, Joseph 13, 172–83, 185
Cotillion (1940–1960) 13, 178, 180
The Creeper (1948) 82
'Cruel Cinema' (Tamil) 12, 166

Dalapathi (1991) 164
Davis, Bette 9, 71–5, 77–9, 82–3
Daayan (2013) 167
Days of Heaven (1978) 27
Deamer, David 145, 155 n.28
Deleuze, Gilles 3, 11, 14–5, 40, 47 n.18, 95, 140–42, 144, 152, 155–56 n.16
Diff'rnt Strokes (1978–84) 98
Do You Remember Dolly Bell (1981) 10, 122, 124, 126–27, 129, 132–137
Doane, Mary Ann 10, 95, 96, 100 n.24
Documents (1929–30) 180–1
Dogsbody (1975) 57
Don't Look Now (1973) 196
Dyer, Richard 10, 96, 100 n.27
Dykes, Tony 196, 200 n.12

E.T. (1982) 94
East of Borneo (1931) 178, 181
Edelmen, Lee 4, 5, 16 n.9
Egan, Michael 213, 218, 219
Egoyan, Atom 8, 28
Eleftheriotis, Dimitris 10, 121
Elite Squad (2007) 147
Ellis, John 105, 110, 114, 116 n.9, 117 n.18
Engelmann, Sasha 6, 16 n.12
Erice, Victor 95, 209, 215
Etre et Avoir (2002) 10, 101, 105–06, 109–13, 115–16

Everyday (2012) 16
Europa di note (1959) 133
Fenichel, Otto 176, 177–78, 184 n.20
The Finishing Line (1977) 192, 200
Fire and Hemlock (1985) 57
Flight of the Red Balloon (2007) 162
Foucault, Michel 127, 137 n.11, 194, 200 n.10
Frank, Herz 96, 179
Freud, Sigmund 14, 21, 23–4, 32, 33. N.4, 34 n.22, 172, 176, 178, 183
Freyre, Gilberto 150, 156 n.49

Garland, Judy 71, 73, 82
Garland-Thomson, Rosemarie 88, 99 n.13
Gates, Racquel 96, 100 n.28
Germany Year Zero (1948) 141
Ghattashraddha (1978) 162, 163
Ghobadi, Bahman 38, 44
Gillespie, Michael Boyce 88, 99 n.6
Giovacchini, Saverio 203, 207, 222 n.1 223 n.10
Girl, Interrupted (1999) 10
Glick, Megan H 6, 16 n.11
Gocic, Goran 136, 137
Goethe, Johann Wolfgang von 13, 172, 175, 176, 178, 184 n.15
Good Morning (1959) 39
Gopalan, Lalitha 10, 12, 157, 168
The Grave of the Fireflies (1988) 38, 44
Gregg, Melissa 39, 46 n.14
Green Cross Code (1970) 194, 195, 196
Guattari, Felix 42, 47 n.27, 95

Halloween (1978) 199
Hamburger, Cao 11, 141, 147
Hastie, Amelie 8, 13, 21
Hauptman, Jodi 180, 185 n.30
Heading for Heaven (1947) 82
Heise, Tatiana Signorelli 147, 155 n.41
Henreid, Paul 72, 73
Henry, Julie 40, 47 n.19
Hibbert, Alex 10, 87–8, 90, 93–4, 97
Hickey-Moody, Anna Catherine 15 n.4, 39, 40, 47 n.18
Hicks, Colin 133, 137 n.21
Hiller, Susan 13, 182–83, 185
Hitchcock, Alfred 80, 95
Holston, James 145, 150, 155 n.30, 156 n.48
Home (2008) 44

The Homeward Bounders (1981) 57
Hopkins, David 12, 171, 185
Howl's Moving Castle (2004) 9, 57–65
Hudson, Liam 183, 185 n.40
Hunt for the Wilderpeople (2016) 87
Huston, John 101, 103, 104

I Was Born But… (1931) 39
Illich, Ivan 41–42, 47 n.26
In Camera (2011) 158
In this World (2002) 44
Iordanova, Dina 122, 137 n.4
It's Love I'm After (1936) 72

Jackson, Michael 4, 98
Jamie, Kathleen 38, 46 n.11
Jane Eyre (1943) 71
Jarecki, Andrew 10, 101, 111–12, 117
Jenkins, Barry 4, 10, 85, 88, 91–3, 96–8
Jones, Owain 3, 8, 13, 35, 38, 46 n.12, 188–9, 199 n.2–3
Jordan, Larry 13, 178
Journey for Margaret (1942) 71

Kaaliya Mardan (1919) 12, 157, 158
Kamlabhai (1992) 158
Kamchatka (2002) 139, 142
Kannada 'new wave' 12, 162, 163
Kannathil Muthamittal (2002) 166
Keay, Douglas 106, 107
Keene, Judith 132, 137 n.9
Keller, Marjorie 175, 176–78, 184 n.14
Kelly, Grace 95, 100
Kilborn, Richard 108, 117 n.14
Kinney, Katherine 92, 99 n.18
Kizirian, Shari 109, 117 n.16
Klevan, Andrew 9, 72, 82 n.3
Koree-da, Hirokazu 3, 16
Kracauer, Siegfried 26, 34 n.15
Krish, John 196, 200 n.13
Krishna 12, 157
Krishna Janam (1918) 157
Ksha Tra Ghya (2004) 158, 159
Kuhn, Annette 25–26, 34 n.11
Kusturica, Emir 10, 121–27, 130–32, 134–36

Ladybird (2017) 10
Larsen, Reif 11, 131, 137 n.6
Laputa: Castle in the Sky (1986) 49
Lebeau, Vicky 34 n.23, 104, 116 n.4

Le Havre (2011) 44
Lesser, Jeffrey 150, 154, 156 n.45
Linklater, Richard 3, 8, 16, 35
The Little Rascals (1934–44) 97
Little Women (1949) 71
Lonely Water (1973) 13, 193, 194, 195
Lopez, Georges 109, 110, 111
Lost Embrace (2004) 151
Lury, Karen 29, 33 n.6, 39 n.17, 46, 81, 82 n.2

Machuca (2004) 139
Mackenzie, John 188, 190
McArthur, Colin 215, 223 n.19
McCormack, Derek 6, 7, 16 n.12 n.14
Madame Curie (1943) 71
Malick, Terence 8, 27
Martin-Jones, David 11, 12, 139, 155 n.15 n.17
Maslen, Robert 8, 49
Maxwell, William 38, 46
Meadows, Shane 4, 216
Medicine For Melancholy (2008) 88
Meet me in St Louis (1944) 71, 215
Mermaids (1990) 2
The Midnight Party (1940–1960) 13, 178, 180
'Mignon' 13, 175–78
Milestone, Lewis 72, 82 n.1
Mind How You Go (1973) 13, 187, 194–96, 198
Minnelli, Vincente 71, 215
Minotaure (1933–9) 177, 180–81, 184 n.25
Miyazaki, Hayao 9, 49, 54, 67
Moonlight (2016) 4, 10, 85–98
My Childhood (1972) 87
My Neighbour Totoro (1988) 9, 50–53, 54, 67
My Reputation (1946) 79, 81

Nancy Drew (1938–39) 72
Naremore, James 91, 99 n.16
Nascimento, Amos 150, 156 n.51
Nausicaa of the Valley of the Wind (1984) 54
Nayakan (1987) 164
News of the World (2020) 87
Nobody Knows (2004) 16
Now, Voyager (1942) 9, 71, 72, 73, 74, 78, 79, 81, 82

O'Brien, Margaret 71, 73, 82, 215
October (1928) 160
Orner, Michelle 204, 220, 221, 222 n.6
The Other Bank (2009) 47
The Owl Service (1969–70) 199
Ozu, Yazujiro 160, 161

Paisan (1946) 203
Paisito (2008) 139
Pan's Labyrinth (2006) 209
Paresh Pather (1958) 161
Paruthiveeran (2007) 166
Pasanga/Children (2009) 167
Pather Panchali (1955) 12, 159, 161, 16
Pender's Fen (1974) 199
Pearson, Mike 37, 40, 46 n.9
Phalke, Dadasaheb 157, 158
Phalke, Mandakini 157, 158
Philibert, Nicolas 10, 101, 109
Phillips, Adam 130, 137, 138 n.29
Philo, Chris 2, 15 n.3
Phuc, Kim 105, 109
Pini, Maria 211, 223 n.16
Pixote (1981) 141
Play Sufficiency Measures (Welsh) 35, 36, 37
Podalsky, Laura 140, 154
Pom Poko (1994) 53
Powrie, Phil 109, 117 n.15
Prasad, M. Madhava 162, 163, 168
Protect and Survive (1975) 200
Public information films 12, 13, 187, 197
Pudhupettai (2006) 166
'Punch and Judy' 13, 182

Quashie, Kevin Everod 10, 88, 89, 90, 97, 99 n.12

Rains, Claude 72, 73
Ratcatcher (1999) 8, 22, 25–28, 87
Ramsay, Lynn 8, 25, 27,28, 87
Ratnam, Mani 163, 166, 168
Ray, Satyajit 12, 159, 161, 168 n.6, 203, 207
Rear Window (1954) 95
Rebecca (1940) 80
The Red Balloon (1956) 162
Reid, Mark 206, 208, 223 n.11
Reynolds, Simon 198, 201 n.17
The River (1951) 159
Robida, Albert 60, 68 n.11

Rocha, Carolina 15, 139, 140, 154 n.1, 156 n.52
Rocks (2019) 99
Rome, Open City (1945) 141
Rose Hobart (c.1936) 178, 181
Rose, Jacqueline 123, 137 n.9
Rossellini, Roberto 141, 203

Said, Edward 204, 222 n.5
Samskara (1970) 162
San Pietro (1945) 101, 103, 105, 106, 115
Sanders, Ashton 10, 87–8, 91–4, 97
Schwarz, Roberto 145, 146, 155 n.31
Scott, Sarah 40, 47 n.22
The Secret Garden (1949) 71
The Selected Works of T.S. Spivet 11, 131–132, 136, 137 n.6
Seven Days of Luke (1975) 57
Sewing Machine (1973) 196, 197,200
Shingler, Martin 9, 10, 71, 86
Shoeshine (1946) 204
De Sica, Vittoria 141, 203
Singleton, Valerie 194,196
Sitney, P. Adams 179, 184 n.28
Skidmore, Thomas E. 146, 155 n.34
Sklar, Robert 203, 207, 222 n.1
So Long, See You Tomorrow (1996) 38, 46
Sontag, Susan 103, 104, 116, n.5
Spelling Bee (2002) 116
The Spirit of the Beehive (1973) 95, 209, 215, 216
Stanwyck, Barbara 71, 79
Starsky and Hutch (1975–79) 190, 199
Steedman, Carolyn 13, 17, 24–6, 33 n.8, 177, 182, 184 n.21
The Strange Love of Martha Ivers (1946) 72, 79, 80, 81
Strike (1925) 160
Subramaniapuram (2008) 166
Summer at Grandpa's (1984) 162
The Sweet Hereafter (1997) 8, 21, 22, 28–33
synchrony 8, 49, 53, 56, 65–7

Tabarne Kathe (1987) 163
Takahata, Isao 38, 44, 53
Tarnation (2003) 10, 101, 105, 111–14, 117
Taylor, Elizabeth 71, 73, 82
Telles, Edward E. 150, 156 n.50
Temple, Shirley 73, 82
Texas Chain Saw Massacre (1974) 199
Thirteen (2003) 10

INDEX   227

This is England (2006) 4
Thomson, Amanda-Jane 206, 211–12, 213, 217
Threads (1984) 200
Time of the Gypsies (1989) 11, 122, 125, 127, 133
Todorovic, Bora 125
Tokyo Story (1953) 160, 161
Traverso, Antonio 142, 155 n.13
Turtles Can Fly (2004) 38, 44

Underground (1995) 121, 122, 136, 137
'Understanding Cinema' (project) 14, 203–11, 214, 216–17, 22–21
United Nations Convention on the Rights of the Child (1989) 8, 14, 35, 36, 41, 123, 137, 185

Veyyil (2006) 166
Village of the Damned (1960) 191

Wagstaff, Christopher 204, 206, 207, 222 n.2
Waiting for Godot (1953) 121
Waldman, Diane 174, 184 n.9
Walk Away Renee (2011) 117
The War Game (1965) 200
War of the Worlds (2005) 94
Ward, Colin 41, 47 n.23

Watch on the Rhine (1943) 71, 79, 81
Watch with Mother (1952–73) 198
Waugh, Thomas 114, 117 n.32
Welcome Home (1945) 82
What Time is it Over There? (2001) 162
When Father Was Away on Business (1985) 10–11, 122, 125–30, 133
Where is the Friend's Home? (1987) 203
Whisky (2004) 151
Whistle Down the Wind (1961) 40
Whisper of the Heart (1995) 9, 53, 54–56, 59, 65
The Wicker Man (1973) 199
Will it Snow for Christmas? (1996) 44
Willett, Rebekah 211, 223 n.17
Williams, Raymond 208, 209
Wilson, Janis 9, 71, 72, 74–82
Winnicott, D.W. 135, 138 n.29
Winterbottom, Michael 3, 16, 44
Wyness, Michael 90, 92, 93, 99 n.15
Wynne-Jones, Diana 57, 68 n.8
The Year my Parents Went on Vacation (2006) 11, 139, 142–151

Yi Yi (2000) 162

Zapruder, Abraham 112, 117
Zizek, Slavoj 121, 136